Courthouse

ALSO BY THE AUTHOR

Lions in the Street
Tiger in the Court
"What the Hell Is Justice?"
To Drop a Dime (with Ira Pecznick)

Courthouse

by

Paul Hoffman

HAWTHORN BOOKS, INC.
Publishers/NEW YORK
A Howard & Wyndham Company

To Kathy
In Memoriam
April 7, 1938–March 21, 1978

COURTHOUSE

 All inquiries should be addressed to Hawthorn Books, Inc., 260 Madison Avenue, New York, New York 10016. This book was manufactured in the United States of America and published simultaneously in Canada by Prentice-Hall of Canada, Limited, 1870 Birchmount Road, Scarborough, Ontario.

Library of Congress Catalog Card Number: 78–65401

ISBN: 0–8015–1790–7

1 2 3 4 5 6 7 8 9 10

Preface

This is the log of ninety-nine days in the life of the world's busiest courthouse, the Manhattan Criminal Courts Building. It cannot pretend to be comprehensive. With nearly one hundred thousand defendants passing through more than fifty different courtrooms every year, compiling a complete record would require an army of observers, and the account would fill several volumes. But I hope it is representative.

Wherever possible courtroom colloquy and testimony have been checked against transcripts; I have not hesitated to repunctuate and reparagraph the dialogue to my style, and in almost every instance the proceedings, of necessity, had to be telescoped. It has not always been possible, because transcripts are not routinely prepared in the New York city and state courts, and much of the colloquy occurred "off the record." Much more occurred outside of court with no stenographer in attendance. In a few instances conversations had to be reconstructed from the accounts of participants and observers. Some names had to be spelled phonetically.

Rather than interrupt the narrative with definitions and explanations, I have included a glossary of courthouse jargon and nomenclature.

Acknowledgments

Compiling this log required the cooperation of many persons. Among those who did more than merely let me sit and observe and whose assistance I gratefully acknowledge are: Geoffrey Abrams, Benjamin Altman, Arthur Bernhardt, Dan Bonanno, Robert Crane, Mary DeBourbon, Herald Price Fahringer, Robert Ferraro, Avon Gresham, David Hackel, Robert Haft, Louis Hulnick, Jonathan Jacobs, William Kunstler, Irving Lang, Frank LaNotte, Robert LaSado, James Leff, Philip Leshin, Leslie Maitland, Peter McQuillan, Charles Meara, Howard Meyer, Robert Morgenthau, John Mulligan, Mike Pearl, Burton Roberts, George Roberts, Ernst Rosenberger, Edgar Ross, Harold Rothwax, James Ryan, Melvyn Sachs, Stephen Shiffrin, Edwin Torres, Pablo Torres, James Vinci, John Walsh, David Worgan, Peter Zimroth, and John Zirinsky. I would also like to thank Bennett Epstein for first suggesting the idea; my agent, Jay Acton; and my editor, Beth Backman, for steering it through to completion.

P. H.

Courthouse

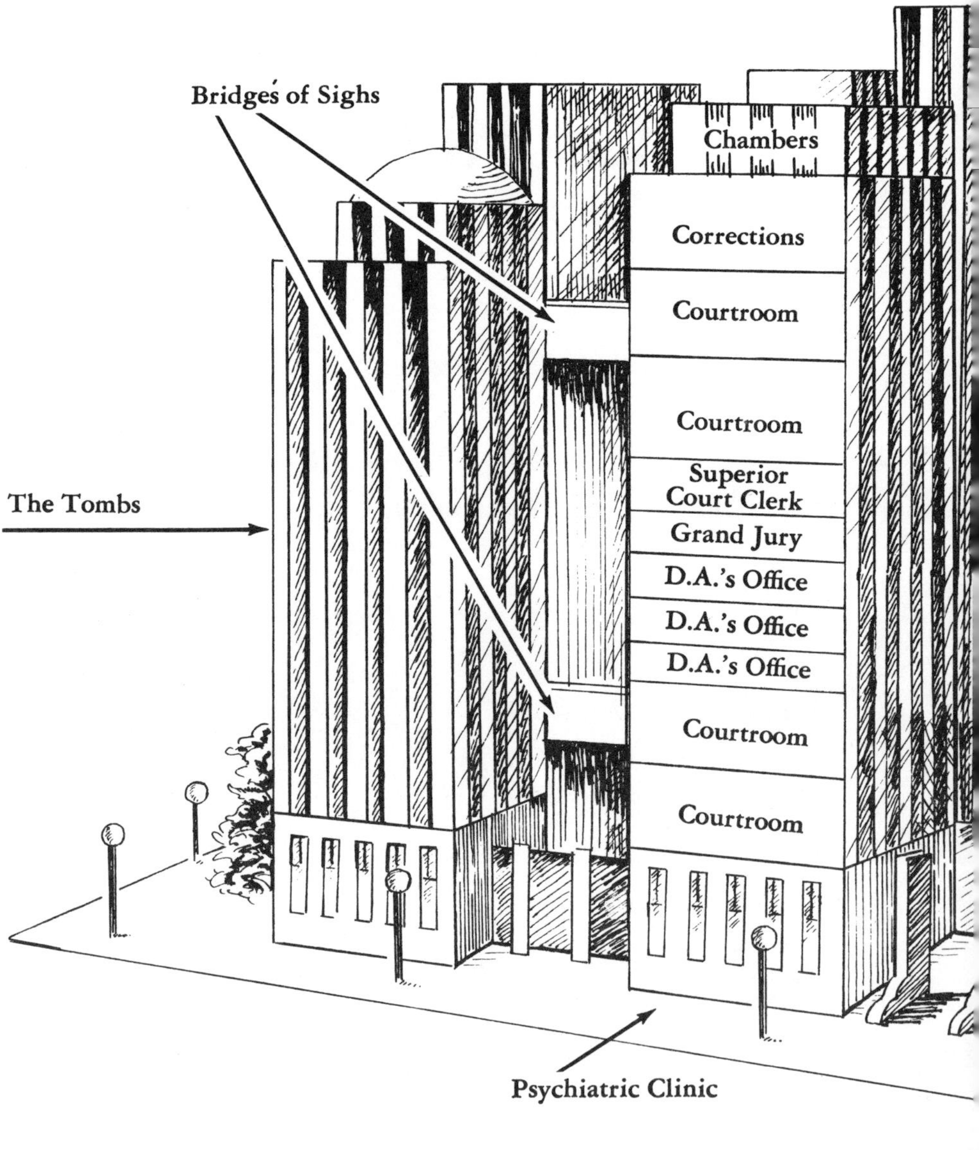
Bridges of Sighs
Chambers
Corrections
Courtroom
Courtroom
Superior
Court Clerk
Grand Jury
D.A.'s Office
D.A.'s Office
D.A.'s Office
Courtroom
Courtroom
The Tombs
Psychiatric Clinic

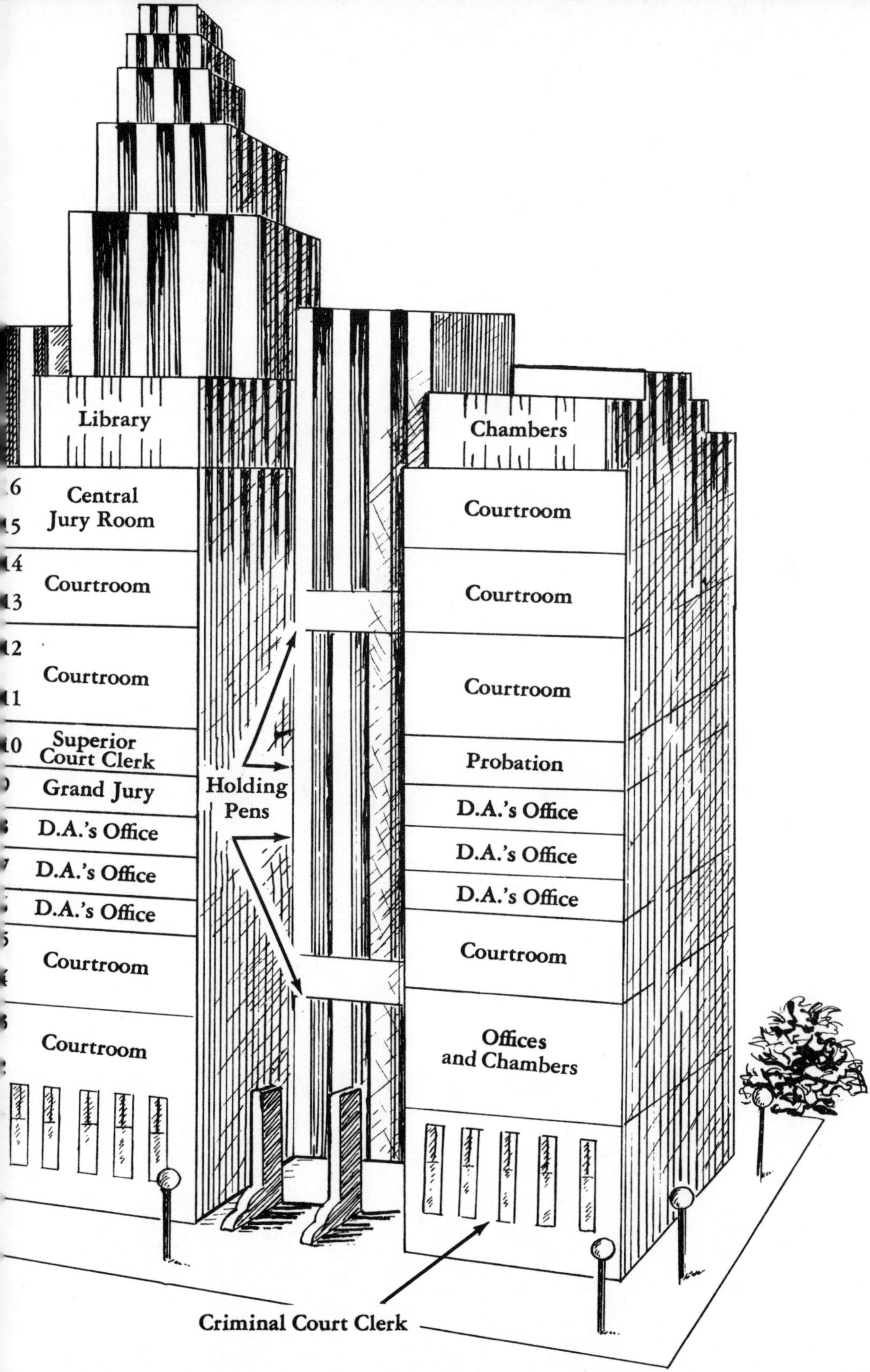
Library
Central
Jury Room
Courtroom
Courtroom
Superior
Court Clerk
Grand Jury
D.A.'s Office
D.A.'s Office
D.A.'s Office
Courtroom
Courtroom
Holding
Pens
Chambers
Courtroom
Courtroom
Courtroom
Probation
D.A.'s Office
D.A.'s Office
D.A.'s Office
Courtroom
Offices
and Chambers
Criminal Court Clerk

Tuesday, January 3

The blue-uniformed bridgeman bangs his hand loudly against the rail. Manuel Sullivan is a barrel-chested black who peers at the world through thick horn-rimmed glasses. Although he's been on his job less than a year, his voice booms with authority.

"All rise! Stand up!"

About fifty persons in the courtroom shuffle to their feet. Just inside the rail are policemen, most of them in the off-duty "uniform" of slacks, flannel shirts, and padded ski jackets. On a bench along the wall, four defendants —three blacks and a white. In the spectator seats, a scattering of complaining witnesses and friends and relatives of the accused—white, black, and Hispanic, a crazy-quilt cross section of the metropolis.

"Hear ye! Hear ye!" Sullivan shouts.

Then his voice takes off at a mile-a-minute clip. "All persons having business before the Criminal Court of the City of New York, held in and for the County of New York, draw near, give your attention, and ye shall be heard! The Honorable Milton L. Williams presiding."

Finally back to the imperative: "Sit down! Keep quiet! Put away all reading matter!"

The crowd takes seats again as the judge enters. The Honorable Milton L. Williams is a rotund black man who paces the bench restlessly, hands thrust in pants pockets beneath his black robe, while the uniformed court officers ready the day's docket.

After conferring with Williams, Sullivan returns to the rail that divides the spectator seats from the well of the court.

"Lopez!" he calls.

A short, stocky man with a black beard comes forward.

"Stand over here, please," Sullivan says, directing him to a place just inside the rail.

Then Sullivan takes his place behind the "bridge," a long table set directly before the bench and piled high with legal papers. Taped to the bench behind him is a poster-sized calendar of 1978. Behind the judge's leather chair are the standard items of New York courtroom decor—an American flag and, on the pine-paneled wall, faded gold letters with the inscription: IN GOD WE TRUST. From the high ceiling hang ultramodern light fixtures that illuminate the dirt caked on the linoleum-tiled floor. On a wall is a sign whose crumbling letters make it read: ALL OFFICERS ST DISPLAY THEIR SHIELDS.

"Raise your right hand," Sullivan tells Lopez. "Do you swear to the truth of this affidavit?"

Lopez shakes his head in bewilderment.

"Andre Lopez?" Sullivan asks.

Wrong Lopez. The right one—a slight, dark-complexioned man—answers Sullivan's second call, quickly attests to the affidavit, and goes about his business.

"Docket number 8-0-0-1-3-4," Sullivan shouts. "Eddie Radcliffe." Then he rattles off a string of numbers listing the provisions of the Penal Law that Radcliffe is charged with violating.

A policeman in plain clothes leads a young black to the bridge. A woman assistant district attorney stands beside the officer.

"Mr. Kravitz!" Sullivan shouts, calling the name of a Legal Aid lawyer. He looks around the courtroom. "You better be here," he mumbles aloud.

Kravitz isn't.

"Second call," Sullivan says, throwing down one sheaf of papers and picking up another. The defendant is returned to the prisoners' bench.

"Docket number 8-0-0-1-3-2. David Hardin," Sullivan calls, rattling off another series of Penal Law listings.

Another black is brought to the bridge. A Legal Aid lawyer—not Kravitz—takes his place beside him.

"Waive reading of your rights?" Sullivan asks.

The attorney mumbles assent. Then he and the prosecutor confer with Judge Williams at the bench. A few minutes later they return to their places, and Legal Aid enters a guilty plea to a reduced charge.

"Defendant ready for sentence?" Williams asks.

"Yes, Your Honor."

"One hundred forty dollars or thirty days."

Hardin is given a month to pay and is led away to complete the processing.

"Docket number 8-0-0-1-3-1. Stephen Francis."

A young white in blue jeans is led to the bridge. Beside him a bushy-haired Legal Aid lawyer—still not Kravitz. Again there's a conference at the bench. When it concludes, Judge Williams directs, "Reduce to misdemeanor."

The Assistant District Attorney so moves.

"Anything to say, Counsel?"

Legal Aid says the defendant has no prior record, lives at home with his parents, and attends a community college.

Williams offers to "A.C.D." the case—adjourn it in contemplation of dismissal. The prosecutor agrees. The Legal Aid lawyer takes Francis aside and explains that if he stays out of trouble the charge will be dropped. There won't even be a conviction on his record.

Eddie Radcliffe is recalled. This time Kravitz stands beside him. Again there's a conference at the bench and again the charge is reduced. Radcliffe pleads guilty.

"Defendant want to be heard before I impose sentence?"

Kravitz points out that Radcliffe has a wife and three children.

"Under the circumstances, I'm only going to impose two hundred dollars or thirty days," Williams says.

Radcliffe also is given thirty days to pay.

"Docket number 8-0-0-1-3-6. Stephen Benjamin."

Another black is brought to the bridge, and the bushy-haired lawyer from Legal Aid rises to represent him. The formalities are completed quickly.

"One hundred fifty dollars or thirty days."

This is the scene on the first business day of 1978 in Part AR1, Criminal Court of the City of New York, Borough of Manhattan. AR1 is an arraignment part. For the defendants haled into it, AR1 is the scene of their first contact with the judicial process . . . and for many their last.

AR1 dispenses assembly-line justice. So many cases come into court every day that the judges, assistant district attorneys, even Legal Aid lawyers, are hard pressed to dispose of them, even summarily. Adjournments, hearings, or trials will only clog the calendars on some later day. So, except for heinous crimes, the procedure is the same: The lawyers "plea-bargain," haggling like traders at an Arabian bazaar until a three-way bargain is struck between prosecution, defense, and judiciary; the charge is reduced, the defendant pleads guilty, and a minimum sentence is imposed—minimum in part because the city's jails are so jammed that making room for a minor miscreant might mean freeing a hardened criminal, but mainly because defendants facing harsh penalties can't be induced to "cop a plea." As a result, first offenders can expect to have their cases A.C.D.'d, and even career criminals—prostitutes, pickpockets, bookies—are usually let off with a fine or "time served." In the parlance of Criminal Court veterans, "They're giving away the courthouse."

In 1977, 63 percent of all cases were "disposed of" at the initial arraignment, and the number would have been even higher but for the District Attorney's "pre-screening," under which certain classes of cases are thrown out even before they come to court—college kids caught smoking a "joint" or teen-agers trespassing in abandoned buildings.

AR1 and its companion, AR2, sit across the hall from each other in what were once the borough's traffic courts on the first floor of the Criminal Courts Building at 100 Centre Street. It's the world's busiest courthouse, handling all arrests in Manhattan—90,746 in 1977—everything from dope dealing in Harlem to Mafia murders in Little Italy, from five-dollar muggings in Central Park to five-million-dollar stock swindles on Wall Street.

The building itself is a seventeen-story Art Deco structure of gray limestone with steel trimming. It was built by the Public Works Administration thirty-eight years ago when Franklin D. Roosevelt was president and Thomas E. Dewey was district attorney. It stands in Manhattan's Civic Center, one block north of Foley Square at the edge of Chinatown, and fills the entire block bounded by Centre, Baxter, Leonard, and White streets. It is laid out like two capital *E*'s set back to back and topped with a horizontal *I*: ≣

The *E*'s are the courthouse proper, the *I* the Tombs—officially the Manhattan House of Detention for Men. Two "Bridges of Sighs"—on the third and twelfth floors—connect the jail with the courthouse. But prisoners no longer sigh sad farewells through their translucent windows. For the past four years the Tombs has been empty—except for emergencies—closed by order of a federal judge as unfit for human habitation.

The courthouse, too, is tattered and tawdry with nearly four decades of use, abuse, and overuse. As crime rates soared in the 1960s and 1970s, so did the volume of court business and the number of judicial, legal, and lay personnel required to cope with it.

When the building was dedicated on June 30, 1941, Mayor Fiorello LaGuardia expressed the hope that it would never be used to capacity. At the time the District Attorney's legal staff numbered 84, and it prosecuted 26,000 cases a year. It now numbers 229 and prosecutes enough defendants annually to populate a city the size of Schenectady.

As the volume of cases soared, clerical offices, witnesses' waiting rooms, even judges' robing rooms were converted into courtrooms to cope with the crush. But the most obvious sign of the increased case loads can be seen not in the courtrooms but *outside* them—in the glass-enclosed bulletin boards designed to display each day's dockets. Since the calendars in some parts usually run to two, three, or even four pages, the bulletin boards are no longer adequate, and the dittoed docket sheets have to be Scotch-taped to the marble walls. And as new parts were added and offices shifted, the building's signs also proved inadequate. Throughout the courthouse hand-lettered signs are pasted over the old ones of engraved glass or metal. Despite the cramming and conversion, the building literally overflowed.

On the walls outside the courthouse are engraved edifying statements about justice. Most prominent—carved in the façade between the twin entrance plazas on Centre Street—is a quotation from Jefferson's first inaugural address:

EQUAL AND EXACT JUSTICE TO ALL MEN
OF WHATEVER STATE AND PERSUASION

It doesn't always happen.

Eleven floors above AR1 the mills of justice grind at a slower pace.

The courtroom is larger and brighter than that of AR1. Again there's an American flag and the inscription: IN GOD WE TRUST. Similar light fixtures hang from the ceiling. Paint peels from the walls and the leather on the chairs in the jury box is worn through.

Only a dozen persons are in the courtroom when the uniformed court officer bangs his hand against the door and shouts, "Remain seated! Come to order! His Honor, the Justice of the Supreme Court."

Actually, Irving Lang is only an *acting* justice of New York State's incongruously named basic trial court, a Criminal Court judge sitting by designation on the higher bench. He's a short, chubby man with thinning brown hair and tortoiseshell glasses. His black robe hangs loosely as he strides to the bench, takes his seat, and starts shuffling through his papers.

Two lawyers sit in the jury box chatting while they wait for their cases to be called. In the second row of spectator seats sits Joseph B. Cortale conferring with his attorney. Cortale is a chunky man of forty-four with dark, wavy hair and dark, deep-set eyes. He wears a bright blue suit and clutches a fur-collared leather coat in his lap. He's charged with the double murder of two business associates—Eugene Acca and Enrico Galietta, president and executive vice-president of Applied Systematics, Inc., a Long Island computer company. The two men were found shot to death in the company's New York office, on the fifteenth floor of 2 Penn Plaza (a modern office building adjoining the new Madison Square Garden) on the morning of June 11, 1976. At the time, Cortale, the firm's former president, was questioned by the police, then released. Not until fourteen months later was he charged with the crime.

Cortale is one of the fortunate few facing criminal charges who can afford to retain private counsel, and he's reached for the top—Richard H. Kuh, the former district attorney of New York County.

As an assistant district attorney and chief of the Criminal Courts Bureau under Frank Hogan, Kuh gained nationwide fame—or notoriety—from his obscenity prosecution of the comedian Lenny Bruce. Kuh made the case a moral crusade and pressed it with the fervor of a Savonarola. Although he won the trial, the conviction was reversed on appeal. Afterward Kuh left the D.A.'s office to write an apologia for his actions, *Foolish Figleaves?*, then entered private practice. In 1974 he was tabbed by interim Governor Malcolm Wilson to succeed the dying Hogan as interim district attorney. He was defeated in a special election that fall in his bid to serve the remainder of the term.

Although his brown hair is silvering, Kuh still looks a decade younger than his fifty-six years and he still has the handsome features of a movie star. Kuh does not intend to plea-bargain; he's pulling out all the stops in Cortale's defense.

The case is on for motions. But Judge Lang has to wait ten minutes until the court stenographer arrives. Then he nods to Kuh. Clutching a bulging briefcase, the lawyer leads Cortale to the defense table.

Assistant District Attorney James Ryan takes his place at the prosecution table next to the jury box. At thirty he is of medium height and rail thin. He has a bristly brown mustache, shaggy brown hair, and an acned face. Like the judge, he wears round tortoiseshell glasses. He's been an assistant district attorney for four years and has tried perhaps a dozen cases. Cortale's will be his first murder trial.

"Quiet!" shouts a court officer.

"Your Honor," Ryan says, "may I make a statement for the record?"

In accordance with Lang's directive of December 16, Ryan says, he delivered various documents to the court, but the grand-jury minutes have not yet been fully transcribed. Over the Christmas holidays he was unable to contact the stenographer and has subpoenaed her for today's hearing.

"Second call," Lang orders, deferring the hearing until the rest of his calendar has been called.

"I don't understand the second call," Kuh protests. "Section 325 of the Judiciary Law makes it quite clear that the stenographer's duties are to the

District Attorney. . . . The prosecutor obviously has troubles and I am moved by the prosecutor's plight."

But, he continues, he moved back in August for inspection of the grand-jury minutes. This is a routine ploy in felony cases. The defense asks the judge to read the minutes and determine if there's sufficient evidence for an indictment. Once in a thousand cases it results in a dismissal. The prosecution, Kuh says, has not produced the full minutes, and now, by his action, Lang is assisting the prosecution.

"I respectfully ask you to grant the motion and dismiss the indictment."

"May I see those sections?" Lang asks.

Kuh hands a copy of the statute to a court officer, who passes it to the judge. Lang reads it, then hands it back.

"I don't understand the purpose of the second call," Kuh repeats.

"Mr. Ryan has subpoenaed the grand-jury stenographer to be here," Lang explains.

Cortale sits silently as Kuh argues: "I suggest that there's nothing in the grand-jury law that says Your Honor has a role in obtaining grand-jury minutes."

"First of all, Mr. Kuh, I disagree with your interpretation of the statute," Lang replies. "My view is . . . that I'm not aiding the prosecution. Rather, I'm aiding you and the court with respect to your motion to inspect the grand-jury minutes. . . . It is my order which is being thwarted by the court stenographer." Kuh stands with his hands in his pockets as Lang chews him out judiciously: "I think your remark is gratuitous and really uncalled for."

"This may seem overly technical, Your Honor," Kuh replies, still pressing the point. "The District Attorney's problems, I respectfully submit, are not the province of the court."

"I disagree with you, Mr. Kuh," Lang rules. "Your motion is denied."

Kuh takes up another motion, concerning an undercover tape recording of Cortale. Like "Rose Mary's Baby" in the Watergate trial, the tape was mysteriously erased. Kuh calls it "willful destruction of evidence" and asks that the case against Cortale be dismissed as a result.

Standing with his arms folded on the back of his chair, Lang replies with a lengthy exposition of recent decisions on missing evidence, including his own opinion in *People* v. *Aviles.*

Kuh is not impressed. "I suggest to Your Honor that what the Supreme Court has termed 'the imperative of judicial integrity' of the court is in danger."

Ryan protests that there's no evidence to show that the tape was "willfully destroyed." Besides, he says, it was "inaudible."

Lang suggests that it was also "inadmissible." But, he continues, "this does not indicate in any fashion that this court does anything but deplore the loss, destruction, or mislaying of any potential evidence in this case."

Ryan argues that the tape was made when the case was "only in the investigative stage."

Now it's the prosecutor's turn to be chewed out. "The target *was* Cortale," Lang says. "That's somewhat ingenuous, Mr. Ryan. . . . I do not in any way sanction this type of conduct. In fact, I deplore it."

Kuh demands a hearing on the issue. "There is reason to believe now that there has been police dishonesty," he shouts, punctuating his point with his forefinger.

"Are you pointing your finger at me?" Ryan asks.

"Yes, Mr. Ryan."

Lang tries to sum up the legal situation: "Let's assume that he did not make admissions."

"He had nothing to admit," Kuh says.

"Then the tape is not admissible," Lang says.

Kuh argues again that there was "willful destruction of evidence." Ryan again asserts that there's no such testimony.

"Why are both of you repeating remarks you made last time?" Lang asks impatiently.

Kuh again demands a hearing on the issue.

"Please, Mr. Kuh," Lang says. "Now may we have second call to wait for the stenographer?"

"How long?" Kuh asks.

"I'll be here all day," Lang says.

"I cannot be here all day, Your Honor," Kuh protests.

"If you don't want to stay here, you don't have to stay here."

"I waive in no fashion my presence at any proceeding in this case," Kuh says. "Counsel should not be punished like a schoolboy—'You sit all day and wait.' "

"I'm going to adjourn for one week," Lang says. "January tenth."

For the record Kuh objects to the adjournment, but says the date is "personally convenient."

There's desultory discussion of the timetable in the case, tentatively scheduled to go to trial on the first Monday of the February Term, when Kuh notices the court reporter still punching his stenotype machine.

"I assume all this is off the record," he comments.

"I want it *on* the record," Lang insists.

This time it's the stenographer's turn to protest: "I'm running out of paper."

"January tenth," Lang rules.

"Is the defendant needed on that date, Your Honor?" Kuh asks. "He's trying to make a living."

Ryan objects. Lang agrees, and Cortale is not excused.

On that note, after more than an hour, the hearing is adjourned. The Cortale case has progressed no further from its status on December 16.

Wednesday, January 4

District Attorney Robert M. Morgenthau has called a press conference. The reporters file into his eighth-floor conference room. Morgenthau, in shirtsleeves, sits at the conference table at the far end of the room sipping coffee from a cup embossed with the Big Apple emblem of New York City. He's a scholarly-looking man of fifty-eight with a hawk nose and sandy hair turning to gray. He wears tortoiseshell glasses and can usually be seen sucking on the stub of an unlit cigar. He stands six feet, but his slim build and thin face make him appear even taller.

Beside Morgenthau sit two assistants—Roger Hayes, the bearded chief of the Frauds Bureau, and John Rieck, Hayes's second-in-command.

Three reporters take seats opposite the prosecutors—Mike Pearl of the *New York Post,* the pint-sized, forty-eight-year-old dean of the building's press corps; John Mulligan of the Associated Press; and Denny Sanders, filling in for the vacationing Bob Crane of the *Daily News.* The reporters for the *Times* and United Press International have not yet arrived, and Morgenthau's announcement is not deemed weighty enough to warrant radio or television coverage.

"We've got two releases," says Mary DeBourbon, Morgenthau's attractive press secretary, as she passes out copies of the indictments and accompanying summaries. Her releases read like society-page notices: "Manhattan District Attorney Robert M. Morgenthau announced today the indictment of . . ."

The first release announces the arrest and indictment of two men on charges of trying to shake down Sotheby Parke Bernet, the art auctioneers, for $100,000. One of the men, James Toohill, was a "confidential informant" for the D.A.'s office who lodged an unfounded allegation against Sotheby Parke Bernet. Toohill and Robert Manfredi—according to the indictment—then informed the art dealer that it was under investigation and offered to sell it inside information about the inquiry for $100,000.

According to the release:

> On November 17 Manfredi telephoned Mr. Marion to make arrangements for the sale of the information. Manfredi told Mr. Marion to place $100,000 in a briefcase and give it to a courier. The courier was to meet a courier for the defendants who would be carrying a briefcase containing the information. They were to meet and exchange briefcases on November 17, 1977, in front of a midtown restaurant. When the exchange took place that day, the briefcase carried by the defendants' courier contained only a copy of the New York Post.

Pearl looks up from his papers. "On page two it says, 'contained only a copy of the New York Post.' Can't we change that to *'Daily News'*?"

"Do we have ages on these guys yet?" Sanders asks.

"Manfredi is thirty-two," Rieck replies. "We're trying to get the other."

"How long has Parke Bernet been under investigation and what are they under investigation for?" Pearl asks.

"Parke Bernet is *not* under investigation," Hayes says.

"Then why would they go along and pay them the money?"

"They didn't," Morgenthau explains. "They called us."

Mulligan asks, "What does Manfredi do?"

"Manfredi is the president of the Westchester News Association, which publishes eight newspapers in Westchester," Hayes replies.

"Weekly papers?"

"Shoppers." Hayes lists them.

Morgenthau looks across the table to Pearl with a twinkle in his eye. "They were going to take the profits from this to start an afternoon newspaper in Manhattan."

"Toohill works for the county of Westchester in parks and recreation, in their arts section," Hayes adds.

Morgenthau absentmindedly picks at his ear with the earpiece of his glasses.

"Why only 'attempted grand larceny'?" Pearl asks.

"Because they didn't get the money," Rieck explains. He says the briefcase carried by the Sotheby Parke Bernet courier contained not the promised $100,000, but only $2,000 wrapped around stage money.

"I think a copy of the *New York Post* is worth a hundred thousand dollars," Pearl quips.

"Are you going to ask for bail?" Mulligan asks.

"We're going to ask for bail on one of them—Toohill," Rieck replies.

"How much?"

"Something."

"This Toohill—is he an actual informant?"

"He had given information to this office in the past," Morgenthau says.

"Was he paid for that?"

"Yes," Hayes says.

"He was a paid informant?"

"A part-time informant."

Morgenthau puts it in newspaper terminology: "A stringer."

"Was the courier one of your informants?"

"I guess that gets into evidence," Morgenthau says, "but the answer is yes."

"What happened to him?"

"He was arrested."

Pearl asks his name. Morgenthau won't say.

"Isn't it a matter of public record if he's under arrest?"

"Yes, but you won't be able to find it."

Pearl quotes from an imaginary news story: " 'Mr. Morgenthau defied the *Post* to find it.' "

"It's a continuing investigation," Morgenthau explains.

Pearl switches the subject. "It says 'midtown restaurant.' Can't we be more specific?"

"Yes," Rieck replies. "It was the Furyus Restaurant—*F-U-R-Y-U-S*—Second Avenue and Fifty-fifth."

"So Parke Bernet can breathe easier?" Pearl asks.

"Yes," Morgenthau says.

"Is it Parke Ber-*net* or Parke Ber-*nay?"*

"That depends on whether you're from the East Bronx or the West Bronx," Hayes retorts.

Morgenthau turns briefly to the second indictment—of John Timoney for commercial bribery. He allegedly paid $2,000 to a claims examiner to get an inflated settlement in a medical malpractice case.

"The insurance industry has been after the guy for years," Hayes says.

Morgenthau quickly cautions, "That shouldn't be a direct quote."

Pearl, his second-edition deadline approaching, casts a nervous glance at the clock. "I gotta get to the phone. Thank you."

With that the press conference ends.

After the reporters and aides leave, Morgenthau returns to the dreary chore of signing his name on every one of a stack of diploma-sized certificates. With his new term starting, all 229 assistant district attorneys must be formally reappointed, and Morgenthau must sign every certificate.

Since the death of Frank Hogan in 1974, Robert Morris Morgenthau—as much as any man—has come to personify the professional prosecutor. The son of the late Henry Morgenthau, Jr., Secretary of the Treasury under FDR, he grew up in affluence and attended Deerfield Academy, Amherst, and Yale Law School. In 1961, President Kennedy plucked him from a Wall Street law firm to be United States Attorney for the Southern District of New York, perhaps the most prestigious prosecutorial post in the federal government.

Although he was an active politician—who ran unsuccessfully for governor against Nelson Rockefeller in 1962—Morgenthau managed a patronage-free office that aggressively attacked organized crime, political corruption, and commercial chicanery. A House Republican task force on crime even urged that he be retained by the Nixon administration. Morgenthau wanted to stay on, saying he had a number of important matters to complete, including the bribery trial of Carmine DeSapio, the former Tammany chieftain, and a tax-dodge investigation into the funneling of funds from Wall Street to Swiss banks. But politics prevailed, and in December 1969 John Mitchell forced him from office.

Morgenthau served briefly as New York's deputy mayor, then in 1974 challenged Richard Kuh in the special election for district attorney. Morgenthau trounced Kuh 86,398 to 28,643 in the Democratic primary and went on to win the general election with 223,084 votes to Kuh's 54,204 and 10,605 for Andrew McCauley, the Conservative candidate.

In 1977 he received multiparty endorsement for a full four-year term and romped to victory with 205,337 votes to 8,750 for David Caplan, his Conservative challenger. A widower with five grown children, Morgenthau was remarried two weeks after his reelection to Lucinda Franks, an author and former *New York Times* reporter.

Morgenthau maintained the Hogan pattern of a nonpartisan prosecutor's office, with assistants recruited from law schools, not political clubhouses. But his style is different. Hogan was an imperial boss, isolated and aloof, dealing with low-level assistants only through the bureau chiefs. He never called on aides; he summoned them to his office. And they always donned their jackets for the occasion. He was "Mr. Hogan" or "Chief." Said one long-term associate, "The only people I ever heard call him 'Frank' were his wife and Tom Dewey."

By contrast, Morgenthau is casual, "Bob" to his boys, and both he and they work in shirtsleeves. He wanders freely through the building, dropping in to chat with assistants in both courtrooms and offices. But where Hogan, for all his public image of a Calvinist crusader, could be a garrulous raconteur, Morgenthau, for all his informality, in public appearances becomes stiff and tongue-tied.

Morgenthau also completely revamped the structure of the office. Under Hogan the office was organized horizontally, with new assistants starting in the Complaint Bureau, listening to witnesses and preparing the simplest of legal forms, and working their way up first to the Indictment Bureau, presenting cases to a grand jury, then to Criminal Court, trying misdemeanors and violations, and finally to the Supreme Court or one of the specialized bureaus —Appeals, Frauds, Homicide, or Rackets.

It was an excellent structure for training assistants who would become career prosecutors—or close to it—but for complaining witnesses it meant dealing with a different assistant at each level and repeated court appearances. For the system it often meant unconscionable delays in bringing a case to trial and building up a backlog of pending cases that was all but unmanageable. And with the high turnover of assistants during the transition from Hogan to Kuh to Morgenthau the training program broke down.

Morgenthau switched to a vertical system, merging Indictment, Criminal Court, and Supreme Court into six trial bureaus. Under the new system one assistant—in theory—follows a case from the initial complaint to the final disposition. Ironically, in the revamping, Homicide, the one truly vertical bureau, also disappeared.

According to Morgenthau, the switch significantly reduced the backlog of pending cases, cut the median time from indictment to final disposition from 44 weeks to 14½, and increased the conviction rate to 85.5 percent. He boasts that now not only are more defendants sent to state prison than in any other county—1,044 in 1974; 1,135 in 1975; 1,340 in 1976; and 1,664 in 1977—but a higher percentage.

The new system, he claims, also cut the C.C.I. rate (Criminal Court indictment, or, alternatively, "cop comes in")—the number of times a case is on the Criminal Court and grand-jury calendars before an indictment is returned. Seventy percent of the felony cases now go directly to a grand jury without a hearing in the Criminal Court—against 10 to 15 percent in the past. The percentage of cases sent back to Criminal Court has been cut from 10 to less than 1. And the percentage of dismissals after indictment has been cut from 20 to 13, while the conviction rate after trial has risen from 65 to 70 percent.

Dealing with the case load is Morgenthau's first priority. Second is money. Of the office's $12 million budget, only $7.7 million comes from city appropriations. About $2.9 million comes from federal grants, and another $1.4 million from the state. Each grant means drafting a specific proposal and lobbying it through the bureaucratic bottlenecks of Albany and Washington —a chore Morgenthau must often handle personally.

The third priority is staff. Aides screen applicants, but Morgenthau conducts the final interviews and decides on hiring. Although there are still more applicants than openings, many observers feel the quality of assistants has slipped sadly since the glory days under Frank Hogan. The office cannot compete on salary scales with private firms or even other government agencies, which steadily siphon off the D.A.'s most experienced men. In the past many young lawyers were willing to make the financial sacrifice because the D.A.'s office was a training ground that qualified them for top-level positions elsewhere. But now so few cases come to trial that assistants no longer get this experience—and Wall Street law firms seek seasoned litigators, not plea bargainers. Also, Morgenthau still holds to the standards he set as U.S. Attorney, seeking the brightest graduates of Ivy League law schools—men who may have been fine for federal office, prosecuting white-collar crimes, but many of whom lack the "street-smarts" needed to deal with the muggers and murderers who are the bread-and-butter business of the District Attorney.

Needless to say, Morgenthau is essentially an administrator—of a 229-man (56 of them women) law office. Only when there are special problems, such as a jurisdictional dispute with another prosecutor's office, does he interfere with assistants' conduct of cases. Only once in three years has he argued in court—to oppose bail in a rape case—and then only because no assistant was available. As he puts it, "You can't try cases and run an office of this size."

Back in the press room off the main-floor lobby Mike Pearl grabs a phone and calls his city desk.

The press room—actually two adjoining rooms—is one of the few in the building that are not bursting at the seams. In past years it was a bustling place, a scene from *The Front Page,* base for a dozen reporters. In the back room the Baxter Street lawyers and bail bondsmen held a running card game, and tabloid photographers posed attractive women witnesses and defendants on the desks, skirts indiscreetly hiked above the knee—and some could be induced into even racier poses that could never make the papers.

Now the regular press contingent has dwindled to the reporters for the city's three remaining dailies. To the wire services the Criminal Courts Building is only a fragment of a larger beat, while radio and television newsmen come only to cover a major story. In the age of *Playboy* and *Hustler,* photographers no longer scramble for cheesecake. And in a burst of journalistic virtue five years back, the lawyers and bondsmen were banished to the lobby.

The misspelled sign on Pearl's desk is a capsule chronicle of New York's newspaper industry:

MIKE PEARL

NEW YORK POST

FORMELY OF

N.Y. MIRROR

JOURNAL-AMERICAN

WORLD JOURNAL TRIBUNE

On the wall behind his desk is a pastiche of headlines, photos of reporters, lawyers, and judges, and Frank Hogan's reelection poster, "You can't play politics with people's lives." On the wall opposite, a framed reward poster for Joseph Force Crater, the Supreme Court justice who mysteriously disappeared in 1930.

Cradling the phone on his shoulder, Pearl sits on the edge of his desk, cluttered with the out-of-date docket sheets he uses for notepaper, and dictates against his deadline:

"Manhattan District Attorney Robert Morgenthau announced today the indictment of James Toohill—that's *T*-for-Thomas, double *O, H, I,* double

L—thirty-five, of Scarsdale. He works for the Department of Parks in Westchester in their arts section."

In the back room a TV camera crew putters with its equipment while Bob Teague of WNBC-TV News mumbles to himself, rehearsing his "stand-up" on the arrest of two men charged with stealing a taxicab and then robbing the passengers they picked up. Preparations complete, they go outside to film the segment against the backdrop of the building.

Mulligan grabs his coat and dashes off to Police Headquarters to cover the swearing in of a new deputy commissioner. Late arrivals Leslie Maitland of the *Times* and Arthur Bernhardt, a stringer for UPI, Reuters, and several suburban newspapers, leave for Mary DeBourbon's office to catch up on the day's doings. Sanders, his deadline hours away, returns to his office to write the story. Pearl, alone in the press room, continues his recitation: "As an inducement, Morgenthau said, Manfredi made several false statements, among them that the investigation was being conducted by the Manhattan D.A.'s office and focused on managerial employees and that presentation of evidence to a grand jury was imminent."

Thursday, January 5

Peter English, a young, mustached Criminal Court officer, stands in the circular information desk. Situated at the junction point of the T-shaped lobby, the desk is a magnet—the only place to lean against, the only place to sit. It attracts the flotsam of the courthouse: defense lawyers schmoozing until their cases are called; cops on overtime swigging coffee from styrofoam cups and catching up on the *Daily News*; people waiting for friends and relatives who've been locked up, invariably including a black or Puerto Rican mother diapering her baby; above all, strangers to the building who need guidance through the legal labyrinths.

"Part Thirty-two?"

"Eleventh floor," English says, erroneously.

"Where the elevators?"

English points to the twin banks off the north and south ends of the lobby.

A woman called for jury duty asks, "Where can you get a paper around here?"

"Next building over," English says, pointing toward the Alfred E. Smith State Office Building across Leonard Street. The Criminal Courts Building's newsstand has been closed since November, when John Murken, the blind proprietor, died.

A woman with a Spanish accent asks, "Room AP1—where is it?"

"Fourth floor, center of the building."

Two black men approach the desk.

"Can I help you?" English asks.

"Yeah," one replies. "We're looking for someone who has a case here. We don't know where he's at."

"When was he arrested?"

"Two weeks ago."

"Go down to Room One-fifty and ask there."

Another voice asks, "AR2?"

"Down the hall, to your right."

A heavyset man in work clothes approaches. "Where can I find my son? He was arrested last night."

"How old is he? Over eighteen?"

"Yes."

"Down the hall. AR1."

A well-dressed young man: "Excuse me. Can you tell me where to go to file a summons?"

"Across the street. Small Claims Court. One-eleven Centre Street."

Someone shouts, "AP5?"

"Fourth floor."

A bearded lawyer asks where Judge Edwards is sitting.

"That's Supreme Court?" English asks, baffled for the first time. He opens a drawer and picks up a phone. A few seconds later he tells the lawyer, "Part Thirty-three on the fifteenth floor."

A heavyset black asks for Legal Aid.

"Eighty Lafayette Street. Out that door and over a block," English says, pointing.

At 10:15 A.M., Judge Benjamin Altman ambles past the information desk. He's a slightly built man with the look of a friendly chipmunk. He likes to boast that playing the violin is the only thing he does well—he merely makes his living at the law. He studied at the Curtis Institute and worked his way through law school by playing with the Philadelphia Orchestra. He served three terms in the state Assembly before being named the city's rent and housing commissioner in 1970. Two years later he became a Criminal Court judge, resigned to become chairman of the city's Criminal Justice Coordinating Council, then returned to the bench. He's now an acting Supreme Court justice and supervising judge of the Manhattan Criminal Courts.

He's starting his daily rounds—and running forty-five minutes late because of a "rocket" from City Hall. On Christmas Day, Mayor-elect Edward I. Koch dined with inmates at Rikers Island, the city prison. One of them told Koch that he'd been locked up for two months without a hearing. City Hall demanded to know why. Altman spent his first hour at work checking and found out that Koch had been conned by a con. There were two "holds" on the prisoner from other jurisdictions in robbery cases, and the prisoner himself kept postponing his hearing so he wouldn't be transferred to face more serious charges.

Altman walks to his courtroom, Part AR2, at the base of the T-shaped lobby. Only a handful of people are in the arraignment part.

"Are we ready?" Altman asks Court Officer Dan Bonanno.

"Yes."

"Legal Aid here?"

"Yes."

"I don't see any lawyers."

"They're in the back"—the bullpen.

"How many do we have?"

"Five. Some have more than one defendant."

At the early-morning hour only a few cases have been processed. There's usually a delay of four to six hours between arrival and arraignment because no prisoner can be processed without a "rap sheet" listing arrests and convictions. It used to be called a "yellow sheet"—from the paper it was printed on—typed out by clerical cops at the Police Department's Bureau of Criminal Identification. As part of building his crime-fighter image, Governor Nelson Rockefeller centralized the process, computerized it, and imposed it statewide—and it's led to interminable delays. The computer in Albany is electronic, but the joke around the courthouse is that there is no computer—only two trucks that meet halfway up the New York State Thruway and swap fingerprint cards for rap sheets.

"I'll tell you what," Altman tells Bonanno. "Let me make the rounds first."

He leaves the courtroom and walks briskly through the lobby. In his hand he carries a mimeographed form on which some of the day's statistics have been penciled:

	AP1	*AP7*	*AP3*	*AP5*	*AP9*	*AP17*
Open	40	30	46	41	68	33
Sentence	5	12	11	13	10	14
Fines	16	42	28	12	5	26
Jail	15	10	23	11	21	—

It's not an exceptionally heavy schedule—Altman has learned not to worry until the case load in a courtroom hits two hundred—but it's lopsided, and one judge is out ill. To Altman the bottom line is . . . the bottom line.

He trots up the north stairway to the second floor, turns left, and enters the corridor alongside Part AP17—for "all-purpose." A woman assistant district attorney greets him: "Hi! I wanted to talk to you."

"That case bothered me," Altman tells her. "I wanted to tell you why."

But he has no time now. He enters the courtroom of Judge Milton Samorodin and approaches the bench. The judge interrupts the proceedings to speak with him.

Altman tells Samorodin about another case that bothers him—an assault involving two neighbors on Roosevelt Island, the state's new middle-income housing development in the East River. Altman wanted to A.C.D. the case, but the complainant refused to drop the charges. So he found the defendant guilty, then suspended sentence.

"These people have to go back and live with each other," he explains. "Our job doesn't start in the courtroom and end in the courtroom. We have a duty to the community."

He turns to the court clerk. "How many jail cases do we have?"

"Seven. Five men and two women."

"We're in good shape," Altman tells Samorodin.

The Criminal Court's all-purpose parts are built in complexes of three: a main courtroom for the calendar call and two makeshift courtrooms converted from judges' robing rooms or witnesses' waiting rooms to handle the overflow of hearings and trials.

Altman peeks into the robing room, but it has yet to receive a case.

He walks down the hall—alongside the metal grille installed after a despondent defendant made a suicide leap from the second-floor balcony to the lobby—and enters Part AP9. Court is in recess and Judge Edwin Torres is taking a break in the robing room. He's a dark-complexioned man with close-cropped hair, dark, deep-set eyes, and an intense expression. He was the first Puerto Rican assistant in Hogan's office, but he's better known for writing two well-received novels about crime and justice, *Carlito's Way* and *Q. & A.*

"You have twenty-one jail cases," Altman says. "You might need some help."

"The problem is the prisoners aren't here yet," Torres replies.

In past years prisoners were brought from the Tombs and were in court by 10:00 A.M. Now they have to be bused from Rikers Island—in the East River opposite LaGuardia Airport—and rarely arrive before noon. And they must be processed by 4:00 P.M. so they can be brought back to prison in time for supper.

More important, under state law prisoners must be granted hearings within seventy-two hours of arrest or be paroled. If judges can't get jail cases heard in time, they may be forced to free dangerous criminals.

Altman leaves the courtroom, continues down the hall, and with a key signals for the judges' elevator. He rides the tiny cage to the fourth floor and walks down the hall to the courtroom of Judge Geraldine Eiber.

"I have mice in my chambers," she tells Altman. "The court officers refuse to catch any more. They said it wasn't in their contract."

Altman chuckles. Catching mice isn't his responsibility either. "How you doing?" he asks.

"Fine."

"Ed Torres may be in trouble by the end of the day," he says, advising her to be ready to handle any overflow.

Then he crosses the hall to the courtroom of Judge Morris Schwalb, who interrupts a hearing to fill in the supervising judge. "We've got three hearings, two sent down. Luckily it broke early today."

"After lunch, check," Altman tells him. "Betty and Torres seem to have the heavy jail cases."

They discuss the problems of scheduling the heavy court calendars. Altman suggests that they might be able to move more expeditiously if they set up separate calendars for jail cases in the morning and afternoon.

"They tried it years ago," Schwalb says. "It didn't work."

Altman leaves and continues down the hall to the courtroom of Betty Ellerin, a Civil Court judge sitting by designation in the Criminal Court. He likes to joke that he keeps her chained to the bench so she can't return to the Civil Courts Building across the street.

"You might be in some trouble later on. You have twenty-five jail cases," he advises her, exaggerating slightly.

"We're moving right along," she assures him.

But before he leaves, Altman cautions the court officer, "You might be in some difficulty here. You have twenty-five jail cases."

Leaving through the main aisle, he crosses the hall to the courtroom of Judge John Leone, brother of a former Brooklyn borough president, who is presiding without a robe. Leone interrupts a hearing while Altman checks his calendar.

"I don't think you're in any great trouble today, but Betty might be."

"We have approximately ten jail cases, none of which have been produced yet. So about twelve o'clock—" Leone says, shrugging. "But if Betty needs any help, shoot 'em in."

His rounds—for the moment—completed, Altman returns via public elevator to the first floor and walks to his courtroom. Bonanno helps him out of his suit jacket and into his robe. Then Altman mounts the low bench.

"Come to order, please!" Bonanno calls. "Remain seated! AR2 is in session. The Honorable Benjamin Altman presiding."

The first case is called, and four blacks are led from the detention pens to the bridge. It's a gun-in-a-car case. The police officer swears to his affidavit. The Legal Aid lawyer, Michael Gold, the bantam blond son of Brooklyn District Attorney Eugene Gold—yet to try his first case—waives a reading of the rights. Then he and the Assistant District Attorney confer with Altman at the bench.

"Your Honor, I don't think that a disposition can be arrived at," Gold says when the conference ends.

"What date, Officer?" Altman asks.

The policeman checks his schedule. "The week of the sixteenth?"

Altman checks his calendar. "Counsel, eighteenth?"

"Yes, Your Honor," Gold replies.

Altman enters the date. "January eighteen. AP5."

Gold asks that 18B lawyers be appointed for three of the defendants because there's "a potential conflict": One defendant may testify against the others.

Under Article 35, §18(b) of the county law, private lawyers are appointed to represent indigent defendants when Legal Aid cannot.

Altman tells Gold that the fees for 18B lawyers come out of Legal Aid's budget, notes the difficulty of getting four lawyers together at the same time, and urges him to reconsider his application.

But Gold presses it. Altman reluctantly grants it, though he observes, "I think it's outrageous in a case like this to have four lawyers."

"Harold Lewis!" Bonanno calls—and another black is brought before the bench.

Friday, January 6

All morning Robert Ferraro has been standing by the information desk waiting until his case is called. He's a handsome man in his forties with a "spare tire" that shows through the turtleneck sweater he wears to protect his infected throat against the winter cold. He was called during the night by the owner of a midtown massage parlor to represent one of his girls who was busted for prostitution.

For two hours he's been passing the time gossiping with other lawyers. As noon approaches, he talks with the arresting officer in his case, Alan Grossman of the Public Morals Squad. Naturally, the subject is prostitution.

Grossman is ruddy faced and red haired. He wears a leather jacket, woolen sweater, and faded denim slacks. He doesn't look like a cop—an asset on his assignment. He's completed the paperwork, the prints have been processed, but the file has yet to be sent to the courtroom. In past years the arresting officer carried the file to the courtroom, but in a jurisdictional dispute the court personnel claimed—and won—the right.

Suddenly, Ferraro breaks away from Grossman's discussion of call-girl operations and grabs a passerby—Albert Feureisen, deputy chief clerk of the Criminal Court.

"Al," he implores, "Karen Fuchs—the case is being docketed now. Go in there and get the papers so we can get out of here."

"Pros case?" the roly-poly clerk asks.

"Yes."

"Where's the gal?"

"She's in."

Feureisen agrees to bring the papers to the courtroom, and Ferraro explains to Grossman, "You have to have a friend in court just to get your case called."

A few minutes later Feureisen returns carrying a stack of legal papers.

"You got it?" Ferraro asks eagerly.

"It's here."

Like a football player who's scored a winning touchdown, Ferraro raises his arms and lets out a yell of triumph. "Maybe we can get out of here by one o'clock."

Grossman leaves to fetch the defendant from the holding pen on the third floor while Ferraro walks upstairs to Part AR2A, where most prostitution cases are heard. In the hall outside, beside a water fountain filled with paper cups and cigarette butts, strut the pimps. They seem stamped from the same cookie cutter—rail-thin blacks wearing porkpie hats and garish suits. None enters the courtroom. Prostitutes with known pimps are not eligible for Legal Aid.

Ferraro enters the courtroom and takes a seat in the first row—reserved for attorneys and policemen. A court officer, alerted by Feureisen, asks him, "Is he here yet?"

"No."

"When he comes, let me know, right?"

It's the customary courtesy. The cases of private counsel usually receive priority over those of the salaried Legal Aid lawyers.

Ferraro dons metal-rimmed glasses to read the complaint and the computerized rap sheet.

"What the hell did she do?" he mutters to himself.

The complaint reads:

> Deponent states that he heard defendant offer and agree to engage in sexual conduct with deponent in return for a fee, to wit: $100.00 for a lay and a blow job, or a greek.

Ferraro notes with satisfaction that it's his twenty-four-year-old client's first arrest.

Six girls—two white, four black—sit on the prisoners' bench along the wall. All are young, none especially attractive. Then Grossman leads in a girl from the bullpen and seats her on the bench. She's a thin, frizzy blond without makeup. She wears a white lamb's-wool jacket, gray sweater, and blue jeans.

Ferraro steps into the well to meet his client for the first time. They have no time to chat, for the case is called immediately. Ferraro, Grossman, and the girl step to the bridge, taking places alongside the Assistant District Attorney.

"Officer Grossman, swear to the affidavit you signed?" the bridgeman asks.

Grossman raises his hand. "Yes."

"Waive reading?"

"Yes," Ferraro replies.

"State your name for the record."

"Bob Ferraro," he tells the stenographer. "Two hundred West Fifty-fourth Street."

The lawyers confer with Judge Leon Becker at the bench. When the conference ends, Ferraro moves to A.C.D. the case.

"State the grounds," Judge Becker says.

"On grounds she has no prior record."

Becker enters the judgment, admonishing Karen Fuchs to "stay out of the business," the Criminal Court equivalent of "Go and sin no more." Usually prostitutes are fined—$50, $100, $200. The only way they can raise the money to pay the fine is by returning to the streets, making the court "the biggest pimp in town."

Ferraro leaves the courtroom with his client. Once in the hall, he raises his arms and lets out a shout of triumph—not over his legal victory, but because "We made it by one o'clock!"

Monday, January 9

In his office deep in the bowels of the building Avon Gresham fields the flak.

To Gresham the Criminal Courts Building is like Forty-second Street. It attracts the scum of the city and it must be properly policed or it will become a slum. But Gresham, the building's custodian, doesn't have the staff to do it.

When the building was opened in 1941, the service staff numbered two hundred, including about forty elevator operators. The elevators are now self-service, but Gresham's authorized staff is down to eighty-one. With emergency layoffs, attrition, and a city hiring freeze, the actual number is fifty.

In the past year the cleaning load per employee was increased from 10,000 square feet a day to 15,000. Since there are roughly 50,000 square feet on each of the seventeen floors, Gresham needs every man merely to keep up with sweeping the floors and dusting the desks, to say nothing of replacing burned-out bulbs, emptying garbage, and fighting roaches and rodents, and on top of it all coping with vacations and sick leave.

The building has only one maintenance man, and most of his time is spent on emergencies. The Baxter Street entrance has been closed for months because the door is broken. None of the building's thirty-two water fountains has functioned for three years.

The city's fiscal crisis forced the Department of General Services to eliminate night work and thus save paying the 10 percent night differential. That means daytime cleaning, with many of the building's employees reporting to work in uncleaned offices. And it means garbage left overnight to attract vermin.

The double-decked basement, uncomfortably warm because of the heating plant, is a subterranean warren of catwalks and pipes, of stacks of court records awaiting storage space, of rubbish awaiting removal, of salt bags in readiness for the next storm. But Gresham's office, with ceramic tile walls and linoleum floor, is neat and spotless. Gresham cleans it himself.

Gresham is a light-skinned black with wispy brown hair and a shaggy mustache. He's dressed completely in green: dark green suit, light green shirt, Kelly green tie. He puffs an unlit pipe.

The day's problems are routine—burned-out bulbs, uncleaned offices, a fuse blown because electric typewriters overloaded the antiquated circuit, and leaks.

The maintenance man pokes his head through the door. "The water's still leaking down there."

"What's leaking?" Gresham asks.

"The toilet bowl."

"Bad?"

"Not too bad."

"What floor?" asks Gresham's deputy, Pablo Torres, a short, dark man with a black mustache and a fringe of beard.

"First floor."

"Well, wipe it up and I'll check on it later," Gresham says.

The maintenance man leaves as Gresham answers the phone. It's started to snow, and that means salting the steps and sidewalks.

In the aerie of the building, Edgar L. Ross presides over another spotless room—the seventeenth-floor law library in the central tower of the courthouse. Ross is a tall, kinky-haired black who served as law secretary to several judges before assuming his present post in 1973. Most of the ninety thousand volumes in his domain are law reports, compilations of the decisions handed down by various courts. Except for current cases, the courthouse files—the clerks' domain—are stored in the city archive in Brooklyn.

But Ross's predecessors salvaged some of the more memorable files for exhibit in the library's glass display cases. There's the docket book with the first case ever brought in New York's Court of General Sessions: November 1, 1683, against Henry Thomassen, a Long Island planter accused of burglary. He was convicted, and the sentence was that he "be branded on the forehead with the letter B and be whipped on the bare back 11 strykes."

There's the docket book of a century later. The last entry on the left-hand page reads:

> May 1776
The King
v.
Hercules Herring — Court adjourned to the first Tuesday in August next

The right-hand page is dated May 4, 1784, and reads:

Minutes
of the Court of General Sessions of the Peace held in and for the City and County of New York since the Independence of The United States of America . . .

There's the report of the coroner's inquest into the death of Alexander Hamilton and the docket book of August 7, 1804:

The People &c v. Aaron Burr	Indictment for fighting a Duel
The People &c v. William P. Van Ness	Indictment for being the bearer of a Challenge
The People &c v. Nathaniel Pendleton	Indictment for being a Second in a Duel

No dispositions are recorded.

There are the programs for the cornerstone laying on June 28, 1940, and the dedication on June 30, 1941. And finally the transcript of the ceremony of August 31, 1962—the last day of the Court of General Sessions. On September 1 the oldest court in the United States was merged with the Supreme Court of the State of New York.

Tuesday, January 10

The Cortale case is on again. The defendant, stout and stolid, sits at the defense table while the attorneys stand before the bench.

Judge Lang rules on pending motions, denying the defense move to dismiss, but granting it certain exhibits and ordering a pre-trial hearing on eyewitness identification. Accordingly, Ryan hands Kuh two tape cassettes.

Kuh notes that the recordings are "copies."

Lang asks if he's objecting to that.

"I just want the record to show that I haven't absconded with the original recordings," Kuh explains.

"Can we agree on a trial date?" Lang asks.

"We can get to that," Kuh says. He still wants a hearing on the "willful destruction of evidence." He accuses the court of indulging in a "rush to judgment."

Lang cuts him off, noting that he read more than seven hundred pages of grand-jury minutes and "the entire D.D. [Detective Division] file." "This matter has been before me for months," he continues. "I can hardly accept your characterization of 'rush to judgment.' "

Kuh admits that he indulged in "dramaturgy" and apologizes.

Lang says it's "fruitless" to reiterate what happened at the January 3 hearing.

"I gather Your Honor is prejudging," Kuh says.

"As to what?"

"As to Your Honor's assisting the prosecution in getting the grand-jury minutes."

Ryan interjects, "The People feel that Your Honor's ruling is correct."

Kuh again asks for a hearing.

"Your Honor, I object to this," Ryan says. "I have made a full record."

Lang agrees.

Kuh calls it "another example of Your Honor's eagerness to see this case tried."

"Can we agree on a trial date?" Lang asks impatiently.

"We may try to agree," Kuh says.

"The People are ready for trial at the earliest possible date," Ryan says.

Kuh says he also seeks an early trial, but there's a problem—he's slated to try a case in Brooklyn's federal court. Then he suddenly switches and asks that the defense be allowed to see the grand-jury minutes.

"I object to that," Ryan says.

"At the least, I ask that we be given Mrs. Robbins's grand-jury minutes."

"I particularly object to that."

Lang tries to sum up the legal situation: Mrs. Robbins's voice was on the tape that was destroyed; therefore, the defense should be allowed to read her testimony. "Is that your point, Mr. Kuh?"

"My point is—"

Lang cuts him off. "Why do I have to get a speech every time I ask a simple question?"

Kuh says that was his point.

Lang says he'll consider it.

Ryan says, "I object to that."

"I understand," Lang replies. "Your objection is overruled. I am going to direct that you turn over the testimony of Mrs. Robbins."

Ryan objects. Kuh starts to speak.

"Why don't you quit while you're ahead, Mr. Kuh?" Lang suggests.

He orders Ryan to turn over the testimony two weeks before trial.

"Why can't we have it now?" Kuh asks.

"When you're right, you're right," Lang says. "Turn it over now."

"Can we have a recess?" Ryan asks.

"You're gonna go to the Appellate Division?" Lang asks.

"We're going to consider it."

Lang grants a recess until 11:00 A.M. Ryan rushes from the courtroom to confer with his bureau chief. Kuh and Cortale take seats on a back bench to study the documents Ryan turned over to them. Lang continues with his calendar call.

In the hall outside, Supreme Court Officer Herb Schwartz mans the metal detector at the south elevator bank.

Since 1970, after Judge Harold J. Haley was taken hostage and killed by Black Panthers in San Rafael, California, persons entering the eleventh and thirteenth floors—where most of the Supreme Court parts are situated—are screened by metal detectors. Men must empty their pockets and women hand over their purses for inspection before they step through the doorway-sized detectors, which emit a high-pitched "beep" if there's metal. The beeps are frequent, since even a belt buckle can trigger the apparatus. If metal is detected, the subject is frisked or screened with a hand-held detector. In thousands of searches Schwartz has found one weapon—a tear-gas gun.

The 10:00 A.M. rush has passed. Schwartz, a squat man with curly gray hair and thick horn-rimmed glasses, won't be busy again until after lunch. While a colleague frisks a Hispanic man, Schwartz examines a black woman's purse as she steps through the detector.

A well-dressed man, bearded and carrying a briefcase, approaches.

"Counsel?" Schwartz asks.

The man nods yes, and Schwartz motions him around the detector. Attorneys and court personnel are exempt from search.

A court officer rushes from the north elevator bank and shines a flashlight into the wastebasket.

"I want to check your grating," he explains to Schwartz—many visitors hide contraband under the radiator grilles before they pass through the detectors. "Somebody on the other side apparently came through with a 'lighter gun' [a single-shot gun disguised as a cigarette lighter]. We found two twenty-two shells in a basket."

In Schwartz's wastebasket he finds nothing—except garbage.

Schwartz walks with the officer to the north elevator bank, then returns to tell his colleague, "Go to lunch."

It's 10:51 A.M.

The officer departs, saying, "Herbie, yell for help if you need me."

The clock reads 11:15 when Ryan returns to Judge Lang's courtroom. Like most of the courthouse clocks, it's ten minutes fast. The Cortale case is immediately recalled and the lawyers resume their places.

"Have you decided to go to the Appellate Division or not?" Lang asks Ryan.

"Your Honor, may we be heard further on this?"

"Would you answer my question?"

"I believe that we have decided not to go."

Ryan argues that Mrs. Robbins is a "sensitive witness." "The court may not appreciate the importance of certain items of interest."

Lang says he's well aware of them and directs Ryan to turn over the testimony. "I want a firm trial date," he adds.

"We're eager to have an early trial," Kuh says.

"Good! I'll give you a trial next week." But Lang schedules another hearing for January 18. By then Kuh should know his schedule.

Ryan returns to the subject of Mrs. Robbins's testimony, saying Kuh "may not be aware of how damaging that witness is."

"I'm not going through this again," Lang snaps.

Kuh asks that the testimony be delivered to him "not later than twenty-four hours."

"I have a copy of it now," Ryan says, handing it to the defense attorney.

Kuh notes that one of the police reports he was given ends in midsentence. He asks if there's another page.

"Either there is another page or there isn't," Lang says. "If there is another page, you'll get it. If there isn't, you won't."

Kuh asks that he be given the police reports on the investigation of other suspects in the case.

"Anything else, Mr. Kuh?"

"Other points."

"Go on."

"Is Your Honor ruling on my motion?"

"My ruling stands."

Kuh argues that the grand jury that indicted Cortale was "not fair and impartial" because the "panel was a far cry from a cross section of Manhattan."

"Denied."

Kuh then asks for any criminal records or records of treatment for alcoholism or mental illness of any prosecution witness. Ryan says there are none.

"Next, Mr. Kuh?"

Kuh has nothing next.

"All right," Lang rules. "January eighteenth."

Wednesday, January 11

Coatless in the twenty-degree chill, Acting Supreme Court Justice Harold Rothwax arrives at the judges' entrance on Leonard Street. In good weather he bicycles to work from his apartment on Central Park West. At forty-seven he has straight black hair flecked with silver. His face still shows the scars of teen-age acne. He clutches the stub of an unlit cigar as he shouts a greeting to Irving Lang.

With a key he directs the judges' elevator to the fourth floor and walks to the chambers he shares with Judge Joel Tyler. Tyler is now sitting in the Bronx, so Rothwax has the room to himself.

He has one chore before he goes into the courtroom—phoning in the grades for a course in criminal justice that he teaches at Staten Island Community College. But he's left the number at home, directory assistance is busy, and his wife has already left home for the day.

So he walks to the third floor, picks up his mail, then takes the judges' elevator—sharing the tiny cage with another acting Supreme Court justice, Dennis Edwards, Jr.—to the eleventh floor. He walks down the dimly lit hall, filled with defendants and lawyers catching a last-minute smoke before the courts convene, and through a winding corridor to the robing room of Part 35. It's a bare room with a desk, three wooden chairs, and two metal file cabinets. On a metal table is an electric coffeepot.

A court officer informs Rothwax that the college called. Rothwax gets the number from him and phones in the grades. Then he doffs his jacket, dons his robe, and walks to the bench. It's 9:50 A.M. by the courtroom clock, but only a handful of people are in the courtroom.

Behind Rothwax is a mural—one of three presented by the artist, Edward Simmons, to the Court of General Sessions in 1896—of Justice, eyes open, draped in an American flag, holding the scales.

"There's gonna be a slight delay," Rothwax announces. "We don't have the calendar."

"Here's today's calendar," says a court officer, handing him the dittoed docket sheet. It lists thirty-three cases—an error, since one case is not numbered—and more may come in during the day.

Rothwax is one of the six calendar judges in the Criminal Term of Supreme Court, Manhattan—along with Lang, James Leff, George Roberts, Robert Haft, and E. Leo Milonas—men specially selected for their ability to move cases. They handle arraignments and motions and conduct much of the plea bargaining. When a case is ready for trial, they usually send it to another judge.

Five of the six—all but Leff—are *acting* Supreme Court justices. Because the justices are nominated at political conventions for political reasons, only a handful are considered competent to preside over criminal trials, even fewer of handling the rapid-fire head banging and plea bargaining essential to moving the case load in the calendar parts. So Criminal Court judges are elevated—supposedly temporarily—to fill the gap.

Ironically, the judges with the heaviest case loads and greatest work loads of legal research and writing are given the least staff support. Supreme Court justices receive the services of a personal secretary, a law secretary, and a law clerk. As an acting Supreme Court justice, Rothwax must make do with the help of one law assistant, whom he shares with Roberts and Lang. As a Criminal Court judge he makes $42,451, plus a $40 per diem up to a Supreme Court justice's $48,998 salary.

Rothwax, for many years a top trial attorney for Legal Aid, knows he'll never be nominated for the Supreme Court and sometimes gets bitter about it, because he considers himself as able as any judge on the bench. But he has no political clout and will not play the political game of going from clubhouse to clubhouse to solicit support or buy a nomination with a "contribution" to a party's campaign coffers.

Rothwax has made up index cards listing the history of every case on his calendar. He pulls out the cards for the day's docket and sorts them into separate piles for sentences, ready-for-trials, hearings, and P.P.I.s (pre-pleading investigations). He studies a memo from the District Attorney's office listing the four cases it wants to move to trial. To Rothwax's right is a pile of motion papers, to his left a stack of probation reports. He sifts through the probation file.

"Captain," he calls to the chief court officer, "can I give you a list of the pre-sentence reports I don't have? Are you gonna have a piece of paper available?"

The court officer comes to the bench and makes notes as Rothwax reads the names.

"Are they on for today?" he asks.

"Yes, they are," Rothwax snaps impatiently. "That's why I'm asking for them."

It's 10:00 A.M., but neither the Assistant District Attorney nor the Legal Aid lawyers have arrived.

"Now we wait," Rothwax says aloud.

Assistant District Attorney Katharine Law, a stocky woman in a blue knit dress, arrives clutching a stack of file folders.

"Counsel, do you have a case?" Rothwax asks a lawyer in the first row. "Can we have a clerk?"

Clerk Frank Lanotte calls the case of José Diaz.

Rothwax beckons the attorneys to the bench. "This is a fellow who was out on bail and got rearrested," he says. "What was he rearrested for?"

"Robbery," the defense lawyer says. He asks that bail be reinstated and then the defendant can be remanded on the new charge. That way, he explains, he can collect his fee from the remitted bail money.

"We'll see if the check was sent to the treasury," Rothwax says, instructing the clerk.

Katy Law submits a handwritten memo objecting to bail.

"How the hell did this fellow get out on bail in the first place?" Rothwax says, scanning the papers. "Robbery with a knife and shooting. No prior felonies." He asks for the D.A.'s recommendation.

" 'C,' Your Honor"—a Class C felony.

" 'C' is a low offer on this," Rothwax says. "It won't go lower."

"The complainant is a sympathetic old man," Katy Law says.

"Most complainants who are shot in the back are," Rothwax says. "I think it's gonna be a heavy sentence on this—three-and-a-half to ten, four to twelve."

"Let me talk to him, Your Honor," the defense lawyer says. "His family's here. Is it possible for him to be brought out?"

Diaz, a young man in a red shirt and slacks, is led from the bullpen to the counsel table. The lawyer sits beside him.

"Yes, Mr. Acciani, what do you want?" Rothwax asks.

Assistant District Attorney Michael Acciani steps to the bench and mentions his case.

"Leone Slate is marked ready," Rothwax announces. "Let's notify Mr. Reaves."

Robert Reaves is the court clerk who serves as the liaison between the calendar judges and the trial parts.

"Mr. Mickenberg, come up," Rothwax tells another lawyer.

"Yes, Your Honor?"

"Where's your client?"

"He's on his way."

Rothwax marks Mickenberg's case ready for a *Huntley* hearing—on the admissibility of a defendant's statements.

"There's Mr. Reaves!" Rothwax calls as a rotund, cotton-haired black enters the courtroom. "Come up, Mr. Reaves!"

Reaves approaches the bench and tells Rothwax, "At this point we have no open parts."

"No open parts?"

"Our only hope is something's about to fall."

Rothwax sighs heavily.

Reaves says the jury in Judge Melia's part might come back with a verdict.

"Melia would be ideal for Slate," Rothwax says.

"Let me get the lay of the land and I'll be back."

Reeves leaves.

The court officer returns with a stack of pre-pleading reports—tomorrow's.

"Mr. Jacobs, would you come up," Rothwax asks a Legal Aid lawyer.

The case of Pedro Rodriguez—Jonathan Jacobs's client—is called. Rothwax reads aloud from the probation report. Rodriguez is charged with manslaughter for stabbing a man in a fight on West Forty-second Street.

"Sit down and talk with Davidson"—the assistant district attorney on the case—Rothwax tells Jacobs.

Diaz is recalled.

Rothwax interrupts the proceeding to say to a Legal Aid lawyer who has just entered the courtroom, "Mr. Sato, your case has been marked ready. We're looking for a part. Check back."

A bearded lawyer interrupts the proceeding again to ask if Rothwax has received a probation report on his case.

"I have *not* received a probation report."

Rothwax returns to Diaz's lawyer. "I can say top of three-and-a-third to ten."

"Let me sell him on that."

"Ed," Rothwax tells a clerk, "second call on José Diaz. Call the next case."

The case of David Grippi is called.

The attorney asks for a one-day adjournment.

"January twelfth on David Grippi," Rothwax orders.

Luis Reyes is called for sentencing for robbery.

"I don't know if you recall much about this matter," his lawyer tells Rothwax at the bench.

"I recall everything about it," the judge replies. "That's why I make out cards."

He reads aloud from the report recommending probation and announces, "I'm willing to place him on probation."

As the lawyers return to open court, Rothwax pounds the heel of his hand on the bench for order. Only in the movies do judges wield gavels.

Rothwax asks the Assistant District Attorney if she has anything to say.

"Your Honor," Katy Law replies, "this was a negotiated plea. The People have no position."

Neither does the defense.

"You have made a favorable adjustment," Rothwax tells Reyes. "You're to be congratulated on that. Keep up a good record on probation."

He sentences Reyes to five years' probation.

Assistant District Attorney Michael Davidson arrives. Rothwax beckons him to the bench. "Find Jacobs, read the report, come back, and we'll discuss it."

The case of Fidel Alvarez, Reyes's co-defendant, is called. Alvarez's probation report is not as favorable as Reyes's. Rothwax tells Alvarez's lawyer, "If he doesn't cooperate, I'm going to put him in jail." The case is adjourned until April 20.

The clerk calls the case of Andrew Cruz.

"Let's hold up on Cruz, Williams, and Clark, because I don't have probation reports," Rothwax says.

The case of Albio Valladarez and Raymond Salo is called. The two are accused of robbing homosexuals in the West Village. Rothwax calls the Legal Aid lawyer and Katy Law to the bench.

"Where are we?" he asks. "Back to ground zero?"

They are.

Rothwax sums up the situation: "The question is whether they're entitled to a hearing, and it seems to me they're entitled. There's no question in my mind that the motion to suppress will be denied, but they're entitled to a hearing. We'll fix a date when we can have a hearing on it."

He asks the attorneys to agree on a date, and the case is adjourned until January 26.

Pedro Rodriguez is recalled. Rothwax lets the jailed defendant meet with members of his family while the lawyers confer with him at the bench.

"What do you know about the decedent?" Rothwax asks Davidson.

"We haven't got a sheet," the prosecutor replies.

"C'mon!" Rothwax snaps, throwing down his pencil in frustration. "How can we evaluate this case without knowing anything about the decedent?"

Jacobs says he was an addict and a dealer.

"Where are you in terms of time?" Rothwax asks Davidson.

"Seven or eight."

Jacobs asks for "zero to five."

"Split the difference," Rothwax says. "Zero to six. Let's sell him on it."

Davidson presses for seven, but Rothwax cuts him off. "Second call on this matter."

Reggie Crumpler is called for sentencing for robbery. Again there's a conference at the bench as Rothwax reads aloud from the probation report, noting that the defendant is working, has completed a high-school equivalency, and is in a drug-treatment program. The report recommends probation.

"There doesn't appear to be any problem with that, Your Honor," the defense lawyer says.

But Rothwax insists that a condition of probation be that he remain in the treatment program.

Then in open court: "Mr. Crumpler, is there anything you wish to say before I impose sentence?"

"No."

Five years' probation.

José Diaz is recalled.

His lawyer tells Rothwax, "We're going to take a plea to possession of a weapon, Class C."

In open court Rothwax recaps the history of the case and asks if the plea is acceptable to the People. It is.

He pounds his hand heel again for order. Then he questions Diaz to make sure that the defendant knows what he's doing. Finally, he asks, "How do you plead to that charge: guilty or not guilty?"

"Guilty."

Rothwax puts his pledge of a maximum sentence of three and a third to ten years on the record and adds that he might consider a lower sentence, but no promises.

In past years judges and lawyers alike went through the "legal fiction" that "no threats or promises" were made. But so many prisoners appealed, arguing that judges reneged on the deal, that most judges now put the plea-bargaining process on the record.

"Do you understand what I've said, Mr. Diaz?"

"Yes."

Clerk Frank Lanotte takes the plea, and sentencing is set for February 28.

"James Campbell!"

Second call. His attorney is absent.

"Steven Williams!"

The defendant, a black in a knit cap, is on for sentence for robbery as a second-felony offender. Under the law, his minimum sentence must be at least one-half the maximum.

"Come up, please," Rothwax tells the lawyers.

The defense attorney asks to see the probation report.

"Why don't we go through it together?" Rothwax suggests. He starts reading aloud from the report, then stops. "What do we have to go through this for? I'm going to give him the minimum. Does he owe any time?"—from his previous conviction.

"I believe not," Katy Law says.

"Let's go with it."

The defense lawyer points to the probation report. "I'd like to take a brief look at it."

Rothwax tells him that it's a waste of time, but the lawyer insists.

He reads the report, then hands it back. "Thank you for indulging me."

"That's all it was," Rothwax says.

In open court Williams is arraigned as a predicate felon. The defense lawyer asks that Rothwax direct that Williams be made eligible for work release.

"I'm not going to interfere with the parole board," the judge replies.

He imposes a term of one and a half to three years.

Pedro Rodriguez is recalled. A Spanish interpreter is summoned for the defendant as the attorneys gather again at the bench. They've agreed on a plea to manslaughter in the first degree.

"I think man-two is a better plea," Rothwax suggests.

But Davidson insists, "I want man-one."

"You're a pain in the ass, Davidson," Rothwax tells the prosecutor. But he agrees to manslaughter in the first degree.

In open court he takes the plea and promises Rodriguez a sentence of zero to six years.

"The defendant wishes to be sentenced today, Your Honor," Jacobs says.

"Arraign the defendant for sentence!" Rothwax orders.

Jacobs asks that Rothwax recommend parole "at the earliest possible opportunity."

Rothwax says he won't recommend one way or the other and imposes the "zip-six" sentence.

"Would it be possible—" Jacobs starts as Rodriguez is led away.

"Brief court visit," Rothwax orders.

"I still don't have a part on this yet," he tells a lawyer at the rail.

Then he beckons Davidson to the bench and asks him about a missing witness in another case: "Who is he?"

"He's an eyewitness—" Davidson starts.

Rothwax cuts him off. "I don't want to know what he saw," he snaps. "I want to know what he does. If he's a pressman for the *New York Times,* then you'll locate him. If he's a Bowery bum, you won't."

Among courthouse regulars such outbursts are called "Waxing Roth."

An attorney approaches the bench and asks if Rothwax can handle a sanity hearing on Friday.

"It's conceivable that would go beyond one afternoon," the judge says. "So I really don't think I can."

"I thought you might want to hear Judge Roberts testify"—not George, but Burton, his older brother.

Rothwax laughs. "I don't think *I* should pass upon his credibility."

A frail blond woman in custody is led to a seat in the jury box to separate her from the men in the bullpen. Then the clerk calls the case of Rose Marie Mitchell, and she's led to the defense table for arraignment. She looks a decade older than her forty-one years.

Rothwax summons Katy Law and Larry Fagenson, the Legal Aid lawyer, to the bench. He reads aloud from the handwritten D.A.'s report, still called a "161" from the days when it was typed on a printed form.

"This is a robbery of a doctor. Defendant's pocketbook was found in the office." He shakes his head sadly. "This gal is a real winner."

A court officer brings Rothwax a mug of coffee.

"She has her picture in her purse," Rothwax continues. "As if her name and address weren't enough! Unbelievable!"

Katy Law hands up another handwritten note urging a "top count" unless Rose Marie Mitchell cooperates by turning in her accomplice. Fagenson argues that she can't cooperate while she's in jail.

Rothwax asks the prosecutor, "Would you be prepared to take an open 'D'?"—a D felony with an open sentence of up to seven years.

The case is adjourned while she ponders it.

The case of Michael Parzini is called. It's on for motions on the grounds of diminished responsibility.

Craig Kaplan, Parzini's Legal Aid lawyer, comes to the bench and explains that he's leaving the office to become president of the Legal Aid lawyers' union.

"If you're as effective there as you are as an attorney," Rothwax tells him, "it may be the end of the labor movement in America."

Kaplan asks for an adjournment until a new lawyer can be assigned to the case.

"I find this a fascinating issue, and frankly I'd like to write on it," Rothwax says.

Kaplan suggests putting it over for a week.

Rothwax suggests three.

"You convinced me," Kaplan says.

"If I convinced you, I'm going to rethink my position," Rothwax says. "January nineteenth."

The clerk calls the case of Timothy Oree. The defendant does not respond.

"Parole revoked. Bench warrant issued," Rothwax orders.

It's an empty gesture. The Police Department's Warrant Squad is so overworked that defendants who jump bail can expect to remain free until they are rearrested . . . on some other charge.

"James Campbell!"

"Case is marked ready."

Rafael Baez is called for sentencing on a gun charge.

Rothwax summons the lawyers to the bench and reads aloud from the probation report. "All right," he rules, "it's more than a year. We'll place him on probation."

Baez is given five years' probation.

"Come up, Mr. Reaves!" Rothwax calls as the liaison clerk returns to the courtroom.

"We may have a part for a hearing at two," Reaves tells the judge. "In Judge Carro's part. Does it meet the guidelines for a six-month case?"

John Carro is one of three judges who sit in a federally funded section handling only cases of defendants jailed six months or more.

Rothwax looks at the file card. "It's pretty close. This is the fifth month."

The judge looks around the courtroom, then tells the clerk, "I see a number of attorneys here. Frank, can we call their cases?"

Luis Lara is called. He's accused of robbing a grocery store. It's a new case and Rothwax starts filling out a fresh file card.

"What's the offer on this?"

"Offer is 'C,' Your Honor," Katy Law replies.

"And you, Counsel?"

"My present understanding is that this is going to go to trial," the Legal Aid lawyer says.

"The longer you wait, the less the offer is," Rothwax advises him. "February two on Luis Lara." Then he stops himself. "I think he has to be arraigned."

Lara is arraigned and pleads not guilty.

Arthur Tyrone Clark is scheduled for sentencing for rape, but Rothwax says, "I don't have a report on him yet." Under the law, a defendant cannot be sentenced until a probation report is prepared. The case is adjourned until January 18.

The law clerk of recently retired Justice George Postel wanders into the courtroom looking for work. Rothwax gives him a stack of motion papers.

"Go through it," he says. "Give me a write-up on it and let me know."

Rose Marie Mitchell is recalled. Rothwax summons Laura Drager, the assistant district attorney in charge of the case, and Fagenson to the bench.

"I know the question," Drager says. "The answer is no."

"Why not an open 'D'?"

"Our position is, it should be a top count unless she cooperates."

"Would you ask Mr. Freed"—her bureau chief—"to come up," Rothwax tells her. And as she walks away, he adds, "And if he's not there, maybe you could ask Mr. Stevens, Mr. Rienzi, Mr. Lowe, Mr. Zimroth, or Mr. Morgenthau"—running through the list of her superiors. "Any one of those would suit my purposes."

The attorney on the next case approaches the bench, and Rothwax tells him, "She's out of her goddamned mind, but I'm constantly frustrated by inexperienced assistants."

The lawyer's client is not in court.

"Parole revoked. Bench warrant," Rothwax orders. "Stay execution, Frank, until—"

"January seventeenth," the lawyer suggests.

"January seventeenth," Rothwax agrees.

The attorney advises the clerk that his client's name is not "Alton Ray," as it's listed on the calendar, but Alton *Mc*Ray.

Lanotte recalls that a Mr. McRay called to say he'd be late because he was stuck somewhere.

The case is put over for second call.

There's no probation report on Ulysses Eaddy, arrested for looting during the July 13 blackout, so the case is adjourned until January 31.

The case of Allan Proctor is called, and a black is led from the bullpen. His lawyer approaches the bench.

"I know what you're gonna say," Rothwax tells him. "It doesn't make any difference to me. He failed to show up for sentence. He's gonna get zip to five."

"He honestly believes that he's getting screwed here."

"I don't give a shit what he believes! Proceed!"

"Can he withdraw his plea?"

Rothwax carefully accents both words of his answer: *"No way."*

Then he spots a lawyer in the courtroom. "Mr. Freed, come up!"

John Freed, a chunky man wearing horn-rimmed glasses, is chief of one of the six trial bureaus in the D.A.'s office. As he approaches the bench, Proctor is led back to the bullpen.

Freed explains the office's position on Rose Marie Mitchell: "I think there's more inducement to cooperate with the 'B' over her head." He says Rothwax's offer is "reasonable," but "sometimes reasonable men can't agree."

"I'm going to change the mixture," Rothwax tells him. "I'm going to parole her. I've spent as much time with it as I want to spend with it. Decide what you want to do."

Proctor is recalled.

"Mr. Proctor doesn't want to appear in the courtroom," his lawyer announces.

"I don't care," Rothwax replies. "We're going to go ahead."

Rothwax recapitulates the history of the case. Proctor pleaded guilty to robbery and failed to show up for sentencing on July 21. He was rearrested in November.

"Miss Law, is there anything you wish to say?"

"No, Your Honor."

"Counsel?"

The defense lawyer says that Justice Postel—now retired—originally promised Proctor a sentence of zero to three years and that Proctor is now "extremely frustrated."

Rothwax calls Proctor "a highly antisocial and dangerous criminal" and sentences him *in absentia* to zero to five years. "If it errs at all," he says of the sentence, "it errs on the low side."

He tells the lawyer to advise Proctor of what has transpired in court. The lawyer leaves for the bullpen.

The case of Vincent Crowe is called, but the indictment has not yet been delivered to court. January 19.

A court officer brings Rothwax a cup of soup—a twelve-thirty ritual.

Proctor's lawyer returns from the bullpen. "Any second thoughts?" he asks the judge.

"I have *no* second thoughts."

The case of Carlos Rivera is called, but the defendant is in Bellevue Hospital.

"January sixteenth on Carlos Rivera."

Rose Marie Mitchell is recalled.

"Has the defendant been arraigned?"

"No."

"Arraign the defendant!"

Rose Marie Mitchell is arraigned. Laura Drager advises against parole or low bail. Fagenson points out that the defendant is the mother of four and that her children are in court.

"I propose to parole her with a view to testing her good faith," Rothwax says, adjourning the case until January 16 and admonishing her to cooperate with the D.A.'s office.

Reaves returns to report. "The situation has not changed, Judge."

"See me at two o'clock."

Segundo Valentino is up for sentence for looting a liquor store during the blackout. Rothwax summons the attorneys to the bench and reads aloud from the probation report. The defendant is thirty-nine, lives alone, and is unemployed. He said he wasn't looting, merely looking for a friend.

"There were no looters—just like there were no Nazis," Rothwax remarks.

The woman from Legal Aid says, "The only thing I can say is he doesn't drink."

But he was a heroin addict and he was shot in the leg three weeks ago.

"They recommend probation," Rothwax concludes. "Well, he did eleven days. We'll try him on probation."

It's 1:00 P.M. Rothwax adjourns court until 2:10. Five cases remain on his calendar.

Before he leaves the courtroom for lunch with his fellow Criminal Court judges—a Wednesday ritual—he gives two bills to a court officer and asks him to buy copies of the *Post, Village Voice,* and *SoHo News.*

Then he adds, "I want change."

At 2:00 P.M., Rothwax stands on the bench in the locked courtroom bantering with Judges Irving Lang and George Roberts.

On the bench beside him are the newspapers he ordered. The *Post* is running a series on the courts. Today's installment notes that Rothwax and Lang were the only judges who could be found still sitting late one afternoon. The *SoHo News* prints a critical comment by Rothwax on the cases brought by "decoy cops"—policemen who pose as drunks and derelicts to lure robbers and muggers. And the *Voice* leads with its annual feature, "The Ten Worst Judges in New York." Rothwax is *not* on the list.

Below the bench Reaves speaks into a walkie-talkie: "Can you take a *Wade* and *Huntley* hearing?"

The answer is audible throughout the courtroom: "Tell 'em to send it right to the part."

Rothwax leans over and yells into the mike, "It's on its way!"

So the case of Steven Charlotten is sent out.

"What are we gonna do with Slate?" Rothwax asks.

"That's the only part we have," Reaves replies. "He's charging."

"Who's charging?" the judge asks anxiously. "Is Carro charging? He'd be ideal for Slate."

Roberts and Lang leave for their courtrooms. The doors of Part 35 are unlocked. Rothwax calls court to order and announces: "James Campbell—ready and passed until tomorrow. Slate is before Judge Carro, Part Seventy-one."

Lanotte tells Rothwax about an "added starter." "We have a violation of probation—one of Culkin's old cases"—Gerald Culkin, a retired Supreme Court justice.

"Why is it here?" Rothwax asks. "Why isn't it in Part Thirty-one?"

The clerk checks the file. "This apparently was before you in October."

Rothwax studies the file, then tells the defendant, "The defendant is restored to probation. Do well now. Don't come back before me. I'm a bad guy to come back before a second time."

Laura Drager returns to court to report on Rose Marie Mitchell. She called the detective on the case and told him, "I have Rose Marie Mitchell in my office." And he replied, "We don't need her. We just picked up the guy."

Rothwax turns to the clerk. "Let's call Anthony Ricco on the writ. I understand he's pleading a constitutional right to escape for a third time."

The case is another added starter.

Ricco is led into court. He's a bearded man who's serving a ten-to-twenty-year sentence for rape and sodomy and awaiting trial for robbery and murder. He's escaped from both Bellevue and Rikers Island.

Rothwax interrupts his study of the papers to tell a lawyer, "He hasn't appeared here, Mr. Blackstone. Any reason why I shouldn't issue the writ?"

David Blackstone can think of none, and Rothwax orders Lanotte to call the case of John Pazivoda.

"Bail forfeited. Bench warrant issued."

He returns to Ricco's application. Ricco claims he's being held in "illegal detention" at the Brooklyn House of Detention.

"This is one of the few facilities remaining from which he has not escaped," Rothwax observes.

Ricco also claims he's been denied medical treatment.

Katy Law hands Rothwax a note from the prison doctor saying that Ricco refused treatment for "ecchymosis left preorbital area."

"That's a black eye," she explains.

Ricco also complains that his life has been threatened by other prisoners.

"If his life is in danger there, maybe we could move him to the Bronx," Rothwax suggests.

Then he notices Michael Acciani standing amid the conferees. "What are you doing here?" he asks.

The prosecutor explains that he has one of Ricco's pending cases and would like to listen to the argument. "Do you mind?"

"Do I mind? *Yes*," Rothwax replies. "Will I tolerate it? *No.* You're on trial before Judge Carro."

He orders Acciani out of the courtroom.

"There goes the Playboy of the Western World," he observes as the attorney leaves.

"Charney, welcome!" Rothwax calls as another lawyer enters the courtroom. "It's three o'clock and here's Charney."

The assault case of Armando Diaz is called. Charney explains that Diaz was stabbed in another fight and is still recuperating. The Assistant District Attorney notes that the victim in the current case is going to Lebanon for forty-five days.

"At the rate Mr. Diaz is going," Rothwax says, "if you put it over for two months, he'll probably be dead from other fights he'll get into."

But the case is adjourned until March 10.

An attorney reports that the lawyers for Kenneth Curtis are on trial in another case. Rothwax adjourns Curtis's case until January 13.

"Have you spoken with Mr. Dorceley?" he asks. "Can we put that on the same day?"

"No problem."

Andrew Cruz is called for sentencing for looting during the blackout. Rothwax reads the probation report to the lawyers, noting that Cruz has previous arrests for loitering and trespassing. "He really doesn't have much of a record."

The report says that Cruz has been living with a woman for seven years, but has "no immediate plans regarding marriage."

"I don't think he has any long-range plans either," Rothwax quips. "They recommend probation. Well, we'll place him on probation."

Cruz is sentenced to five years' probation.

"All right, Frank," Rothwax tells the clerk. "That's the calendar except for the Ricco writ."

The bench conference resumes.

"Why can't he be put in the infirmary?" the woman from Legal Aid asks.

"Because it's easier to escape from the infirmary than maximum security."

She says other prisoners are threatening Ricco.

"Generally, the guys in maximum security are not nice guys," Rothwax observes. "That's why they're in maximum security."

They're also grimacing at Ricco, she adds.

"You want me to issue an order: 'There shall be no grimaces'?"

Rothwax wants a report on Ricco's situation from someone in the Department of Correction. "Call him down," he tells the prosecutor. "We'll talk about it informally and then we'll do something."

Katy Law returns a few minutes later. "Apparently, the correction officer is not available now. He's out to lunch."

Rothwax does paperwork at the bench until 3:46 P.M., when Captain

Reginald Lee arrives from the Correction Department office on the fifteenth floor. Rothwax beckons him to the bench.

Lee explains that Ricco can't be transferred to the Bronx because that's not a maximum-security facility.

Legal Aid says Ricco is being threatened in Brooklyn.

"If we can substantiate it, we will have the person moved from that area," Lee tells her.

"Do you have specific names?" Rothwax asks.

"Not in my possession."

Rothwax points to the bullpen. "Go! Ask him!"

She leaves to confer with Ricco and returns a few minutes later.

"All six," she says—the entire cellblock. "And the officer who sits in the gallery—he was a witness. It's in his logbook."

"Look into it," Rothwax tells Lee. Then he stands. "On the record. . . . The writ is denied with leave to renew. Good afternoon, everyone."

Thursday, January 12

Acting Supreme Court Justice Peter McQuillan has summoned the press to hand down his opinion in the Miguel Pinero case. Mike Pearl and Bob Crane, the red-bearded reporter from the *Daily News,* enter his makeshift chambers on the sixteenth floor—a stark, bare room with a wooden desk and a metal file cabinet.

Clutching an unlit cigar, McQuillan, a short, handsome man of forty-eight with bushy black brows and black hair streaked with silver, hands them copies of his 108-page opinion from a stack on his desk. He's a former assistant district attorney who served as counsel to the Penal Law Revision Commission which drafted New York's current criminal statutes. He's regarded by many lawyers as the best "law man" on the criminal bench.

"I apologize for my lengthy prose," McQuillan says. Then he launches into a lengthy exposition of his findings. His voice is clipped and tinged with the classic accents of the New York Irish. His eyes blink as he speaks, and he chops the air with his hands to punctuate his points. He bears a slight resemblance to Peter Falk as Columbo.

Pinero's is a controversial case. On the evening of December 20, 1976, a cabby named Larry Williams drove his eighteen-year-old girl friend Tina Arnone, a heroin addict, to get a "fix." She bought forty dollars' worth of heroin on the Lower East Side, shot up at a "shooting gallery" around the corner, then went to visit a friend in a building next door. She left her purse in the cab.

In the hallway of the building she was accosted by three men. One of them fetched Williams from the cab and at gunpoint took his wallet and coat and made him take off his shoes. The three also frisked Arnone, but apparently found nothing worth stealing. They then drove off in Williams's cab, which was later found abandoned.

A few hours after the robbery police accosted three men in another taxi on Eldridge Street, a few blocks away, and ordered them out of the cab at gunpoint. One of the men was Miguel Pinero, a thirty-year-old ex-convict and author of *Short Eyes,* a searing drama of prison life, which Pinero was then filming on location in the Tombs. The second was Andrew Butler, twenty-five, who had acted in *Short Eyes* under the stage name of Tito Goya. The third was Ernesto Rivera, twenty.

The police searched the cab and found a gun, seven tinfoils of heroin, along with a syringe and a needle, and a fur coat, in the pocket of which was Tina Arnone's driver's license.

At the Elizabeth Street station in Chinatown, Arnone and Williams identified the three men as the bandits—first from photographs that night and then at a lineup the following morning.

In addition, the arresting officer claimed that while they were awaiting arraignment in Criminal Court he'd asked Pinero, "Miguel, I can't understand you. A guy who makes a lot of money, you know, how can you get involved in a stupid robbery like this?"

"Well, I'll tell you the truth," he claimed that the playwright replied. "We were helping you guys."

"What do you mean, you were helping us guys?"

"We were down there ripping off all the junkies and all the pushers."

Pinero, Butler, and Rivera were charged with armed robbery, larceny, and possession of drugs and a gun. Their attorneys moved to suppress the physical evidence, Pinero's admission, and the eyewitness identification on the grounds that they had been obtained illegally—the decision McQuillan is handing down.

Pearl cuts short the judge's rambling exposition. "The bottom line is what?"

"The motion to suppress the physical evidence is granted. Pinero's motion to suppress his statement is granted. The motion to suppress the identifications of the girl and her boy friend is granted."

"So you dismissed just about all the evidence?"

"That's fair to say."

"What do you think really happened?" Crane asks.

"Oh, shit!" the judge replies. "In a fact-finding hearing you can never learn the true transcendental reality."

"Where are you gonna be today in case after reading—"

"Up here," McQuillan tells Crane. "I've got another hearing."

"What's your number up here?" Pearl asks.

McQuillan has to look at the phone to tell him.

Pearl and Crane return to the press room to file their stories. It's crowded with TV cameramen, radio reporters, and newspaper photographers—in the courthouse to catch Robert Norton, a Texas store detective who the night before shot and killed a mugger in the New York Hilton. " 'Ah figured it's either them or me,' " screams the headline in the *Post.* But none of the newsmen knows what Norton looks like. Worse, he's supposed to go before a grand jury and the press isn't even allowed on the ninth floor, where the grand-jury rooms are located.

Gerald Lefcourt, Pinero's bushy-haired lawyer, enters the press room to inform the reporters of the ruling. He's one of the younger, rapidly rising radical lawyers in New York, the successful defender in the Panther 21 case. He's followed by Pinero himself—a short, shaggy-bearded man wearing a green trench coat and a cloth cap set backward like a baseball catcher's.

"You got it?" Lefcourt asks, seeing the thick sheaf of papers in Pearl's hands.

Pearl nods yes and turns to Lefcourt's client. "Mr. Pinero, can I get a statement from you?"

The playwright's reply is couched in the inarticulate accents of the streets. "Talk to mah lawyer, man. That's why I got a lawyer. I'm a writer. I can't rap."

While Pearl talks to Lefcourt, John Mulligan of the Associated Press grabs a phone and tries to get a line on Norton's whereabouts, but the D.A.'s press office knows even less than he does. He hangs up and mutters aloud, "It's gonna be another one of these fuck-up days, I'm afraid."

Friday, January 13

Wearing a trench coat that looks as if it had gone through the battle of Vimy Ridge, Geoffrey Abrams slogs through the snow to his office at 80 Lafayette Street. At thirty-five he's tall, thin, and shaggy-haired, a senior trial attorney for Legal Aid.

In past years Geoff Abrams's trip from courtroom to office was by elevator. But the Legal Aid staff overflowed its office off the courthouse lobby and the new union of Legal Aid lawyers made adequate facilities one of its first demands. So two years ago the Manhattan Criminal Defense Division moved to a building a block from the courthouse.

Abrams takes the antique operator-driven elevator to the fifth floor, where a handful of shabbily dressed blacks wait in the foyer. The receptionist buzzes him through the door and comes out of her booth to greet him.

"I got a funeral order waiting for you"—an order directing the temporary release of a prisoner to attend a relative's funeral.

She leads Abrams down a narrow corridor. He pauses to drop off a file in the cubicle he shares with Helen Sadow—even in its new quarters Legal Aid is cramped for space—then follows her to the end of the corridor, where there's a desk piled with papers. Abrams glances at the top sheet and signs the last—on each of three copies.

"No, no," the receptionist says, "you've gotta sign three times."

Abrams riffles through the forms and signs at the appropriate places.

"I'll run it over this afternoon," he tells her.

Then he peeks into the office of James V. Vinci, attorney in charge of the Manhattan Criminal Defense Division. Vinci is a short, chunky man with silver hair and a hawk nose. He, Milton Adler, a cadaverous man in his sixties who gave up Vinci's job to return to the tumult of the trial court, and Russel Bowman, like Abrams a senior trial attorney, are schmoozing and sharing a Friday-afternoon schnapps. Abrams joins them.

Now fifty-one, Jim Vinci kicked around a bit before he found his niche at Legal Aid. He started his legal career in a Madison Avenue law office, but soon got bored with the paperwork of corporate practice. He tried his hand at general practice upstate, then returned to do trial work for a firm that represented an insurance company in personal-injury cases. After five years he became disillusioned with the law and, in effect, dropped out for fifteen months and lived a bohemian life in Greenwich Village.

Marriage spurred him back to the daily grind. In 1961 he applied at Legal Aid and was interviewed by the then attorney-in-charge, Anthony "Chick" Marra—soon to become a Criminal Court judge—and Adler. Vinci was hired and has been at Legal Aid since. "Best job I ever had in my life," he boasts. In 1972 he succeeded Adler as attorney-in-charge.

Vinci presides behind a disorderly desk in a tiny office overlooking White Street. He directs a staff of 125 lawyers and 91 support personnel. He estimates that his office handles 93 percent of the criminal cases brought in Manhattan, including many it shouldn't.

Technically, there are guidelines as to whom Legal Aid can and cannot represent. A rule of thumb is that it will not represent a defendant who can raise $1,500 bail. But often such clients claim that the money was raised by friends or relatives who went into hock—Vinci calls it "Bail Defense No. 23"—and the judge directs Legal Aid to remain on the case.

In addition, the courts are so clogged that judges are loath to grant adjournments—even to permit defendants to retain counsel. Private counsel, Vinci notes, are often reluctant to come to court at night or on weekends and know that Legal Aid does a "bang-up job" on arraignments, so Legal Aid handles virtually all arraignments. Sixty-three percent of the cases never progress beyond that.

Of those that do, Vinci estimates, Legal Aid is counsel in 80 percent. In 1977 it defended in 160 Supreme Court trials and 45 in Criminal Court.

One of Vinci's greatest pleasures in his job is not having to worry about money. Neither he nor his staff ask for fees—often the grubbiest part of criminal practice. Nor does he have to bother with a budget, which is handled by Legal Aid's executive office. Although the Legal Aid Society is a private charity, run by a board of directors made up mostly of Wall Street and Park Avenue lawyers, the bulk of its funds comes from city, state, and federal government grants. Of its three divisions—Civil, Criminal, and Juvenile—Criminal and Juvenile are wholly government funded. The Criminal Division consumes $21.5 million of Legal Aid's $28.8 million budget.

But Vinci *does* have to worry about staff. There's a high turnover, largely because Legal Aid salaries can't compete with those of private law firms. First-year lawyers start at $15,500, and after thirteen years can earn $29,500; Wall Street lawyers start at $24,000. But perhaps a more important reason is that Legal Aid—like the D.A.'s office—is no longer a training ground for the trial lawyer of tomorrow, because so few cases come to trial. Vinci estimates that it used to take a year to teach an attorney to try a case in Criminal Court; now it takes three.

Vinci's pride is S.T.A.B., the Senior Trial Attorney Bureau, originally set up to counter the District Attorney's federally funded Career Criminal Program, which focuses special attention on second and third offenders. Now S.T.A.B. is primarily a reward for its six members, who are relieved of the routine chore of handling arraignments and thus avoid night and weekend assignments. But they do defend the most difficult cases, and Vinci boasts, "The worst offenders get the best representation."

Monday, January 16

Some four dozen elderly Chinese men sit silently in the thirteenth-floor courtroom of Part 70, awaiting the start of a trial that is of special interest to the Chinese community. Chik Keung Pang, a twenty-five-year-old native of Hong Kong, is charged with attempted murder in the stabbing of Man Bun Lee, a restaurant owner, president of the Chinese Consolidated Benevolent Association, and honorary "Mayor of Chinatown," who led the fight to end the extortion of Chinatown merchants by marauding youth gangs.

Pearl of the *Post* and Crane of the *Daily News* sit in the jury box, along with four attorneys for the papers—corporate lawyers who rarely come to the city's criminal courtrooms. The case is of more than routine interest to the press because the defense has made a *Gannett* motion, the first in New York City. A few weeks before, in the case of *Gannett* v. *DePasquale,* New York State's highest tribunal, the Court of Appeals, ruled that a judge may bar the press from a pre-trial hearing if publication of the evidence could prejudice potential jurors.

Ironically, the motion to bar the press is on before Justice Burton B. Roberts, a boozing buddy of columnist Jimmy Breslin and perhaps the most publicity-hungry judge in the courthouse, constantly calling reporters to tout his trials and frequently visiting the press room—usually to "borrow" Mike Pearl's copy of the *Post.* For years Roberts was the most flamboyant of Hogan's assistants, then went on to serve as chief assistant and district attorney in the Bronx before he was elevated to the Supreme Court in 1973.

A second irony is that the *Gannett* motion has had a boomerang effect. Ordinarily, the metropolitan media report the criminal judicial process only at indictment, verdict, and sentence. Only in a sensational case, such as "Son of Sam," are pre-trial hearings covered. Pang's case does not fall into that category, but the *Gannett* motion brought out the press.

Red-haired and ruddy-faced, Roberts, fifty-five, sits on the bench, waiting impatiently for the proceedings to begin.

"Is Mr. Linzer here?" he asks.

"He's now with the interpreter," the clerk says, nodding toward the bullpen.

"Bring him out."

A court officer fetches Robert Linzer, a short man with dark, close-cropped hair, and the defendant. Pang is dark, long-haired, and sports a drooping Fu Manchu mustache. He wears a white sweater and blue jeans.

Linzer and Nancy Ryan, the assistant district attorney, confer with Roberts at the bench.

"Mr. Linzer requests permission to continue to speak to him inside," Roberts reports for the record.

Linzer and his client return to the bullpen, while Roberts runs through the rest of his brief calendar. When he finishes, he continues to sit on the bench, scratching his nose, wringing his hands, nervously donning his black horn-rimmed glasses and taking them off again . . . waiting.

Finally he asks, "Captain, are Pang and Mr. Linzer coming out?"

The court officer checks the bullpen and reports, "Judge, the attorney requests two more minutes."

Roberts waits five.

"Are they ready?"

Without bothering to check, the clerk replies, "In a minute, Judge."

Another wait.

"Is he ready?"

"He's putting the question to him right now," the clerk replies.

Finally Linzer returns to court and confers again with Roberts at the bench.

"Do you want to talk to him a bit more?"

"I do."

"Step back."

Roberts again puts the delay on the record. Linzer returns to the bullpen while Roberts continues to fiddle . . . and wait. Finally he can take it no more.

"Let's go!" he orders.

Linzer and his client are brought out, and Laura Ho is sworn as interpreter for Pang.

Roberts asks Pang if he wants Linzer to continue as his counsel. Despite his inability to speak English, at his last hearing Pang demonstrated that he'd learned the latest trick of Rikers Island inmates—the delaying tactic of trying to switch lawyers.

"For the time being, yes," Pang replies through the interpreter.

Roberts chuckles. "I don't know what that means. I shall preside over this case—*for the time being*."

The judge asks Linzer if a *Huntley* hearing—to determine the admissibility of Pang's statements—can be held without revealing prejudicial material and, if not, how such a disclosure would make the impaneling "of a fair and impartial jury difficult. Not impossible. Difficult."

Linzer replies that it is possible to hold the hearing without revealing the prejudicial material.

"I understand that you're withdrawing your motion?" Roberts asks.

"That's right."

"And you're saying, 'Let the courtroom doors be opened'?"

"Yes."

Disappointed because he's been denied the opportunity to pen a precedent-setting decision, Roberts swivels and addresses his captive audience of newsmen and newspaper lawyers in the jury box. He notes that it would be "extremely difficult in New York County to show taint." Although it wasn't spelled out in the Court of Appeals decision, he says, there's a "difference between a community consisting of thirty-six thousand citizens"—Seneca County, where the *Gannett* case originated—"and one consisting of one-point-eight million."

Then, reversing like a broken-field runner: "I would hasten to add that, indeed, there could be cases even in a county as large as New York County where, indeed, it would be necessary in the course of a pre-trial hearing to exclude the press." But such cases, he adds, would be "extremely rare."

"The court should strive always to make sure that the courtroom doors are always standing open," he concludes—in another reversal.

Roberts thanks the newspaper attorneys for their briefs and oral arguments and they leave.

Then, instead of starting the *Huntley* hearing, Linzer pleads Pang guilty to attempted murder.

"The plea is acceptable to the People," Nancy Ryan says.

Roberts notes that at the bench conference the lawyers agreed on "a unique recommendation"—a sentence of four to eighteen years. It's unique because the minimum term of a sentence is rarely less than one-third of the maximum. Defendants become eligible for parole after serving the minimum, and Roberts knows that the extra six years are pap to make the Chinese community think Pang is getting a long sentence. He indicates that he'll impose a sentence of four to twelve.

He asks about Pang's prior record.

Nancy Ryan says that Pang was arrested in Hong Kong for an "affray" and served a few days in jail.

"An 'affray' sounds like a Chinese version of disorderly conduct," Roberts observes.

Roberts asks Pang about the stabbing. "Are you pleading guilty to stabbing Mr. Lee in the stomach three times with intent to kill him?"

"I stab him not with intent to kill him," Pang replies through the interpreter.

"What did you intend to do—conduct an appendectomy operation?" Roberts bellows.

"I do not know what my intent was," Pang replies. "I was very confused at that time. I didn't know what was going through my head."

Shouting—as if that makes his words more comprehensible—Roberts demands to know the reason Pang stabbed Lee. He's frustrated because, under the law, he can't accept a guilty plea unless the defendant admits his guilt—and Pang is not admitting "intent to kill."

"I just wanted to hurt him a little," Pang says. "I had no intention of killing him. I was confused."

"What were you confused about?"

"I don't recall what the confusion was about."

Roberts asks Pang how big the knife was. There's more confusion because Pang apparently is unfamiliar with American measurements. Finally, at Roberts's urging, he marks a distance on the table with his forefingers. Roberts assesses it as "eight inches."

"The court will infer that a person knows the natural and inevitable consequences of his actions," Roberts finally rules. "The court will accept the plea."

Orating to his Chinese audience, Roberts says, "It's quite clear . . . that the plunging of an eight-inch knife into a person's abdomen three times indicates an intent to kill." He calls Pang "a hired killer imported from Hong Kong to assassinate Mr. Lee."

Nancy Ryan corrects him, noting that Pang was already in New York.

"Alien or no," Roberts continues, "he is going to spend time in a United States prison—many years in a United States prison—before he is deported from these shores."

He thanks the Chinese community for its cooperation and orders Pang held without bail for sentencing on February 22.

Tuesday, January 17

Wearing his turtleneck sweater, Bob Ferraro waits for his client beside the deserted newsstand in the lobby. Fernando Ruiz is late. To Ferraro every Hispanic coming through the revolving door resembles him. Finally, Ferraro phones Ruiz's home, but there's no answer.

He continues to wait.

At 10:20 A.M. Ruiz arrives—a short, dark man with a shaggy mustache. He's a Mexican who works as a waiter at the Vesuvio Restaurant. He's charged with criminal possession of a weapon—for carrying a .22-caliber revolver he claims he needed for his own protection.

"Hey! What happened?" Ferraro asks.

"I fell asleep."

Ferraro and Ruiz take the elevator to the eleventh floor and walk to Part 35, the courtroom of Judge Harold Rothwax. Ferraro checks with the clerk, but Ruiz's case is not on the calendar.

"You better stay here," Ferraro tells his client. "I gotta check with the clerk's office. This might be an all-day thing."

At the tenth-floor office of the clerk of the Supreme Court, Ferraro is told, "Don't have anything on him."

"Whadda ya mean you don't have anything on him?"

"No record."

The clerk tells him to check with the clerk of the Criminal Court. So Ferraro descends to the first-floor office, where a clerk feeds Ruiz's name into the computer.

"Counsel, I have an indictment number," he says, writing it on a slip of paper.

"Thanks a lot," Ferraro replies, taking the slip and returning to the Supreme Court clerk's office. The clerk checks again and informs Ferraro that the case is on today—not in Part 35 but in Part 106.

"There goes my good judge," Ferraro says, sighing.

He had hoped to "cop a plea" before Rothwax, a judge he felt certain would not send Ruiz behind bars. And by pleading to a misdemeanor Ruiz would not face the possibility of deportation.

"What judge you got in 106?" he asks the clerk.

The clerk checks the roster. "Haft."

Ferraro shrugs. He still might be able to cop a plea.

He picks up his client in Part 35, descends with him to the first floor, walks through the lobby, and heads out across the snow-swept street to the Civil Court Building at 111 Centre Street.

Symptomatic of the burgeoning volume of criminal cases, new parts had to be created in the Civil Court Building, many of them presided over by Court of Claims judges imported from upstate, to handle the backlog. The summons parts of Criminal Courts—which try offenses such as littering, smoking on the subway, and peddling without a license—had to be moved to an office building at 346 Broadway, two blocks from the courthouse.

The Civil Court Building is a stark modern structure of limestone and glass built in 1960. On the seventh floor—now devoted entirely to criminal courtrooms—Ferraro finds two court officers barring the door to Part 106, where Judge Robert Haft is conducting a closed-door pre-trial hearing in the Washington Square riot case. The officers tell Ferraro that the Part 106 calendar is being heard in Part 109 on the tenth floor.

"What judge?"

"Goodman."

Ferraro and Ruiz walk away.

"That judge is an anathema to me," Ferraro tells his client. "I'm not going to take a plea before him."

They ride to the tenth floor and enter a small courtroom, brightly lit, with marble paneling and plastic bucket seats instead of the usual wooden benches. IN GOD WE TRUST is inscribed on a cardboard sign—like a barbershop's.

Ferraro checks with the clerk, then returns to tell Ruiz joyfully, "Finally found it!"

Budd Goodman, a Civil Court judge sitting by designation in the Criminal Term of Supreme Court, is a bald, bespectacled man. He looks up from a lengthy bench conference, notices Ferraro—a former colleague in Legal Aid—and silently mouths the words, "You're getting fat."

The bench conferences drone on. Not until noon is Ruiz's case called. Ferraro learns that there's an indictment number but no indictment yet.

"May I have February tenth on this, Your Honor?"

"February ten. Bail continued."

Ferraro and Ruiz walk out. Ferraro explains his new strategy: Ruiz testified before a December grand jury in hopes that the panel might be sympathetic to a working man with no prior record. But the panel's term ended before the District Attorney's office could submit the ballistics report. So, Ferraro says, Ruiz will have to return to testify before a February grand jury.

"For this I came three thousand miles and spent four hundred dollars," Ruiz complains. "I could have stayed in Mexico a few more days."

Late in the afternoon District Attorney Morgenthau meets in his office with a delegation of about a dozen members of the Chinese Consolidated Benevolent Association concerned about the Pang case. They sit with Morgenthau at the conference table, while a group of younger Chinese, reporters for the Chinese press, stand behind.

Puffing a cigar, Morgenthau assures his callers that his office will conduct a "thorough and vigorous" investigation to find out who hired Pang. But so far "we do not have the basis for prosecuting anyone else."

Speaking sometimes in English, sometimes in Chinese translated by members of the group, the delegation questions the District Attorney.

Does he have any evidence?

"I can't comment on evidence," Morgenthau says—a principle understandable to American lawyers, but lost on his Chinese audience.

Does he suspect anyone?

"Suspicion is not sufficient to form the basis of a case."

Eyes closed, one elderly Chinese man launches into a long speech in his native dialect. Among other things—according to the interpreter—he wants to make sure that Pang receives a "weird sentence."

"Weird sentence?" Morgenthau asks incredulously.

Nancy Ryan translates: "*Severe* sentence."

"We want your office to find the mastermind," the man continues.

Morgenthau notes that his office has already convicted about twenty persons for crimes in Chinatown, mostly attacks on merchants. He pledges, "We will not give up these efforts."

He notes that his office recommended a sentence of four to eighteen years for Pang, but Justice Roberts plans to reduce it to four to twelve. It's a disingenuous argument, since Morgenthau does not tell the delegation that Pang is certain to be released—and deported—after serving the four-year minimum.

The reporters—more Americanized and aggressive—take over the questioning.

One notes that Pang was an illegal alien without a job, yet had enough money to escape—first to San Francisco, then to the Canadian border, where he was captured—and to hire a lawyer. Obviously, someone is paying for it. "Why can't you find out?"

"This is not Formosa," Morgenthau snaps. "Or Mainland China," he quickly adds, for political balance. He explains that American prosecutors must follow certain rules of procedure. "We need your help. We can't prosecute without evidence. We need people to come forward."

Another Chinese reporter asks if Pang is cooperating.

"I can't disclose that."

There's a desultory discussion about the differences between American and Chinese law. Then one member of the delegation asks Morgenthau how his assistants are assigned.

Some catch-as-catch-can, the District Attorney explains, some on the basis of experience.

Will Miss Ryan continue on the case?

"Yes."

But she's so young—and a woman—the Chinese man protests.

"She's experienced in prosecuting Chinatown cases," Morgenthau insists.

One visitor tells Morgenthau that the Chinese community will "lose faith" in law enforcement if the mastermind behind Pang is not brought to justice.

On that note the meeting of East and West ends, having amended Kipling's adage. The twain may meet, but they don't understand each other.

Wednesday, January 18

Cortale again.

"Are we ready to set a trial date, Mr. Kuh?" Judge Lang asks.

"We are, after a fashion."

He explains that he's slated to go to trial in February in Brooklyn's federal court. But there's a motion for *certiorari* pending before the U.S. Supreme Court. If the high tribunal takes the case, he'll be free in February. He should know by February 9 or 10.

"If that's O.K., Mr. Ryan?" Lang asks the prosecutor.

It is—and the case is continued to February 10.

"If Your Honor please," Kuh adds, "I have several other items."

Ryan protests that he's on trial before Judge Gabel and is due in court at ten o'clock. Lang orders him to remain.

First, Kuh says, he's been unable to understand portions of the tape Ryan gave him; so Ryan gives him another copy. Second, Kuh notes that he's joining a new law firm on February 1 and files a notice of substitution, listing the new firm as Cortale's counsel. Third, he wants to know if Ryan has the rest of the "incomplete" DD5.

"There is nothing further," the prosecutor says.

Next, Kuh observes that portions of Mrs. Robbins's grand-jury testimony are "virtually incomprehensible" without the exhibits. Ryan agrees to show them to the defense.

"I am not infallible—" Kuh starts.

Lang cuts him off, turning to the jury box to make sure that the reporters covering the case heard him.

Kuh again asks for a hearing on what happened to the missing tape.

"Do you know what happened to the tape?" Lang asks Ryan.

"I can't tell you right now, Your Honor." But he promises to check.

Kuh asks for any charts that Ryan intends to introduce at the trial. Ryan agrees to deliver them. Normally, these are matters that can be arranged informally between the defense and prosecution, but Kuh believes in going "by the book."

Finally, Kuh asks Lang to "recuse" himself from presiding at the trial—for "multiple reasons."

Lang tells him to state them.

Kuh asks that it be done out of the hearing of the press.

"Denied."

Kuh lists the reasons: First, Lang had *ex parte* contact with the prosecutor.

Only to get the grand-jury minutes, Lang replies.

Kuh presses the point, but Lang cuts him off. "Please don't repeat yourself."

"Your Honor is repeating himself and I think I might be given a similar privilege."

"That's one of the privileges of a judge," Lang tells him.

Second, Kuh continues, Lang had improper contact with the press.

Only to advise them of "adjourn dates," Lang says, and in one instance he let a reporter examine papers that were part of the public record.

Kuh contends it's "improper for a judge to curry favor with the press by communicating with them even on adjourn dates."

Suddenly Supreme Court Justice Hortense Gabel storms into the courtroom. She's a short, stocky woman with fire in her crossed eyes. As she approaches the bench, Lang raises a hand to still her.

"Judge Lang—"

Lang cuts her off, explaining that they're in the middle of a hearing.

"Whatever it is, this is inexcusable!"

Justice Gabel stands at the side of the bench for a few minutes as the hearing resumes, then returns to her fifteenth-floor courtroom.

Kuh contends that Lang is "biased" against the defense counsel, because he recalled that Kuh as district attorney had "blasted" him over a sentence in a rape case.

Lang laughs.

"Your Honor may laugh. Your Honor may have his jollies about it—"

Again denied.

Lang says he'll decide who the trial judge will be when he sets a final date for trial.

The hearing is adjourned, and Ryan rushes off to Justice Gabel's courtroom.

By noon he has completed a *Wade* hearing—to determine the admissibility of eyewitness identification—in the grand-larceny case of Philip Carlo, a slight, olive-skinned real-estate salesman who is charged with obtaining building materials for his West Side brownstone with forged certified checks. Justice Gabel bars Ryan from presenting testimony about a police lineup, but permits the witness to identify Carlo in court.

Then a panel is brought from the central jury room down the hall, and Ryan starts the *voir dire,* the questioning of prospective jurors, a chore he considers "the most unpleasant part of a trial."

Thursday, January 19

Enid Gerling sits in the ground-floor coffee shop conversing with another woman lawyer.

"I got a case on today you won't believe," she says. "Two lesbians got in a fight in a gay bar, pulling hair. They won't A.C.D. it, so I gotta go to a jury trial. These woman D.A.s are unbelievable! I thought it was maybe because I'm a woman, but I understand the men are having trouble too."

Enid Gerling is the queen of the Baxter Street lawyers, a feisty woman known for her flamboyant hats—her "trademark," she calls them. Indeed, fifteen years ago when the late Justice Irving R. Saypol found her in contempt of court for withdrawing from a case, he devoted the bulk of his decision to a denunciation of her millinery. Her legal specialty—strange for a spinster—is kinky sex cases.

The Baxter Street lawyers occupy storefront offices across the street from the courthouse. Theirs is—or was—a volume business, copping pleas and making motions in the lower courts. Rarely do they go to trial. Many lack the skills to try a case before a jury, and none can afford to be tied up on one case for a week or longer. Their clients, in the main, are petty criminals—gamblers and prostitutes, the professionals whom Legal Aid will not represent.

They are also a dying breed. First, the police have all but stopped arresting the bookmakers and numbers runners who were their bread-and-butter business: According to a study conducted for the federal Law Enforcement Assistance Administration, numbers and bookmaking arrests in New York City fell from 11,467 in 1965 to only 1,394 in 1975. Second, Legal Aid now handles almost all arraignments—and the bulk of the cases are disposed of there. Symbolically, the loft building on White Street that housed Gerling's office was razed for a parking lot; she now operates out of her apartment in Greenwich Village.

Gerling glances at her watch, gulps the last swallow of coffee, clutches her purse and briefcase, and dashes upstairs to catch the calendar call.

Eleven floors above, William Kunstler, the radical lawyer best known for his defense of the Chicago Seven, sits on a front-row bench in Part 31 spinning legal pipe dreams: "If we ever get an evidentiary hearing here, Alex Haley is coming, Clarence Kelley is coming, Senator Church . . ."

And weaving conspiracy theories—especially as to the death of William Sullivan, former No. 3 man in the FBI, in a New Hampshire hunting accident on November 9. Sullivan's testimony before Senator Church's committee was cited by Kunstler in his motion papers. Now he won't be able to call him as a witness.

"That's why Sullivan was killed," he says. "If that's not a murder, I never heard of one."

Kunstler has moved to reopen the Malcolm X murder case.

El-Hajj Malik El-Shabbazz, born Malcolm Little, better known as Malcolm X, was, perhaps next to Martin Luther King, Jr., the most dynamic figure of the Black Revolution that swept the United States during the 1960s. A thief, dope peddler, and pimp, he converted to Elijah Muhammad's Lost-Found Nation of Islam while in prison and after his release rose to become the most potent of Muhammad's ministers and a rival to Muhammad himself.

In 1963 he broke with Muhammad and the following year formed his own Organization for Afro-American Unity and started to move away from the Black Muslims' policy of strict separation of the races. He believed himself marked for death for his apostasy. Indeed, on February 21, 1965, as he started to address a rally of about four hundred followers in the Audubon Ballroom on West 166th Street, he was shot to death.

Malcolm X's bodyguard wounded one of the assassins, who was taken into custody by the police outside. He was identified as Thomas Hagan, also known as Talmadge Hayer. Within a week two more men were arrested for the murder—Norman 3X Butler and Thomas 15X Johnson. All three were Black Muslims.

They were brought to trial a year later. Hagan admitted his own guilt, but said neither Butler nor Johnson was involved. Nevertheless, on the basis of eyewitness identification, all three were convicted and sentenced to life imprisonment. The appellate courts found their guilt was "overwhelmingly established."

Kunstler, retained to represent Butler and Johnson, obtained a handwritten affidavit from Hagan in prison. In it, Hagan again asserts that Butler and Johnson are innocent. For the first time he identifies his confederates in the crime, but only as "Lee," "Ben," "Willie X," and "Wilbour." In his own affidavit Kunstler adds that Hagan is willing to tell the court their full names and last known addresses.

About forty Black Muslims sit in the courtroom when the clerk calls, "On the motion calendar, Norman Butler and Thomas Johnson."

Kunstler steps forward to the lectern before Judge George Roberts. At fifty-eight he's a big shaggy dog of a man, his long hair unkempt, his suit loose and rumpled.

"I have your papers, Mr. Kunstler," Roberts observes. "I have not yet received papers from the District Attorney."

Assistant District Attorney Allen Alpert asks for an adjournment until February 10. He starts to explain why.

"Can we wait until the defendants are here, Your Honor?" Kunstler asks.

A few minutes later the defendants are led in from the bullpen—two bearded blacks, one wearing a green sweater and black skullcap, the other a brown sports jacket and green knitted skullcap. In prison they have changed their names to Muhammad Abdul Aziz and Khalil Islam.

In this courtroom, the courthouse's original arraignment part for felonies, defendants literally stand "at the bar"—not at the defense table beside their counsel. Both Butler and Johnson are impassive as the attorneys argue.

Alpert briefly traces the history of Kunstler's application, notes that he has a heavy case load, and asks for more time to answer. "We're as interested in seeing that justice is done as he is," he explains. But he says the matter requires "thorough investigation."

"Are you opposing his application?" Roberts asks Kunstler.

"I am." He adds that he too has a heavy case load.

"I consider that the least compelling reason cited by the People," Roberts says.

Kunstler says the defendants don't want to remain in Rikers Island. They've been shifted there from state prison for the hearing.

"They won't," Roberts assures him. Then he adds, "I am going to grant the application."

The District Attorney's office is given until February 10 to reply.

Jim Ryan has prepared a minor coup. His case against Philip Carlo hinges on the credibility of the eyewitness identification. Frank Scaduto is the only man who can identify Carlo as the person who passed one of the bad checks. On cross-examination defense attorney Lawrence Hochheiser tested his memory for faces by asking Scaduto to describe the court stenographers who sat a few feet in front of him the day before. One was a man, Scaduto said, but he didn't remember anything more about him. The other was "a heavyset woman . . . tall, taller than I am," with "hair falling down."

On re-direct Ryan brings the female stenographer into court.

"I ask you if you recognize that woman?"

"No, I don't," Scaduto replies.

"You never saw her before?"

"No."

Ryan doesn't let the setback show. He excuses Scaduto and calls his next witness.

Friday, January 20

New York is buried under a blanket of snow—thirteen inches, the worst blizzard in nine years. Peggy Kerry, a "paratroop" in Jim Ryan's trial bureau, has skied to work. But many lawyers, jurors, witnesses, and court employees cannot get to the courthouse and Correction cannot transport prisoners from Rikers

Island. Administrative Justice David Ross has closed the city's courts for the day. Only the arraignment parts remain open. New prisoners must be housed overnight at the Tombs.

District Attorney Morgenthau is home, ill with the flu. But his office chooses this day to announce an indictment in "the case of the green lasagna."

The case has been cooking since September—when the D.A.'s office received an anonymous tip that someone had stolen cash from a trunk that had been gathering dust for more than twenty years at a Manhattan warehouse. During the fall some $313,570 was recovered from various safe-deposit boxes. So was another $17,200, which Terrance Hart allegedly gave to Richard Lynch with instructions to hide it. Lynch's wife, Alice, did—between the layers of a homemade lasagna in the family's freezer.

The indictments charge three former warehouse employees—the brothers Terrance and Raymond Hart and John Hughes—variously with conspiracy, grand larceny, and possession of stolen property. But they do nothing to clear up the mystery of how much money was taken—some estimates run into the millions—who stashed the cash in the first place, or who can claim ownership now.

Judge Harold Rothwax has a sentencing scheduled for 3:00 P.M. Although the courts are officially closed, all the parties show up, so he decides to proceed.

The sentencing illustrates the problems caused by "the Dolkart decision."

Joel Dolkart was the general counsel of Gulf + Western Industries and a partner successively in two of Wall Street's largest and most prestigious law firms. In 1974 he was indicted on charges of stealing $2.5 million in legal fees which Gulf + Western had paid the firms—Strasser, Spiegelberg, Fried & Frank and Simpson Thacher & Bartlett.

Two years later he pleaded guilty to forgery—one of the eighty-nine counts against him—but sentencing was stayed while he cooperated with both the District Attorney's office and the Securities and Exchange Commission in investigations of Gulf + Western. Finally, in June 1977, Justice James Leff imposed a three-year prison term.

In December the Appellate Division, splitting three to one, overruled Leff and reduced Dolkart's sentence to five years' probation. The majority said Leff "did not give adequate consideration to [Dolkart's] extensive cooperation" or to "the fact that he did effectuate restitution." It also noted that Dolkart was sixty-one years old and had been disbarred after practicing law "for over thirty years with an unblemished record."

Many judges and lawyers believe that the Dolkart decision sets a double standard of justice—one set of punishments for crime in the streets, another for what Ralph Nader has termed "crime in the suites."

The case before Rothwax involves another attorney—Jerry Lee Brammer, who admitted embezzling $1.5 million from his employer, Champion International Corporation. Under terms of his plea bargaining, Brammer faces two years in prison. But, citing the Dolkart decision, his attorney, John Martin, has moved for probation.

Tall, blond, well dressed, and handsome as an Arrow-shirt ad, Brammer

stands beside Martin as Chief Assistant District Attorney Peter Zimroth argues against probation. He says the Dolkart case differs from Brammer's because Dolkart cooperated with the authorities and provided "extraordinary information."

Brammer himself protests: "The only difference between Mr. Dolkart and me was that I worked for an honest company and had no information to give up."

Rothwax says disbarment is not severe enough punishment in Brammer's case. "There ought to be a presumption of jail for any lawyer who commits a felony."

He sentences Brammer to two consecutive one-year terms and enters a recommendation against early release. But he stays the start of the sentence—until January 31—to give him time to appeal.

Monday, January 23

The problems of the Dolkart decision are posed again—in the flesh.

Joel Dolkart—sixty-two, chunky, his silver hair still showing a trace of yellow, obviously a man of property—is in court for resentencing. The Appellate Division directed that the terms of his five years' probation be set by a judge other than Leff. So the case has been assigned to Dennis Edwards, Jr., one of the few blacks on the bench.

Edwards summons counsel to the bench. Dolkart, an attorney apparently more used to boardrooms than courtrooms, stands beside the prosecution table.

"Excuse me, sir," a court officer says—with unusual civility—directing him to a seat at the defense table.

When the lengthy conference breaks up, Edwards asks, "Has the case been called?"

"No, Your Honor," the clerk replies. "I'll call the case. Joel Dolkart, for resentence."

Edwards briefly summarizes the Appellate Division order. Then Peter Zimroth asks for "the usual conditions of probation—with one addition, that Mr. Dolkart be required to cooperate honestly and fully with the Securities and Exchange Commission, the New York County District Attorney's office, and any other agency . . ."

"We have no problem, Your Honor, with that condition," says Dolkart's attorney, Bernard Nussbaum.

Edwards says he's received an oral update of Dolkart's probation report from probation officer Charles Cushing. "I see no significance in belaboring the record," he says—and imposes the probation.

Dolkart walks out of court.

Jim Ryan sits on a cushioned seat in the jury box beside Detective Daniel O'Neill, waiting for court to reconvene after lunch. He tells O'Neill that he spent the weekend waxing his skis.

From the defense table the beefy, mustached Hochheiser bellows, "You went skiing this weekend?"

"I was going to."

"Your case is in shambles and you went skiing!"

Ryan's case *is* in shambles. Not only is Scaduto's identification of Carlo suspect, but on direct examination O'Neill admitted that a prosecution witness, under subpoena, had disappeared. Francis Fleetwood, the contractor who worked on Carlo's brownstone, was the witness Ryan felt would tie all the loose ends of the case together.

When court reconvenes, defense attorney Hochheiser launches into his cross-examination of O'Neill. It's punctuated by Ryan's frequent objections —usually sustained—and finally Justice Gabel herself denounces the line of questioning as "a fishing expedition."

O'Neill soon steps down, and Ryan rises. "Your Honor, that is the People's case. The People rest."

Hochheiser rises. "Your Honor, the defense rests at this time."

Tuesday, January 24

Jim Ryan rises and spreads the sheets of white legal paper on the shelf in front of the jury box. It's a few minutes past noon. He sat up until 2:30 A.M. preparing his closing argument in the Carlo case.

Left hand thrust in his pants pocket, gesturing with his right, he directs his remarks at the juror he's least sure of—No. 2, a blond man in a turtleneck sweater who walked into the courtroom day after day whistling jauntily and who reacted to much of the testimony by making faces.

"The issue in this case is relatively simple," Ryan says. "It's a question of identification."

The case is really two cases, he continues, one for each check. "One case is stronger than the other, and I'd be less than frank with you if I didn't deal with it in that manner."

He admits the weakness of Scaduto's identification, but calls the testimony of Fred Glickstein, the merchant bilked by the other bad check, "devastating." He can't tell the panel what the court clerk told him—that Glickstein was the most impressive witness he'd ever seen. Nor can he tell the jurors that Carlo faces a series of bad-check charges in other counties. Instead, he asks the jury not to let the weakness of one case "taint" the other.

He finishes a few minutes after one.

Justice Gabel charges the jury after lunch. The panel retires at 3:30 P.M. and Ryan returns to his sixth-floor office to prepare a case for presentation to the grand jury the following day.

At dinnertime he slogs through the slush to the World Trade Center in search of a seafood restaurant he heard about. He can't find it, so he settles for a Burger King.

He returns to his office, working . . . and waiting.

At 8:30 the call comes. Ryan returns to court to hear the jury's verdict: guilty on the Glickstein count.

Wednesday, January 25 In a driving rain William Depperman passes out leaflets at the doors of the courthouse. He's a long-haired man with a drooping mustache, wearing a black raincoat and holding a dripping umbrella. The leaflets say:

> TOTAL MEDIA BLACKOUT
> With Trumped-up Charges
> Capitalist State Harassing William H.
> Depperman, Coordinator of the Assassination
> Information Committee of New York:
>
> FIRST ASSASSINATION
> RESEARCHER ARRESTED
> For Exposing That Photo-Overlays Along
> With the Canfield-Sturgis Tapes Prove
> Without Doubt that C.I.A. Agents, Nixon's "Plumbers,"
> E. Howard Hunt and Frank Fiorini Sturgis, Both Assassins,
> Were the Triggermen in the J.F.K.
> Assassination, and for Revealing the U.S.
>
> NUMBER ONE STATE SECRET
> Namely, that the J.F.K. Assassination
> Was Part of a Rockefeller Dynasty-Led
> Ruling Class Takeover (Coup D'Etat) Based on
> A Consensus Agreement Including the C.I.A.,
> The Pentagon and the Mafia. This Takeover
> Continues Today as David Rockefeller's Present
> Unconstitutional Tri-Lateralist Brzezinski-"Carter"
> Administration! The Truth About the J.F.K.
> Assassination is the Achilles Heel of
> Gov't Credibility Because it Destroys
> The Illusion of "Democracy" in the
> United States. People Start to Realize
> *Socialist Revolution is Inevitable!!*
> DEMONSTRATE

Later, in the fifth-floor courtroom of Criminal Court, Jury 1, Depperman appears *pro se*—acting as his own attorney.

Wearing half-glasses, Judge Benjamin Altman reviews the thick sheaf of papers in the case.

Assistant District Attorney Catherine Reid notes that at the last hearing the D.A.'s office successfully protested that Depperman earned too much to be represented by Legal Aid.

"Legal Aid makes its own determinations as to who is eligible," Altman rules. He says one woman assistant once protested to him about Legal Aid's representing a woman because she was better dressed than the assistant!

Altman summons Legal Aid attorney John Zirinsky to the bench and asks him about Depperman's status. When Zirinsky calls it "a borderline case," Altman reassigns him to the defense.

"The People are ready for trial," Reid announces.

"The court is adjourning this," Altman says. He's always loath to grant adjournments in Jury 1 because the Jury parts are outside the tracking system under which cases, assistant district attorneys, and Legal Aid lawyers move together from the arraignment to the all-purpose parts of Criminal Court, then to the calendar and trial parts of Supreme Court. Usually he must "crack heads" to get the lawyers to set trial dates for misdemeanor cases. But because of the snowstorm all the calendars for the week are overcrowded with the cases originally scheduled for Friday, and jail cases have priority. Depperman's case is continued until February 14.

The charge that prompted the protests: defacing public property by stenciling slogans on the Washington Square arch and the nearby Bobst Library of New York University.

Thursday, January 26

Five black men are led from the bullpen into the thirteenth-floor courtroom of Justice Clifford Scott. Like John Carro and Burton Roberts, Scott sits in a federally funded section designed to speed the cases of those jailed six months or more. In this case, the defendants have been in jail for more than a year.

The spectator seats are deserted, but the well is crowded with uniformed court officers, for the defendants are deemed dangerous. The five—Alfred Plummer, Paul Pitts, Carl Dukes, McArthur Nelson, and Curtis Brown—are accused of felony murder, for killing a customer during the stickup of a Harlem supermarket. Plummer, the alleged gunman, is a veteran of the 1971 riot at Attica State Prison. His co-defendant, Brown, went through the Tombs riot the year before.

In lawyers' lingo, the case is "a can of worms"—complex, tangled, messy. When the police arrived after the shooting, the robbers scattered through the crowded store and tried to blend in with the customers. It took hours for the cops to discern who was who. As a result, Assistant District Attorney Eugene Porcaro has a list of more than one hundred potential witnesses, both police and civilian, none of whom knows more than a fraction of the total picture. And he may have to call most of them to fill in the mosaic.

Naturally, neither Porcaro nor the court-appointed defense attorneys was anxious to try the case. According to courthouse scuttlebutt, Plummer was offered a sentence of fifteen to life and the other four manslaughter pleas if they admitted their guilt. But the prosecution insisted that it be all five or none, and the deal fell through because Brown balked. He had been paroled for robbery and, if returned to prison, might have to serve out the remaining eighteen years of that sentence. Brown, highly regarded by his fellow prisoners as a "jailhouse lawyer," is conducting his own defense.

So the *Wade* hearings continue into their second day. The pre-trial phase of the case alone is expected to last at least a month. And the proceedings will be even more protracted because Pitt is a Black Muslim and the court will not sit on Fridays, the Muslim sabbath.

At the other end of the hall the bribery trial of Martin Geruso is in its second day of testimony. Geruso, a stocky man of forty-six with a high forehead and a neatly trimmed beard, is accused of accepting more than $20,000 in bribes while he was an assistant attorney general and later an assistant counsel in the state's Office of General Services. In return, he allegedly appointed a favored accountant to audit claims against the state and gave inflated settlements to a contractor with claims arising from construction of the South Mall in Albany—the billion-dollar boondoggle resulting from Governor Nelson Rockefeller's "edifice complex."

Geruso is the first of three former assistant attorneys general to be brought to trial for bribery in the investigation. Vera Bocco, personal secretary to Attorney General Louis J. Lefkowitz, has already pleaded guilty to perjury in the probe. It's an election year and, obviously, the case has political implications.

Beside Geruso sits his attorney, Herald Price Fahringer of Buffalo. Slim, slick, and white-haired at only forty-nine, Fahringer has built a reputation as one of the nation's leading criminal lawyers. His celebrated clients include literary critic Leslie Fielder, New York State Assembly Speaker Stanley Steingut, and *Hustler*'s Larry Flynt.

Since Geruso admitted receipt of most of the money, Fahringer has his work cut out for him. His strategy is threefold: first, to show that the payments were "loans" that Geruso repaid; second, to show that Geruso's superiors—not he—appointed the accountant and approved the settlements; third, to show that those above Geruso were even more indebted to those he dealt with—in his opening remarks Fahringer pointed out that two of the contractors gave $35,000 to the 1974 campaign of then Governor Malcolm Wilson.

The prosecutor is Stephen Shiffrin, an assistant in the Rackets Bureau, which investigates organized crime and political corruption. He's slightly built, bearded, and somewhat prissy in manner. He likes prosecuting white-collar crimes because there's no question as to the defendant's being "a victim of society."

Shiffrin calls his second witness—Assistant District Attorney Peter Benitez, his colleague in the Rackets Bureau. Benitez is tall, dark, and suavely handsome.

Shiffrin asks him about the investigation. Did it have a code name?

"Roadgang," Benitez says.

"Objection!" Fahringer shouts at the same time—so loudly that the stenographer cannot hear Benitez's answer, even though he's sitting only two feet away.

"Sustained," rules Acting Supreme Court Justice Aloysius Melia.

Shiffrin asks for a conference at the bench.

Melia, a white-haired man of sixty-two, who served as an assistant district attorney and deputy police commissioner before his appointment to the bench, shakes his head sadly. "I can see very early in the game that we're going to break the record of the U.N. for conferences."

The conference is held, but Melia's ruling stands.

Under Shiffrin's questioning, Benitez tells how he questioned Geruso in the District Attorney's office. He asked if he'd ever received money from Bernard Landers, a Syracuse accountant.

He quotes Geruso's reply: " 'The first time I did anything wrong with Mr. Landers was when Mr. Landers offered me one thousand dollars for every case I assigned to Mr. Landers.' "

In all, Benitez says, Geruso admitted to taking $4,200 from Landers. Then, according to Geruso, Lefkowitz found out about the payments—to Geruso and Assistant Attorney General Joseph Hopkins—and ordered them to repay the money. Geruso said he'd borrowed the funds for repayment from Peter Bratti, a marble contractor on the South Mall with pending claims against the state.

Benitez tells of other favors Geruso admitted receiving from Bratti—paying off $2,000 in markers he'd run up on a Las Vegas trip; a gift of $5,000 that Geruso, in turn, gave to a prostitute named Pixie; and picking up the $1,800 tab for Pixie's "shopping spree."

The thirteenth-floor courtroom of Part 37 is all but deserted during Benitez's testimony, but there are three very interested spectators—Geruso's wife, Patricia, a sultry brunette in a pants suit, and two Treasury agents.

Friday, January 27

The last of four alternates is picked in the Washington Square riot case, rounding out a jury of seven men and five women. In a case with racial overtones the panel includes three blacks.

The nine defendants allegedly were part of a gang of eighty to one hundred that swept through the park on the night of September 8, 1976, attacking blacks and Hispanics with baseball bats, pipes, and chains. Fourteen persons were injured, one of them fatally—Marcus Mota, a twenty-two-year-old native of the Dominican Republic.

With nine defendants, nine defense lawyers, and panel after panel of prospective jurors, the courtroom at 111 Centre Street was so crowded that five days earlier the trial was moved to a larger courtroom on the eleventh floor of the Criminal Courts Building. A cardboard sign on the door indicates that the courtroom is now Part 106 and that Part 44 has been moved down the hall.

Now, with the jury picked, the courtroom is almost deserted. Only the sixteen jurors and alternates in the box, Assistant District Attorney John Moscow at the prosecution table, the defendants and defense attorneys seated *around* the double-length defense table, the court functionaries, and a handful of spectators listen as Acting Supreme Court Justice Robert Haft gives the jurors their preliminary instructions.

"You are the sole judges of the facts, just as I am the sole judge of the law," he says.

Haft, a short, slim man of forty-six with wavy black hair and black horn-rimmed glasses, admonishes them not to discuss the case, not to form any opinion about it, not to read about it in the newspapers or visit the scene. But they should report immediately any attempt to influence them improperly.

Normally, he continues, the Assistant District Attorney would now deliver his opening, but—as the jurors may have noticed—two of the defendants are absent, out ill.

"So we're going to recess the trial at this time to Monday morning at ten o'clock."

He tells them that trial sessions will run from ten to one and from two to five each day. The jurors will not be allowed to take notes, but he asks them all to pull out pencil and paper now and record the days when the trial will *not* be on—some legal holidays, some days when he will hear other matters. The dates run into March, for the trial is expected to last at least two months.

"So, all I want to say now is, have a very good weekend and I'll see you again on Monday."

Monday, January 30

It's the first day of the February Term. The judges play musical chairs and everyone else plays hide-and-seek.

A woman lawyer from Legal Aid wanders down the eleventh-floor hall asking, "Where the hell is Part Forty-four?"

Simple. Part 44 is in the courtroom marked Part 35. There Jim Ryan is handling the calendar call before Judge Irving Lang.

Part 35 is in the courtroom marked Part 31, the original arraignment part which courthouse old-timers still call "Part 30." There Judge Harold Rothwax is impaneling the six grand juries that will sit during the month, three each morning, three each afternoon.

Part 31 is across the hall in the courtroom marked Part 44.

Down the hall in Part 106—in what a week before was Part 44—Assistant District Attorney John Moscow is slated to deliver his opening address to the jury in the Washington Square riot trial. But there's a hitch: one of the defendants is still ill. As the attorneys pore over the statute books in Judge Haft's robing room to determine if the trial can proceed without him, Ernest "Harry" Hammer, one of the nine defense lawyers, conducts business from a pay phone in the hall.

Suddenly Moscow dashes out the courtroom doors.

"John, what's your prognosis?" Hammer shouts.

"I don't know," the prosecutor replies. "I'm going down to check with my Appeals Bureau. I don't like it."

Two floors above—in Part 37—Herald Fahringer cross-examines marble contractor Peter Bratti in the Geruso case. He elicits that Bratti not only made payments to Geruso, he had financial dealings with Geruso's superiors—Major General Almerin C. O'Hara, former commissioner of the Office of General Services, and former Governor Malcolm Wilson. He gave $5,000 to O'Hara's favorite charity, the New York Military Academy, and offered the general a job doing public relations for the Bratti companies in Saudi Arabia and Iran. He and another contractor gave a $35,000 campaign contribution to Wilson—$10,000 of it from Bratti—and the governor, he says, promised "to see what I can do" about settling their $21 million claim against the state. And when Wilson and his wife visited Rome, a Bratti employee served as their guide and took them to an audience with the Pope. But, hedging his bets, Bratti also made a $10,000 contribution to the campaign of Wilson's Democratic rival, Governor Hugh Carey.

Then the jury is excused as the attorneys argue over whether Fahringer can question Bratti about his meetings with O'Hara. Shiffrin argues that Fahringer should not be allowed to.

What about meetings at which Geruso was present? Fahringer asks.

"That's a different kettle of fish," Shiffrin says.

"I think we've fried this fish long enough," Judge Melia rules. He orders the jury brought in, and testimony resumed.

Judge Haft stops in the press room to report on the unusual proceeding he conducted this morning—going to the home of Carlos Boutureira with a stenographer and counsel for both sides to receive the youth's waiver and let the trial proceed without him. Moscow, he says, will open at 2:00 P.M.

It's 2:20 when Moscow—chunky, curly-haired, sleepy-eyed—rises to address the jury.

First, he runs through the nine defendants. "None of you have scorecards," he says, "but I'm sure that by the end of the trial you'll be able to distinguish them."

The nine defendants are a 1970s reincarnation of the Dead End Kids, down to the token black. There's Michael Andriani, twenty-one, husky and blandly handsome; Rocco Areena, twenty-one, stocky and curly-haired; the absent Boutureira; Edward Burns, eighteen, short, blond, and bouncy; Joseph Chiapetti, at twenty-three the oldest of the group, a pint-sized Air Force veteran; Michael Doyle, seventeen, thin, blond, and wispy; Robert McLamb, eighteen, the only black defendant, short and stoical; Anthony Paolini, eighteen, thin and bushy-browed; and Andres Sanchez, nineteen, chunky and sullen. Of the nine, only Paolini graduated from high school; only Doyle and Paolini were regularly employed.

Moscow tells the panel that on September 8, 1976, "a group of youths entered Washington Square Park. . . . They were armed with pipes, chains, mostly baseball bats. They struck black youths."

He says one pregnant black woman was kicked in the stomach. A man was blinded in one eye. Another was fatally injured.

"These people did not come together spontaneously," he continues. The conspiracy was hatched two days before to drive blacks and Hispanics from the square. White youths were rounded up at parks and playgrounds throughout Greenwich Village. They gathered before the attack in Leroy Street Park. There McLamb was stood on a table.

"Don't hit him," the white youths were told. "He's a good nigger. He's one of us."

A red bandanna was tied around McLamb's head to identify him.

"The People will prove that the intent was to strike what the people there called 'niggers,' " Moscow continues. He notes that some went along "for what they thought was the legitimate purpose of driving the [drug] dealers out of Washington Square Park." But the "most undesirable" of the dealers were forewarned and were not in the park when the attack came.

Moscow says that Marcus Mota was struck while he was standing beside his bicycle, knocked out, hospitalized, and "without regaining consciousness died a couple of days later."

"As regards that blow, you will hear testimony that Robert McLamb—perhaps bragging—said—"

Defense attorney Michael Direnzo, a rotund little man with silver hair and a gravel voice, interrupts. "Your Honor, may we approach?"

There's a conference at the bench, then Moscow resumes.

"As to Mr. McLamb, you'll hear testimony that he told people close to him that he struck a man hard in the back of the head with a baseball bat."

Moscow runs through the charges in the indictment—conspiracy, riot, manslaughter, and six assaults. He cannot tell the panel that this is the second indictment in the case. Judge Haft dismissed the first because of the twenty-nine-year-old prosecutor's "prejudicial behavior, excessive zeal, and inexperience" before the grand jury. Nor can he tell them of McLamb's and Boutureira's extensive records of arrests for assault and robbery. Nor that Chiapetti tried to plead guilty at the outset of the trial, and that Boutureira, McLamb, and Sanchez admitted their part in the assault. Judge Haft refused to accept Chiapetti's plea and suppressed the statements, because the defendants had not been adequately advised of their rights. Originally there were ten defendants, but when Michael Durnin's admission also was suppressed, Moscow was forced to drop the charges against him.

The prosecutor concludes, "The People will prove this case through the testimony of victims. The People will prove this case through the testimony of accomplices. The People will prove this case through the testimony of persons horrified by what they saw and persons curious enough to follow along."

There's another bench conference. Then Judge Haft announces that all nine defendants waive opening statements.

But Direnzo has another point. An attorney often retained by minor-league *mafiosi,* he has grown hard of hearing with advancing age and, as a result, has been seated closest to the jury box. But he complains that because of the seating arrangements he cannot confer with his client, Andriani, during the testimony.

Judge Haft excuses the jury while the attorneys confer again at the bench. The other defense lawyers prefer the present seating arrangements, and Haft declines to change them.

As the lawyers return to their seats, Direnzo suddenly wheels and explodes at a co-counsel, "I don't have to apologize to you or anyone else! I'm only doing my job—the only way I know how!"

Tuesday, January 31

Moscow calls the victim's mother. Alminda Heredia is a small black woman in a black floral-print dress who testifies through a Spanish interpreter.

There's some confusion as to how she spells her last name—with or without an *H.*

"Sometimes with the *H,* sometimes without," she says in English.

Sobbing, she testifies that her only son, Marco Antonio Mota, was born in Santo Domingo on January 25, 1954. She came to the United States in 1966.

"And your son, Marcus—did he come with you then?"

"That is objected to, Your Honor."

There's another conference at the bench, and Judge Haft excuses the jury while the attorneys argue. At the end it's stipulated that her son was the man fatally injured in the riot.

Upstairs in the Geruso case there's another hearing with the jury excused. Jotting on a blackboard, Herald Fahringer lists the payments Bernard Landers made to Geruso, the one charged in the indictment in one column, those not charged—because there was no jurisdiction in New York County—in another.

"Now here's my concern," he says. "Mr. Landers taking the stand and testifying to an actual bribe transaction. . . . When the jury hears that, we feel that he could be convicted on these transactions which are not charged in the indictment."

Shiffrin argues that the testimony goes to "motive" and "intent."

"As to what?" Judge Melia asks.

"Count three and count nine of the indictment."

Fahringer cites a string of cases in which testimony of other crimes was barred.

"But, Mr. Fahringer," Melia says, "in none of those cases was the crime connected with the crime on trial." He rules that the testimony is "related" and "material." "They show the background, the motivation, and the intent. . . . Bring in the jury."

"Are we ready for Brammer?" Judge Rothwax asks.

"Yes."

"Call Jerry Lee Brammer," he tells the clerk.

The case is called, and Brammer stands at the bar. In contrast to his sentencing eleven days before, the usually dapper defendant wears a sweater and blue jeans.

"Does the defendant wish to appeal?" the judge asks.

"He has neither the emotional nor financial resources," says defense attorney John Martin.

The lawyer asks Rothwax to reconsider his sentence. "At least, Your Honor, make these sentences concurrent."

"I did what I thought was right," Rothwax says. But he notes that the Appellate Division might feel differently. "I felt strongly then and I feel strongly now," he continues, "that criminality of this nature requires a prison sentence. . . . I'm acting in good faith. I believe that this is a proper and appropriate sentence and I'm not going to modify it."

He asks if Brammer has anything more to say.

"No."

"The defendant is remanded pursuant to the sentence of January twentieth."

Brammer is led away to the bullpen.

Wednesday, February 1 In Judge Melia's robing room Steve Shiffrin and Herald Fahringer go over transcripts of conversations with Geruso that Bernard Landers recorded to determine what portions may be played to the jury.

"Judge, do you have to leave in 'the Internal Revenue Service'?" Fahringer asks.

"No, I don't."

"Your Honor," Shiffrin protests, "I just think this is becoming a little silly in that we are chopping so much out of this that the jury has no way of understanding anything. We are taking everything out that is not immediately related to the indictment, and now we are chopping every other sentence that *is* directly related to the indictment and leaving gibberish."

"Unfortunately," Melia rules, "that's the way the cookie crumbles."

In the Washington Square trial Andres Sanchez's attorney, Robert Cohen, cross-examines Carl Warren, a big, bearded black who bears the appealing nickname of "Bonecrusher." Warren, one of the fourteen injured in the attack, identified Sanchez as one of the youths who struck him.

Cohen is short, gravel-voiced, and has a profile that belongs on a nickel.

"I believe you testified that you incurred the loss of your right eyesight as a result of something that occurred in the service?" he asks.

"Yes . . ."

"And has that impaired your vision in the right eye?"

"I'm blind in my right eye."

"You're blind in your right eye?" Cohen repeats, making sure the jurors hear. "I notice that you're wearing glasses. Are they prescription glasses?"

"They are."

"Could you tell us . . . what is your eye problem with your left eye?"

"Well, I wear the glasses to keep from putting too much strain on my left eye. The vision in my left eye is so badly strained that the vision had come to twenty-forty and it's still the same."

"Are you nearsighted or farsighted? If you know?"

"Nearsighted," Warren replies. "I have difficulty without my glasses making out things at a distance."

The cross-examination continues. Eventually, Cohen brings out that at a lineup at the D.A.'s office Warren identified Assistant District Attorney Rod Brown, not Sanchez.

Thursday, February 2 A tape recorder and loudspeakers have been set up in Part 37 as Shiffrin and Fahringer continue what Judge Melia calls "haggling over minutiae." The jury is still excused as the attorneys check transcripts of Landers's conversations against the tapes.

"Let's play it," the judge orders.

A D.A.'s detective plays a few seconds of tape—a babble incomprehensible to anyone without a transcript.

"I didn't hear 'yeah,' " Fahringer says.

"I didn't hear it," Melia agrees.

"Can we have that stricken out?"

"Yes."

"Yeah" is deleted from the transcript.

Bernard Jones takes the stand in the Washington Square trial. He's a short, well-dressed black who works as a physical therapist and is in an alcohol-rehabilitation program. He says he was walking through the park on the night of September 8 when he was struck with a baseball bat, first on the head, then on the arm. Forty-two stitches were required to close the wound over his right eye. He didn't see the face of his attacker.

In the fourth-floor hall Channel 5's Gabe Pressman, the pioneer among New York television reporters, and a camera crew are covering Marty Evans's latest case.

Evans, forty, is short, pudgy, bespectacled, long-haired, and mustached. He lists his occupation as "computer consultant," but his preoccupation is seduction. He boasts that he's "made love to 3,769½ women."

Three years before, he was the defendant in a celebrated case, charged with the rape of a Wellesley student. But Justice Edward Greenfield ruled:

> Bachelors and other men on the make . . . have no fear. It is still not a crime to feed a girl a line to get her to say yes about going to bed with you if she says no the first time. You may make promises you have no intention of keeping, exaggerate, or assure any trusting female that the ugly frog is indeed the handsome prince. Force or threat of force is of course out of bounds. But what Marty Evans did is truly conquest by con-job. He can be aptly called "the abominable snowman." But the "abominable snow-job" is not rape.

Evans returned to his old ways. One night last fall he picked up three members of an all-girl punk-rock band and took them back to his room in the Chelsea Hotel, a celebrated hangout for artists and writers. According to Evans, he talked the girls into taking off their clothes . . . and let nature take its course.

But two of the girls—Marlane Panarites and Debbie Bianchi—found out who Evans was and let him know what Women's Lib is all about. Evans filed an assault complaint.

Pressman has filmed an interview with Evans. Now he's trying to get the defendants or their lawyer, Linda Nussbaum of Legal Aid. She refused—and refuses—to let her clients appear on camera.

"All he wants to do is get a story about himself, and we're not gonna help him do that," she explains.

So Pressman waits, conferring with Evans.

"I'm surprised that they haven't filed a counter-complaint," he says.

"What are they gonna charge me with?" Evans replies. "Assault with a friendly weapon?"

Pressman's persistence has produced one result. Nussbaum, in panic, has summoned her superior, Elliott Cook, and the more experienced lawyer works out an accord with the newsman: Pressman and his crew can film the defendants leaving the courtroom—that way there won't be a chase scene embarrassing to both sides—and ask Nussbaum a question, which she'll decline to answer.

The day before, Pressman filmed three stories before noon. It's now nearing 1:00 P.M. and he hasn't put one in the can.

Finally the case is called. Panarites, a tall, thin brunette, and Bianchi, a short, bosomy brunette in a halter top, stand beside Nussbaum at the defense table. Evans stands at the rail.

Both sides know the case will be adjourned, but Stephen Cronin, the prosecutor, is elsewhere and the assistant handling the calendar call won't adjourn it without him.

"Two o'clock," Judge John Leone orders.

Evans calls out, "May I approach the bench?"

Leone glares at him. *"No way."*

In the hall Pressman's crew films the defendants' departure and the newsman leaves for other assignments musing on the old adage: You meet two kinds of people in the business—those who want their names in the paper when they should be out and those who want their names out of the paper when they should be in.

Friday, February 3

There's another robing-room conference in the Geruso case.

"You want to take up Sabo?" Judge Melia asks.

Fahringer outlines the situation: After Geruso left the Attorney General's office, a file he had worked on was assigned to Alvin Sabo, who found $160 in it.

"Your Honor, my position is that that is entirely too remote to be received in . . . evidence as an inference that this is—"

Melia cuts him off. "Mr. Shiffrin."

"Your Honor," the prosecutor replies, "the claim in question was the Torrington claim. Martin Geruso admitted taking two hundred dollars from Bernard Landers for the Torrington claim."

"Judge," Fahringer protests, "that doesn't mean that the money that was in the file is *the* two hundred dollars."

"I think it's a little remote, Mr. Shiffrin," Judge Melia rules. "I will exclude it."

After more verbal sparring, the lawyers return to open court and the People rest.

John Moscow is questioning Diana Brown, a teen-age Greenwich Village girl, about the incident that provoked the Washington Square riot.

She and Teresa Cowan were in the park on September 7 when Andres Sanchez and Frankie Vales got into a fight with Larry Warner, a drug dealer known as "Blue."

Starting a colloquy that could come from the theater of the absurd, Moscow asks, "What color is Blue?"

"Blue is black," Brown replies.

She goes on to describe the incident. "Evidently Blue sold them a 'joint' and they didn't think it was a good smoke. They wanted their dollar back."

"And what did Blue say?"

"He said he wasn't going to give them back their dollar."

"What happened after that?"

"Well, they started fighting," she continues. "There was a commotion and a crowd. . . . The little one struck at Blue and struck him across the face. And Blue kept backing off, telling him to cool down, and he just kept swinging at him, so finally he hit him once too often. Blue backed off and messed him up."

"Was the guy bleeding after Blue struck him?"

"Yes, he was."

"Where was he bleeding from?"

"Cut under the lip, I believe. Either that or he busted his lip."

It turned out that Vales's jaw was broken and Sanchez was bloodied.

Monday, February 6

Heavy snow is falling, but the courthouse continues to function.

For the first time all nine defendants in the Washington Square trial are in court, and the jury gets its first look at Carlos Boutureira, twenty, tall and dark, sitting slumped in his seat as lifeless as a zombie.

Moscow continues his prosecution by calling Gary Cangelosi, a seventeen-year-old participant in the assault who was given immunity from prosecution.

"Seven o'clock came and everybody went through the park," the slim, long-haired youth tells the jury. "I personally went into the park and yelled, 'All niggers and Spanish, get out of the park!' "

"And what did you do then?"

"I just started swinging and hitting people."

But Cangelosi is not a good witness. He's not especially intelligent or articulate, and he has a memory like a sieve. It's like pulling teeth to get a simple statement from him.

Cangelosi says the group consisted of eighty to one hundred people with "bats."

"What else?"

"Pipes."

"What else?"

"That's it."

And: "Who else did you see outside the park?"

"All my friends."

"What were their names?"

"I dunno."

"You do not know the names of your friends—is that your testimony?"

"Yes."

In the afternoon Judge Melia's thirteenth-floor courtroom is crowded with reporters and artists from the television stations while TV camera crews and newspaper photographers mill in the hall outside—not for the Geruso case, which is in recess, but for what columnist Murray Kempton has called a show that's run longer than *Grease,* the saga of Bernard Bergman.

Bergman, sixty-seven, an Orthodox Jewish rabbi, became the largest proprietor of nursing homes in New York. After an Assembly committee exposed their squalid conditions—some likened them to Nazi concentration camps—investigations of his operations were launched, one by the federal government, another by the state under Special Prosecutor Charles J. Hynes.

Bergman pleaded guilty to stealing $367,000 in federal Medicare and Medicaid funds (Hynes estimated the total thefts at $2.5 million) and served four months at the federal prison farm at Allenwood, Pennsylvania. In state court he pleaded guilty to offering "unlawful payments" to Assembly Majority Leader Albert Blumenthal to speed state licensing of his homes—the charges against Blumenthal were dismissed—but for seventeen months dodged the start of his one-year sentence. Today is the final deadline set by Judge Melia.

Over the weekend Bergman's lawyers applied to U.S. Supreme Court Justice Thurgood Marshall for a stay of sentence, and there were rumors that Bergman might flee the country or check into a hospital to avoid going to jail. But, despite the weather, he came to court and waits with his attorney, Jack Littman, in the witnesses' waiting room.

Melia mounts the bench. "Would you have counsel and Dr. Bergman come in."

A court officer calls through the open doorway, "The judge is waiting."

"Let's go," Littman says to Bergman.

Bergman enters the courtroom—a tall man wearing a black overcoat and a black *yarmulke* over his gray hairs. He carries a black hat.

Littman, who successfully prosecuted "rogue cop" William Phillips for murder and has since acquired a reputation as one of the city's leading defense lawyers, addresses the court with his trousers tucked into his galoshes. He tells Melia that the snowstorm kept Justice Marshall from getting to court to rule on his application. He pleads for "one more day."

Melia notes that the case was subjected to "intense judicial review" since he imposed sentence on September 13, 1976—by the Appellate Division, state Court of Appeals, U.S. District Court, U.S. Court of Appeals, U.S. Supreme Court, again by the U.S. Court of Appeals, and again by the Appellate Division.

"I think there has to be a finality," he rules. "The application is denied. Execute the sentence."

Bergman sits for a few moments longer conferring with Littman. Then he stands—and court officers lead him to the bullpen.

The saga has ended. Monday the rabbi went to jail.

Tuesday, February 7

New York City is buried under seventeen inches of snow. Once again the courts are closed. Only the arraignment parts are functioning, and they're jammed with hundreds of cases. As in the July blackout, many in the ghettos took advantage of the disaster to rob and loot.

Wearing a suit jacket over khaki trousers tucked into his galoshes and clutching a burning cigar, District Attorney Morgenthau walks through the deserted lobby and enters the courtroom of AR1.

Judge George Roberts tells him that the system is slowed because many staff members of the Criminal Justice Agency, Inc., are absent. The federally funded agency conducts the R.O.R. (release on own recognizance) interviews. Under the law, a judge cannot set bail without an R.O.R. report.

Morgenthau suggests that the interviews be waived during the snow emergency.

Roberts asks the Legal Aid lawyers if they'll accept that.

One will, the other won't.

"All right!" Roberts bellows. "Let 'em stay in jail!"

Judge Irving Lang chooses this day to file his decision in the case of John Williams, one of approximately one thousand arrested in 1977 for playing "three-card monte." Three-card monte is a hustle similar to the "shell game," except cards are used instead of cups and a pea. The bettor must pick the red card from the two black. "The question to be resolved by this court [Lang writes], previously undecided in this state, is whether it is a known confidence game under New York's fraudulent accosting statute."

He notes that the laws of other states and countries differ on whether it is or isn't. A confidence game, he says, involves "the taking of money by fraud . . . by means of trick or deception after the victim's confidence has first been secured through some false representation or deception." By contrast, in monte the bettor pits his eye *against* the player's sleight of hand.

> In sum [he concludes], merely alleging the operating of three-card monte does not constitute a crime under the statute. . . .
>
> The defendant's motion is granted and the complaint is dismissed.
>
> Lest this opinion be viewed as the emancipation proclamation for the monte sharpie playing his skills on Broadway to an unwary public, his conduct would in my view be a clear violation of Penal Law section 240.35(2)—loitering for the purpose of gambling.

For Williams—as for other monte players—it means a maximum of fifteen days in jail instead of one year.

Wednesday, February 8

The city remains snowbound. In Supreme Court only the calendar parts are functioning, but many lawyers and defendants are absent. Judge Lang interrupts the proceedings in Part 44 to take a phone call from Maurice Mathis, a Columbia law student who helped him research the three-card-monte decision.

Lang notes ecstatically that the decision was reported by both the *Times* and the *Daily News* and made the front page of the *Law Journal.*

Mathis also has news for the judge: He's received a notice from Columbia informing him that he won't be allowed to graduate until he returns an overdue library book Lang used in his research.

Lang tells Mathis that he's lent the book to Judge Rothwax. Then he adds, "Don't worry, Maurice. If I have to, I'll issue a writ of *mandamus* to let you graduate."

Not until late afternoon can enough grand jurors be corralled to hear the evidence in the Klein kidnap case. The District Attorney's office planned to move it the first thing Monday morning, but the storm forced a two-day delay.

The case hit the headlines over the weekend. On Friday Marci Klein, the eleven-year-old daughter of the famed fashion designer Calvin Klein, was kidnaped and ransomed for $100,000. On Saturday the Kleins' baby-sitter, Paule (Christine) Ransay, twenty-three; her half brother, Dominique Placide Ransay, nineteen—both natives of Martinique—and a neighbor of theirs, Cecil Wiggins, twenty-four, were arrested for the crime. All but $100 of the ransom was recovered. On Sunday Paule was held in $50,000 bail and the two men in $100,000 after Assistant District Attorney Thomas Demakis told Judge E. Leo Milonas, "All three defendants have made full tape-recorded confessions to me."

At 4:00 P.M., District Attorney Morgenthau calls a press conference to announce that the grand jury has returned an indictment. There's nothing new in the indictment, and the press conference is too late to make the six-o'clock newscasts or even the "bulldog" edition of the *Daily News.*

Its real function is not to announce an indictment but to end reports of a rift between the FBI and the New York City police. Flanking Morgenthau are J. Wallace LaPrade, assistant director of the FBI and special agent in charge of the bureau's New York office, and Robert McGuire, New York's new police commissioner. The three are all smiles and handshakes. LaPrade calls newspaper reports of a rift "outrageously inaccurate."

Thursday, February 9

It's standing room only as more than three hundred persons jam the eleventh-floor chapel in the Tombs. A metal gate stands open at the narrow entrance. The room is bare, the only decoration a grille design behind the altar, the only flash of color red valances (without drapes) over the eight barred windows. The pulpit is a plain wooden lectern embossed with the seal of the Department of Correction.

The occasion is swearing-in ceremonies for eight civilians and nine promoted members of Correction's uniformed force.

The department's new commissioner, William Ciuros, Jr., a heavyset man with black, wavy hair, welcomes the audience to "the Manhattan House of Detention for Men, otherwise known as the Tombs." Then he asks the audience to stand and pledge allegiance to the flag. The uniformed correction officers snap to a salute.

Father Charles Repole, Catholic chaplain of the department, delivers the invocation. Then Ciuros introduces New York's new mayor, Edward I. Koch.

"First of all," Koch says, "it's a pleasure to be here today and I have been in this building many times, some of them painful. This one is very pleasant."

Tall, thin, and bald, Koch speaks in a piping voice. Some have likened him to Frank Perdue of the chicken commercials.

The Mayor says he interviewed many people before he chose Ciuros as his correction commissioner and that Ciuros has been given "carte blanche" to pick his own staff.

He briefly reviews the department's responsibilities—housing 60,000 men and women a year in its eighteen facilities. On any given day, he says, there are 7,000 prisoners—5,000 of them awaiting trial.

"Public safety is the main job of the department," he asserts. "The Department of Correction stands between a just, orderly society and chaos."

"The Tombs today is only a chapel," he continues. "I believe that it must be reopened."

Judge Haft summons the prosecutor to the bench.

"Mr. Moscow," he says, "I think I should inform you that the judges have a pool on when I'm going to be forced to declare a mistrial in this case."

Moscow returns to the prosecution table, ponders for a few moments, then returns to ask Haft, "Judge, you're not in on that, are you?"

Most of the judges consider Moscow brilliant but erratic. They're convinced that at some point—as he did before the first grand jury—he'll go off the deep end and blow the case. Moscow's demeanor does nothing to dispel such doubts. He has a nervous tic that causes him to *daven* like an Orthodox Jew in prayer when he stands. When he sits, his legs flap like a cricket's. In the defendants' street-corner society, where everybody has a nickname, Moscow has been dubbed "Retard."

Moscow's chief witness of the day is Randy Haber, a tubby fifteen-year-old, who says he followed the rioters from Leroy Street Park to a block from Washington Square. Then "Chuckie [Carlos Boutureira] came over to us and said for us to go home."

Outside AR2 a black derelict stands stupefied. His clothes are tattered, his dirty hair hangs in strings. He leans, balanced on one leg, one hand against a heater grille, the other clutching a Styrofoam coffee cup. He doesn't move. He's a courthouse regular, seen in the same position day after day. No one knows who he is, where he comes from, or where he goes.

Inside AR2 a television studio has been set up for a New York first—the videotaping of a witness's testimony. The courtroom floor is littered with wires and electric apparatus, while two klieg lights and a tiny camera focus on the witness box.

Criminal Court Judge Elliott Golden mounts the bench. He looks like a TV judge, his chiseled features tanned, his dark brown hair streaked with silver.

He recapitulates the ground rules: the defense foots the bill; the D.A.'s office keeps custody of the tape; the court reporter will be present; the camera will concentrate on the witness; the use of the tape at trial will be subject to the same rules of law as a transcript; both sides must agree to its introduction.

The case involves simple assault. Anthony Stone, a Port Authority policeman, is charged with kicking Anthony Jenkins in the head in the Port Authority bus terminal.

Leonard Richardson, an eyewitness to the incident, is leaving town before the trial, and the D.A.'s office moved to perpetuate his testimony by the normal procedure of transcribing the Q. and A. Defense attorney Mel Sachs then moved to have the testimony videotaped so the jurors could observe Richardson's demeanor. Golden agreed, and the Appellate Division gave its stamp of approval.

The lights are flashed on and Assistant District Attorney Gary Black, tall and blond, a microphone strapped around his neck, calls Richardson to the stand.

Richardson is a bearded black with long hair that puffs out from his head. He wears a white turtleneck sweater and a large gold cross. Large rings adorn his fingers. He appears glassy-eyed.

He says he was a New York City policeman for twelve years—until he was retired for a mental disability. At 4:00 A.M. on the morning of August 15, 1977, he went to the bus terminal to meet a friend. While he waited for the bus to arrive, he saw two Port Authority policemen—one white, one black—approach a black man sitting on a seat. The black policeman reported an "assault in progress" over his walkie-talkie. Then he handed his radio and his hat to his white colleague, grabbed the man, and threw him on the floor.

Richardson says the black policeman said, "You want to fight me? I've been fighting all my life."

"What's this all about, man?" the other replied.

The black cop, he says, kicked the man in the head.

The man on the floor repeated, "What's this all about, man?"

The black cop kicked him again and the man shouted, "Oh, my eye!"

Then other policemen arrived and took the man away.

Black asks him to identify the man who did the kicking, and Richardson points to Stone—a husky, clean-shaven black in a black pin-striped suit.

Then Black asks him to demonstrate the kick, and Richardson prances in front of the witness box like an awkward ballerina.

Sachs takes over for cross-examination and quickly elicits the nature of Richardson's mental malady.

"I was likely to explode and hurt someone without even knowing I did it."

Sachs also elicits that one of Richardson's "favorite pastimes" is observing people in states of mental boredom and that he once likened Stone to "Son of Sam," the killer who terrorized New York during the summer of 1977.

As Sachs presses his questions in an effort to get Richardson to "explode," the blond director flashes cards with the countdown numbers: 3 . . . 2 . . . 1.

A minute later Judge Golden announces that they've run out of tape. "We'll recess for two minutes." It's the judicial equivalent of Johnny Carson's "We'll be right back after this message."

Friday, February 10

Joseph Cortale is not in the courtroom when his case is called. Judge Lang summons the attorneys to the bench. Richard Kuh steps forward from a first-row seat, Jim Ryan rises from the jury box.

Kuh tells Lang that the Supreme Court has denied *certiorari* in his federal case. Therefore, he'll be going to trial on February 27. That trial should run about three weeks, he says, and he'll need an additional week to prepare for the Cortale case. Then he adds, "I have a slight problem with Justice George Roberts."

"I will take care of Judge Roberts," Lang assures him.

"Our position is, we're ready, Your Honor," Ryan says.

Cortale arrives and takes a seat at the defense table as the lawyers return to open court.

"Have we agreed on March twenty-seventh for trial?" Lang asks. "Is that correct, gentlemen?"

"Yes, Your Honor," Kuh says.

"Yes," Ryan agrees.

Kuh dons his glasses to note the date in his appointment book.

Ryan observes for the record that he had a detective check at Police Headquarters, and the DD5 there is the same as the copy delivered to Kuh. He also gives the defense attorney copies of the grand-jury exhibits he requested.

Kuh is not satisfied. He asks that the detective who prepared the report be called and asked, "Is that the end of the report or is it not?"

Ryan protests. "There is no further substance to that report and no reason to believe that there's anything improper here."

"I certainly trust his good faith," Kuh says of Ryan, but "my experience has been . . . each time he learns something else [the police] haven't told him."

Lang denies Kuh's request, and the defense attorney returns to the issue of the missing tape.

Ryan says it was returned to the file and apparently rerecorded in another investigation.

Kuh again asks for a hearing on the matter.

"As a practical matter—" Lang starts.

"I'm trying to be practical, Your Honor."

"I've heard you on this before, Mr. Kuh," Lang says. "Your motion is denied."

"I do not believe in the game-playing mode of trial," Kuh snaps. He again asks Lang to "recuse" himself, saying his ruling "suggests to me a degree of interest and unfairness in the case." He notes that Lang hasn't presided over a trial in months.

"Mr. Kuh," Lang replies, "I'll say this one time and one time only: Mr. Kuh, you shoot from the hip and from the lip."

Kuh starts to speak, but Lang cuts him off. "I listened to you. Now you listen to me!"

Lang notes—and he says the court clerk will back him up—that he charged a jury "only last week."

Kuh again starts to speak.

"If you interrupt again, I will take appropriate action," Lang warns him.

He reiterates the counts of Kuh's motion that he recuse himself and again denies them. But he says they reflect a "paranoid ideation on your part" that "may very well affect your ability to protect your client's interest. Therefore, I will not try this case."

"I thank Your Honor for his ruling—for whatever reason," Kuh says.

Actually, it's no concession on Lang's part. His calendar is too crowded to permit him to preside over a lengthy trial. But Ryan is distressed. It's an indication to him that Kuh's persistence pays off and permits him to "judge-shop."

"One more thing," Kuh adds, and again asks for the police reports on other suspects.

"I have made my rulings," Lang says. "I don't think there's anything further to add."

Moscow's witness—Anthony DeFranco, a Greenwich Village youth known as "Dif"—has not shown up in court. Judge Haft excuses the jury until Wednesday—Monday is Lincoln's Birthday, a legal holiday, and he has other matters scheduled for Tuesday.

Once the jurors leave, Moscow rises. "I ask the court to inquire of the defendants who the next People's witness is."

Several of the defense lawyers seem stunned.

"Is that a serious request?" Haft asks.

It is. Moscow says that one of the defense lawyers, who learned the witness's name from the *Rosario* material he turned over the night before, must have inadvertently disclosed it to the defendants, who then ensured that the witness would not appear. He asks that McLamb, Chiapetti, Sanchez, and Boutureira—the four defendants who would have been implicated by the witness—be remanded "to dissuade elements in the community . . . from engaging in rash and improper steps."

"That's one of the most drastic remedies I've ever heard," Haft says. "There's no evidence that any one of those you've named has committed any unlawful act."

"The alternative is to lock up the witnesses and let the defendants go free, which is a far more drastic remedy," Moscow says.

One by one the defense lawyers rise and state that they did not disclose the name. Ronald Degen adds that it's obvious from the testimony who the next witness will be.

"I could tell you the next ten witnesses, the next twelve witnesses—"

"I wish you'd tell Mr. Moscow so we could proceed," Haft says.

Moscow withdraws his application, asking that only Boutureira be remanded—because he pleaded guilty in November to burglary and petty larceny in an unrelated case, breaking into a gas station during the July 13 blackout.

"His respect for the law is minimal," Moscow says.

He adds that even though he won't be allowed to present the evidence in court, Boutureira "is in fact a man who has confessed the crimes with which he is charged."

Haft rules against him. Except for the days when he was ill, the judge says, Boutureira appeared for trial and "I do believe he's going to appear."

He tells Moscow, "If you produce any evidence of threats or misconduct by any of the defendants . . . I will be very prompt and remand that defendant —or all of them."

He admonishes the defendants and adjourns the trial.

"If it please Your Honor," Herald Fahringer says, "I call Martin Geruso to the witness stand."

Geruso is sworn and Fahringer quickly elicits that he is forty-six years old, the father of four teen-age children, a church usher, former president of the Glens Falls Jaycees, and had open-heart surgery. He asks Geruso to trace his career from Union College to the Attorney General's office. Geruso admits that when his wife was ill with meningitis—"We thought she was going to die"—he asked Landers for a loan.

He produces travel vouchers and hotel receipts to show that he was not at the Manhattan hotel where Landers said he'd made a bribe payment to him.

Months later, he said, Landers came to his office in Albany and threatened "to blow his brains out" unless he got more work from the state. Landers even walked to the window and pulled out a gun.

"The guy was in such bad shape that I felt I had to do something for him," Geruso says. "Mr. Landers at that point was a pitiful character. He had been a friend, a good friend, and, yes, I tried to help him."

Tuesday, February 14

It's snowing lightly as members of the Assassination Information Committee pass out leaflets protesting the arrest and trial of William Depperman. It always seems to rain or snow whenever Depperman's case is on the calendar.

Herald Fahringer winds up his examination of Martin Geruso: "Before we conclude, is there anything you'd like to say?"

"Well, I just want to say I worked for the state for seven years to the best of my ability," Geruso replies. "I never took a bribe in my life. I never sold the state out or down the river. It's not in my nature."

Wednesday, February 15 Over the holiday weekend there were newspaper accounts about the missing witnesses in the Washington Square trial. When the case is called, Michael Direnzo asks Judge Haft to examine the jurors *in camera* to determine if they read any of the articles.

Haft denies the request. "There is no reason for me to believe that the jury has disregarded my very specific instructions not to read anything about this case," he explains.

Harry Hammer rises. "Before we go to a new area—"

"The new area I was hoping to go to was the trial," Haft says.

Hammer asks Haft to direct Moscow not to talk to the press.

Haft will not go that far. He directs Moscow not to tell the press anything about the case that has not transpired in court.

Before the jury is brought in, Moscow calls his next witness—Gerald Botros, a bearded youth in shirt and slacks.

"Mr. Botros," he asks, "were you present at an incident in Washington Square Park on the evening of September eighth?"

"Do I have immunity?" Botros asks.

"You don't have immunity now," Judge Haft tells him. "Do you refuse to answer the question?"

"Yes, I do."

"And what is the reason for your refusal?"

"On the grounds that it may tend to incriminate me."

Botros is given immunity and the jury is brought in to hear his account of how he recruited for and participated in the attack.

District Attorney Morgenthau has called a press conference. It's his long-awaited announcement of the results of his year-long investigation into corruption in the Civil Term of Supreme Court. For weeks there has been public speculation that prominent lawyers and sitting judges will be named.

Morgenthau's investigation started with a lawyer's complaint to the Grievance Committee of the Association of the Bar of the City of New York. Wiretaps were placed on the phone of Abram Brown, one of the law assistants in the Supreme Court Building at 60 Centre Street on Foley Square. Brown himself was indicted on eight counts of bribery, but died before his case could be brought to trial.

The final result is something of an anticlimax. The only "name" netted in Morgenthau's probe is that of S. Samuel DiFalco, for twenty years one of Manhattan's two Surrogates—the judges who preside in the courts that handle wills and estates. It's a powerful post, for the Surrogates are lavish dispensers of patronage plums to political pals and personal cronies—with the fees paid from the estates, a circumstance that caused Mayor Fiorello LaGuardia to call the court "the most expensive undertaking establishment in the world." During the Roosevelt-LaGuardia years, when Tammany was out of favor at City Hall, Albany, and Washington, it survived largely on appointments from Surrogates Court.

DiFalco reached the mandatory retirement age of seventy in 1977 and returned to the private practice of law. The censored transcripts of his conversations with Brown give an inkling of how justice is bought and sold in New York City:

DIFALCO: Hello.
BROWN: How are you, sir?
DIFALCO: Abe!
BROWN: You know, when I left yesterday, at lunchtime, I stopped by my cousin, ashes to ashes.
DIFALCO: Yeah.
BROWN: He's going to keep me posted.
DIFALCO: Okay.
BROWN: This morning, much to my surprise, er . . . there's an announcement.
DIFALCO: Yeah?
BROWN: And this is as of yesterday, lunchtime.
DIFALCO: Yeah.
BROWN: I would say— If I called anybody names I would say he's a no-good fuck. But he said he did the next best thing. He sent it along to a friend of mine. So, you want to take a look. Look by page four if you have er— you, you get National Geographic? I think it's on page four today.
DIFALCO: Yeah. Okay.
BROWN: Er . . . but no harm. He . . . he said he's let, letting my friend take a look.
DIFALCO: Yeah. How about that er— the— the twenty-sixth of er . . .
BROWN: The twenty-seventh.
DIFALCO: Twenty-seventh, yeah.
BROWN: Twenty-seven, he still has a note there.
DIFALCO: All right, okay.
BROWN: So, er, but this yesterday, I'm telling you on the way up I went into, you know, just before lunch, I stopped. "Any news?" "No, not yet. I'll keep you posted." So . . .
DIFALCO: Right.
BROWN: Strange world, but no harm.
DIFALCO: Okay.
BROWN: All right, take a look.
DIFALCO: Right.
BROWN: Right. See you. Right.

The investigators established that this coded conversation involved the case of *Kanterman* v. *Cohn,* in which DiFalco's firm appeared as counsel, and that *National Geographic* was in reality the *New York Law Journal.*

DiFalco was questioned before the grand jury about this and other conversations with Brown and charged with contempt—not for refusing to answer, but for repeatedly saying he had "no recollection" of what they were talking about. His answers, the indictment charges, were "equivocal, evasive, conspicuously unbelievable, and patently false."

In addition to DiFalco, a Supreme Court referee, a law secretary to a

Supreme Court justice, six attorneys, a businessman, and a bail bondsman were indicted. The reprinted conversations indicate that some justices were so lazy, overworked, or incompetent that they let their law secretaries do all the work for them. One judge reportedly "would sign anything that Brown put in front of him."

And as one attorney said of Brown, "Abe Brown, do you know Abe Brown? . . . Abe Brown is one of the chief opinion clerks in er Special Term in er New York County. . . . He's a crook. . . . Er whatever you want down there we could have it. . . . You want the motion lost in six months, it will be lost in six months. You want it decided in three weeks, it will be decided in three weeks. Sounds crazy, right? . . . Well, it happens to be the truth."

For more than an hour the courthouse reporters pore over the eleven indictments in Mary DeBourbon's office, trying to fathom the sixty-three counts of bribery, conspiracy, perjury, and criminal contempt of the grand jury. The indictments total 443 pages.

Having digested the documents, the reporters file past the policeman—a member of the "rubber-gun squad" assigned to guard duty at the D.A.'s office—down a narrow corridor once adorned with the portraits of all the men who served as Manhattan's district attorney. When the corridor was last painted, the pictures were taken down—and never replaced. Then they pass through the office of Ida Van Lindt, Morgenthau's attractive secretary, into the conference room, where the radio and television newsmen are already assembled. Morgenthau sits at the conference table, flanked by the assistants who worked on the case and by Sergeant John Vobis of the D.A.'s Squad and Sheldon Oliensis, chairman of the Bar Association's Grievance Committee. The reporters sit on folding chairs, drawn up in rows.

"Have they been booked yet?" Mike Pearl asks.

Sergeant Vobis says the defendants will be taken to the Elizabeth Street station.

"We have them handcuffed and shackled to a steampipe upstairs, Mike," Morgenthau quips.

Morgenthau formally opens the press conference. The first part is devoted to fielding questions, primarily from the print media.

"I'm not going to read it for you now," he says. "You've all had a chance to read them."

"Do the indictments say who the lawyer was who made the initial complaint to the Grievance Committee?" Pearl asks.

"No."

"When was that?"

Morgenthau checks with his aides. "January of seventy-seven."

How many cases were involved?

"At least a dozen."

How much money changed hands?

Morgenthau confers again. "There are some bribery counts, but most of these are criminal contempt."

"In the bribery counts?"

"At least eighteen hundred dollars," Morgenthau says. Then he adds, "One of the targets of this investigation, Abram Brown, is dead."

"Is the investigation continuing?"

"Yes, it is."

One radio reporter, who obviously couldn't tell a civil suit from a civil war, asks, "What kind of cases were involved—burglary, robbery, or what?"

"All civil," Morgenthau says, explaining that they included matrimonial, real-estate, and commercial cases.

Claire Spiegel of the *Daily News* asks how long the phones were tapped.

"That's not a matter of record."

Whose phones?

"That's not a matter of record."

Leslie Maitland asks, "Was Roseman a law secretary to a particular judge?"

"That's not a matter of record," Morgenthau says. "But I imagine you could find that out."

"Why aren't you identifying those judges, except by use of numbers?"

"Because we don't want an inference to be drawn that those judges were guilty of a crime."

Arthur Bernhardt asks, "Can you say if there are going to be more indictments?"

Morgenthau shakes his head. "No."

"The life of the grand jury has been extended," Claire Spiegel asks. "How long?"

Morgenthau confers again. "December 31st, 1978."

Then he nods to the television newsmen. "All right."

John Mulligan steps to the desk. "Can I ask one question about the Washington Square case?"

"The case is proceeding," Morgenthau says. "We're still looking for some of the witnesses."

Then the radio and television newsmen gather around Morgenthau, their microphones thrust in his face, as he reads the formal announcement:

"The Manhattan grand jury has voted indictments . . ."

Some three dozen Black Muslims sit in Part 35 to hear the arguments in the Malcolm X case.

"You indicated to me that you wanted to argue orally," Judge Harold Rothwax says to William Kunstler, "and I'll hear you."

Kunstler, wearing a rumpled gray suit, a beaded Indian bracelet circling his left wrist, reiterates the history of the case.

"Our motion," he says, "is based upon two fundamental points." First, "because of his religious convictions and feelings, [Thomas Hagan] is now prepared to name his confederates." He didn't do it in his affidavit, Kunstler explains, because he felt his life was in jeopardy.

"Wouldn't his life be in jeopardy at a later time?" Rothwax asks.

"I think that was all part of a gradual letting go," Kunstler says.

Rothwax is not impressed. "Before I can hold a hearing, I have to have more than what's contained in Hagan's affidavit," he says. "It may be that he's prepared to do that, but it's also clear that he has not yet done it."

"If he were brought down, away from a prison environment, he would divulge everything," Kunstler says. He adds that the defense has located one of the four men Hagan named, but he will not yet divulge his identity.

"I'm frank to tell you, in its present posture this affidavit is not more significant than what Hagan said at trial," Rothwax says. "It does not assist anybody in locating these people."

Kunstler says that Hagan is torn between an obligation toward his confederates and his indignation at the jailing of two innocent men.

Rothwax says that's a conflict Hagan himself will have to resolve.

Kunstler asks that Hagan be "brought down." "If Your Honor would do that, I will secure another affidavit."

Rothwax says that, as it stands, the affidavit is "almost frivolous."

Kunstler asks Rothwax to "hold it open." His motion, he explains, has a "double-barreled approach." One is Hagan's affidavit; the other is that at the trial the prosecution withheld the fact that Gene Roberts, an undercover policeman, had served as Malcolm X's bodyguard and that Reuben Francis, another bodyguard, was then in FBI custody. "Roberts might have exonerated these two defendants."

Rothwax notes that Roberts testified in the Panther 21 trial in 1969 or 1970, "so this information is not newly discovered."

Kunstler replies that the defendants did not know that. "They discovered it when I told them."

Rothwax adds that the Francis case came up in 1965, so both it and that of Roberts are "old cases." "That's a relevant concern to me in terms of the wording of the statute." He suggests that Kunstler get statements from the defendants' counsel at their 1966 trial.

"All right, Judge, I can do that."

"It seems to me you're proceeding on two contradictory theories," Rothwax observes. First, that Hagan and his confederates acted as "faithful soldiers" of the Black Muslims. Second, that Malcolm X was killed as part of a "police plot." "It can't be both."

"We don't think they're contradictory," Kunstler says. He suggests that Hagan and his confederates may have acted under FBI orders.

"A lack of facts leaves one free to speculate," Rothwax observes. "I would like my range of speculation to be limited."

Kunstler notes the lack of police protection at Malcolm X's last speech.

Rothwax says that was raised at trial. "I'm precluded . . . from reviewing such evidence."

"It's clear that the matter is going to have to go over," he adds.

"Can I leave you with one thought, Judge?" Kunstler asks. "It's very important. When they were trying this case in 1965, they couldn't have conceived in their wildest imaginations what the Church report discovered." He says it was an FBI tactic to sow dissension—even lethal rivalry—among radical groups.

Rothwax says there's "no proof that it was a tactic used in this particular case."

"There's a lot of work to be done," he adds. He suggests an adjournment of two months.

"Will the case stay with you?" Kunstler asks. He's anxious that Rothwax, whom he considers "the best judge in the building," keep the case. He thinks that Rothwax wants to rule on it, but "doesn't want to go out on a limb."

"It should stay with me now," Rothwax says.

After some discussion over procedure, the case is adjourned *sine die.*

The attorneys depart—Assistant District Attorney Allen Alpert having scarcely said a word—and Rothwax continues with his calendar call. The next case is the arraignment of the three confessed kidnapers of Marci Klein.

All three plead not guilty and Rothwax continues the case until February 27. "Same bail," he orders.

The defense attorneys protest Rothwax's continuance of the high bail. They call it "legal ransom."

"It seems to me the bail fixed by Justice Milonas is reasonable, and I won't disturb it," Rothwax rules.

Outside in the hall television cameramen film the arrival of the defendants in the Supreme Court corruption case. The cameras focus on DiFalco—short, white-haired, always natty, usually jaunty. Unlike some of his co-defendants, DiFalco does not cover his face. He marches straight ahead, his nose buried in the shoulder blades of the man in front of him, until he is safe in the courtroom. He takes a seat on the aisle beside his attorney, Joseph Marcheso.

"All right, call them all," Rothwax orders.

As the defendants line up in a row at the rail, a messenger from the District Attorney's office wheels a shopping cart into court. It's filled with the documents that the prosecution must turn over to counsel for each of the ten defendants.

Rothwax notices Marcheso sitting with his arm in a cast, beckons him into the well of the court, and asks what happened.

Marcheso says he broke it playing with his four-year-old granddaughter on a sled over the weekend.

Assistant District Attorney Anthony Ferrara rises to make a "voluntary disclosure." First, the prosecution will turn over to the defendants the wiretap orders and search warrants. Second, it will turn over uncensored copies of the indictments, but he asks for a "gag order" barring the defense from divulging names not on the published record. Third, he invites both the defendants and their attorneys to the District Attorney's office to listen to the wiretap recordings and, fourth, to read any of the court files subpoenaed by the D.A.'s office. Fifth, he'll give the defense attorneys the entire transcripts of their clients' grand-jury testimony. Finally, the District Attorney's office will agree to parole the defendants, but they'll have to return tomorrow to complete processing for fingerprints and mug shots.

Rothwax orders that the defendants be arraigned one by one—DiFalco first, because of his attorney's injury.

DiFalco pleads, "Not guilty."

"Forty-five days for motions," Rothwax orders. "We'll put the matter on for April third, and the defendant will be paroled."

Thursday, February 16

Herald Fahringer sums up in the Geruso case. He has set up an easel behind the prosecution table and a blackboard beside the judge's bench. On the blackboard he has drawn the scales of justice, tilted toward the defendant by the weight of the presumption of innocence. The prosecution's job, he says, is to amass enough evidence to tilt the scales the other way.

As he speaks, he sheds his jacket and rolls up his shirtsleeves. He quotes Carl Sandburg: "The best witness is a written paper." And he displays blowups of various documents on the easel, explaining how they show Geruso's innocence, each time skipping to the blackboard to add another weight to the defendant's side of the scales.

Once again he lists the benefits that Governor Wilson, Attorney General Lefkowitz, and Commissioner O'Hara received from Bernard Landers and Peter Bratti.

"They didn't indict Wilson, Lefkowitz, O'Hara, or any of the other high-ranking politicians who received political contributions and gifts," he says. "But they're making Martin Geruso the scapegoat."

"Martin Geruso doesn't have the most pleasant personality in the world," he admits. "He was rude. He was at times, I think, abrupt with Mr. Shiffrin."

Geruso's wife, Patricia, and three of his teen-age children sit in the nearly deserted spectator seats as Fahringer cites the travails the family has gone through. "I'm not asking you for sympathy," he says, in an obvious play for sympathy. "I'm asking you for justice."

Then, in a highly unusual ploy, he cites the possibility of a hung jury: "Those of you who stand with me in believing that this case has not been proven beyond a reasonable doubt must stand steadfast. . . . You cannot fail yourselves and you cannot fail him."

Judge Melia leans forward and whispers, "Time." He limited each side's summation to two hours.

Fahringer concludes, "If any man can be convicted on this evidence, then I say to you, no person is safe."

After the noon recess Shiffrin addresses the jury of eight women and four men. He makes no attempt to emulate Fahringer's histrionics. Instead, he stands stiffly at the side of the prosecution table reading from notes placed atop a black attaché case.

He congratulates Fahringer for his performance. "I have never tried a case against a lawyer as gifted, as able, as competent, as eloquent as Mr. Fahringer."

But a trial, he says, is not a contest between lawyers—it is a search for truth.

He notes that Fahringer tried to make it a trial of Governor Wilson and General O'Hara. Even if they took bribes, he says, that doesn't absolve Geruso. "Don't be sidetracked."

Shiffrin calls Geruso's claim that he did nothing in return for the benefits he received "something conjured up for this trial to get him off the hook." "Geruso has no respect for the truth," he continues. "His entire testimony constitutes a carefully constructed fabrication to eliminate his liability."

He quotes a remark Bernard Landers made on one of the tapes: " 'I've helped him, he's helped me, and it's worked out.' "

"Ladies and gentlemen," he concludes, "I suggest to you that the evidence in this case is overwhelming. I suggest to you that the only defense left is sympathy. . . . I ask that you find this defendant, Martin Geruso, guilty of the crimes as charged."

In the Washington Square trial George Sewell, an eighteen-year-old art student, sits sullenly in the witness chair, his head bowed. His father, Dan, an actor who appeared on Broadway in *Oliver* and *Equus,* sits in the spectator seats. His two brothers wait their turn to testify in the witness room.

Under Moscow's questioning Sewell says he was at Leroy Street Park on the night of September 8, 1976, and saw "a lot" of kids there, "over fifty."

"Ronnie McLamb went up on a table," he adds.

"Do you see the person known to you as Ronnie McLamb in the courtroom?" Moscow asks.

"Yeah."

"Would you point him out?"

For the first time Sewell looks up. "Last one in the second row."

Moscow asks whom else Sewell saw in the park.

No one he knew, the witness replies.

Moscow shows Sewell his grand-jury testimony and asks if it refreshes his recollection.

"I seen names," Sewell says. "It doesn't become clear to me now."

"Mr. Sewell, are you reluctant to testify?"

Sewell sits silently, staring at the floor.

Judge Haft leans over. "Will you answer that question?"

"Yeah."

Michael Direnzo pops up. "I move for a mistrial."

"The motion is denied," Haft rules.

After a lengthy side-bar conference Moscow asks a few more questions in a futile attempt to extract further evidence from Sewell. Then the jury is excused for still more questions. When Sewell says he'd like to see the defendants acquitted, he's declared a "hostile witness." The action permits Moscow to ask leading questions and, in effect, cross-examine him.

Friday, February 17

After hearing Judge Melia's charge, the jury retires at 11:30 A.M. to deliberate Martin Geruso's fate.

George Sewell returns to the witness stand as sullen as before. Moscow asks him what he saw when he was across the street from Washington Square.

"I didn't see nothin'," Sewell says.

Judge Haft excuses the jury. As soon as they file from the courtroom, he turns to the witness. "Mr. Sewell, do you have an attorney?"

"Yes."

"Have you consulted with your attorney prior to your testimony today?"

"No."

Haft warns Sewell that he may be committing perjury. Under New York law, if a witness gives conflicting testimony on two different occasions, that's *prima facie* evidence of perjury. It isn't necessary to prove which is true and which is false. Haft calls a ten-minute recess to allow Sewell to call his counsel.

Forty-five minutes later, when the trial resumes, Sewell reports that he's been unable to contact the lawyer, who's in another court on another case. Haft excuses him until Tuesday morning and advises him to consult with counsel over the Washington's Birthday weekend.

At 10:00 P.M. the Geruso jury is locked up for the night.

Saturday, February 18

At 9:00 A.M. the Geruso jury returns to court, filing into the corridor alongside Part 37 for the last time, past a sign whose missing letters make it read incongruously: PEN DOO SLOWLY.

At noon the panel returns with its verdict. Geruso stands impassively as it's read—guilty on the eight Bratti counts, not guilty on the one Landers count.

As soon as the jurors leave, he collapses into his seat and buries his face in his hands. His body trembles.

Tuesday, February 21

Bald and bespectacled, Dominick DiMaio, New York City's chief medical examiner, testifies in the Washington Square trial. He says that Marcus Mota died of a skull fracture and contusions of the brain caused "by a blunt instrument."

"Would that be consistent with striking with an object such as a baseball bat?" Moscow asks.

"Yes."

For once there is no cross-examination. Most of the defense lawyers tangled with Dr. DiMaio before and learned not to tangle again.

Moscow's next witness is more casual. Clad in a blue sweat shirt and jeans, Richard Rizzo sits in the witness chair and plops a sneaker-shod foot on the rail. He says he's nineteen years old and has been unemployed since he was laid off by the Radio City Music Hall. He doesn't say what he did; he surely wasn't a Rockette.

Rizzo says he went to Leroy Street Park on the night of September 8, 1976. "I always go there," he explains.

"I seen a large number of people gathered around in the park," he continues. "I seen people with baseball bats and there was talk that there was going to be a fight in Washington Square Park."

Then, he says, Joseph Chiapetti stood Robert McLamb on a table and told the crowd, "Don't hit him. He's with us."

Soon after, Rizzo continues, Carlos Boutureira handed him a baseball bat. "I didn't want to be accused of ducking a fight, so I took it."

Rizzo says he walked with the crowd to the edge of Washington Square. Then there was a rumor that "the cops was coming" and everyone threw away his weapon.

"I threw mine under a car and didn't bother to pick it up again."

Boutureira, he says, called to the crowd, "Are we gonna do it or not?" And they voted "Aye!"

Rizzo says he left without fighting.

Moscow elicits that Rizzo was taken into protective custody the night before and lodged overnight in a hotel.

Michael Direnzo pops to his feet. "Objection! I move for a mistrial."

"The objection is sustained," Judge Haft rules. "The motion for a mistrial is denied."

John C. Hill, the lone black among the nine defense lawyers—he represents McLamb—leads the cross-examination.

"Did anyone ever say to you that if you did not testify you could go to jail?" he asks.

"Yes."

"Who said that to you?"

"Mr. Moscow."

Correction officer John Walsh—in mufti—shows Darryl Simcoe, a town justice from upstate Van Etten (population 1,375), through the Tombs. Like many town justices—formerly justices of the peace—Simcoe is not a lawyer. He's a blond, bearded man of only twenty-six. When he was elected at the age of twenty-three, he was the youngest judge in New York State.

Walsh explains that the city's jails house about 7,000 prisoners at any given time. About 2,000 of them have been convicted of offenses and misdemeanors and are serving sentences of up to one year. The rest are detained to await trial, most of them hardened criminals with high or no bail.

"What we get is the bottom of the criminal barrel," Walsh says. "We get the worst."

As they approach the entrance of the Tombs at 125 White Street, Walsh says, "This jail, when it was built, cost ten million dollars. The foundation alone cost two million."

They enter through the outer door and climb a half-dozen steps. A guard lets them through a second door of steel mesh and thick glass and locks it behind them. Walsh stops in an anteroom to pick up the heavy keys he'll need on the tour. Then the guard lets them through a metal gate and another steel-mesh-and-glass door to the elevator bank.

As they ascend to the fourth floor, Walsh explains that the jail is now closed for prisoners, but a few facilities are still in use—the laundry, the kitchen to provide meals for prisoners brought to court, and the Correction Academy, where new jail guards are trained.

On the fourth floor Walsh opens a door to the double-decked cellblocks and they step inside. The floor is dark and gloomy.

"As you see, this place is built in the form of an *H*," Walsh says. "This is a typical housing floor."

They step through an open gate into one of the cellblocks.

"As you see, this is a complete maximum-security facility," Walsh continues. "You'd be going through six gates before you ever hit a cell."

They sit on one of the built-in metal picnic tables opposite the cells.

"Now these are your cells," Walsh tells Simcoe. "These cells are five foot eight inches wide by eight by eight. If these cells could talk . . ."

Each of the 120 cells on the floor contains a bed, a sink, a toilet without a seat, a small shelf, and a tiny mirror. The cell walls are solid steel plate. The only variation is the color—blue, orange, green, yellow.

"I think the effect of the color was helpful to the men's psyche," Walsh says. "It certainly helped the psyche of the correction officers."

As Simcoe pulls out a pad and takes notes, Walsh explains that the cells were built to house one man, but usually held two. During the early 1970s some held as many as three.

Simcoe, who during his career on the bench sentenced fewer than a dozen men to the Chemung County Jail, asks Walsh about conditions in the jails, about the salaries and pensions of correction officers.

Walsh fills him in, then stops. "Let me ask something. All these questions—"

"This is for my own knowledge," Simcoe says. "I'm not gonna go back and criticize."

When the jail was in use, Walsh continues, all visitors and packages were screened by metal detectors and fluoroscopes. The prisoners and their cells were searched every day. In thirty-four years there was only one escape—in 1974 when seven inmates broke out.

"What sort of weapons would you find in a search like that?"

"Homemade pig-stickers," Walsh says. "Maybe a sock with a weight in it. Maybe a razor blade broken in half and stuck in a pencil. Maybe a spoon with a point on it."

"What are your personal feelings about [Governor Hugh] Carey and the death penalty?"

"Off the record?"

Simcoe agrees.

Walsh notes that New York's first-degree murder statute—ruled unconstitutional by the state Court of Appeals—provided the death penalty for the murder of a policeman or a prison guard.

"What makes me better than you?" Walsh asks. "What's sauce for the goose—"

Walsh says he's philosophically against the state's taking a human life, but would not oppose a death penalty for mob hit-men or political terrorists.

Then he asks, "Want to go to another floor?"

Simcoe agrees.

As they ascend to the ninth floor, Walsh relates the history of the lawsuit that led Federal District Judge Morris Lasker to order the Tombs closed in 1974.

Again Walsh unlocks a steel-mesh-and-glass door and they enter the floor.

"Now, as you can see, this is an entirely different setup," Walsh says. "These floors have only one hundred cells. In the seventies this was the methadone-detox floor. Everybody who came here was being detoxed with methadone."

Unlike the cells on the third through eighth floors, those on the ninth and tenth do not have barred gates. They have steel-plate doors, bolted from the outside, with a slot for food trays. The barred windows look out on the guards' observation ramp.

One cell is still covered with graffiti left by its occupants:

MOUSE & CARMEN
COCAINE IN MY VEINS
LONG LIVE HEROIN
KILL ALL THE PIGS

Walsh tells Simcoe that in the 1960s city jails did away with "the hole" and bread and water as punishment. "Now the only thing [a prisoner] loses is mobility," he explains. "There is nothing punitive in this system. Correction officers here don't carry clubs. They don't carry canes. They don't carry blackjacks. They don't carry guns inside."

As they wander about the floor, Walsh describes the disadvantages of the Tombs's vertical layout: The kitchen is on the second floor, and all the food had to be transported to the cellblocks by elevator. The four elevators couldn't cope with the demand. All the work, Walsh adds, was done by prisoners from Rikers Island, since Tombs inmates, detained to await trial, couldn't be forced to do labor.

As they leave, Walsh explains that it was easier to control prisoners a decade ago than it is today. "They didn't know they had civil rights," he explains. "They didn't know they were being treated—and this is off the record—like sentenced prisoners."

Again they ascend—this time to the twelfth-floor roof. They turn to the left.

"Now, whatever you see on one side, you'll see on the other," Walsh says. "This is what cost us three hundred and seventy-four thousand dollars—on both sides."

He leads Simcoe into a recreation room covered by wire mesh and a plastic bubble. The floor is green composition. At the far end is a basketball backboard. At the near end, two Ping-Pong tables.

Walsh explains that the recreation rooms were designed to provide prisoners with places where they could exercise year-round. The irony is that they weren't completed until *after* the Tombs was closed. The work continued because the city could not renege on its contracts.

They descend to the third floor for a brief glimpse of the "Bridge of Sighs"—one of the two bridges connecting the Tombs to the courthouse. Just across the bridge are twin holding pens, large cells where prisoners are still held until they can be led, a dozen at a time, to the courtroom bullpens.

Then they descend to the first floor and walk to the main entrance.

"Judge, is there anything else I can do for you?"

Simcoe shakes his head no. "I appreciate it very much."

Wednesday, February 22

Three dozen Chinese silently slip into Justice Burton Roberts's courtroom to follow the case of Chik Keung Pang. But nothing is happening.

Roberts addresses the audience. "I want to explain to those of you in attendance on the Pang case that apparently he did not submit to an interview by the Probation Department."

Under the law, he explains, a prisoner cannot be sentenced until a probation report is prepared. He has arranged for Pang to be interviewed in court, but there will still be a delay of a week or two before the report is completed.

"I just wanted to explain to you the reasons for the adjournment."

The Chinese, still silent, are undeterred. Roberts continues to wait until a man walks through the double doors of the courtroom.

"Mr. LaSado?"

"Yes."

"What did you do—go around the cape to get here?"

Probation officer Robert LaSado confers briefly with Roberts at the bench.

"All right, bring out Mr. Pang," the judge orders.

Pang, in the same white sweater and blue jeans he wore at his last hearing, is led from the bullpen. He's accompanied by interpreter Laura Ho and attorney Dennis Sekaloff, filling in for Robert Linzer, who is on trial elsewhere.

"Mr. Pang did not submit to an interview by the Probation Department," Roberts says.

Sekaloff explains that Pang did not know the function of the Probation Department and was reluctant to speak to anyone without Mr. Linzer's being present. Sekaloff says he's now explained it to him.

"Mr. Pang," Roberts asks, "do you understand what has been said?"

"Yes," Laura Ho replies for him.

"Is Mr. Pang willing to submit to an interview?"

"Yes."

Pang, Ho, and Sekaloff return to the bullpen, this time accompanied by LaSado.

The audience rises.

"If the spectators are interested," Roberts says, "this won't take too long. I'll give you the adjourn date."

But this time the Chinese audience departs.

Down the hall, in the bullpen behind Part 32, Geoff Abrams confers through the bars with his client. Peter Muniz is a balding, dark-skinned Puerto Rican of fifty-six who is charged with assault and possession of an illegal knife. He stabbed Pedro Cintron twice during a summer beer-drinking argument—a battle that erupted when Muniz returned from the store with Miller's instead of Budweiser.

Abrams, a senior trial attorney for Legal Aid, won eight of his last nine trials, but this case looks like a loser. He's been offered three to six on a plea and, in English laced with an occasional Spanish phrase, urges Muniz to accept.

Muniz, facing a second felony conviction, holds out for two to four. Otherwise, he says, he'll go to trial.

Abrams warns him that he'll get five to ten or six to twelve.

Muniz says he wants to see the witnesses against him and hear what they have to say.

"The price of hearing the witnesses is going to be an extra three years in jail," Abrams warns.

Two other prisoners in the bullpen shout so loudly in Spanish that Abrams can hardly hear his own words. But he hesitates to hush them for fear of provoking their anger. Instead, Muniz, who because of his age has acquired some sort of prison prestige, shouts at them in Spanish . . . and they quiet.

"Peter, imagine you're a juror," Abrams says. "You saw all these people there"—the potential jurors. "Some of them are older. Some of them are younger. You could be one of them too." He recaps the evidence the prosecution will present—the victim's testimony, that of two eyewitnesses, Muniz's own admission to the police. "How would you vote?"

Muniz doesn't answer.

After a long pause he says that he may testify in his own defense. He'll decide after he hears the witnesses against him.

Abrams asks what he'll say.

"You will wait," Muniz replies. "You will hear when I testify. There will be a lot of surprises in store."

Abrams replies in Spanish: *"Tienes una sorpresa. Gracias. Pero no me gustan sorpresas."* ("You have a surprise. Thanks, but I don't like surprises.")

George Sewell is recalled in the Washington Square trial.

"Is there anything about your testimony that you'd care to change at this time?" Moscow asks.

"No."

"Objection!" screams one of the defense lawyers.

"Sustained," Judge Haft rules.

Moscow tries a different tack. "Since you testified on Thursday and Friday, have you had occasion to look at your grand-jury minutes?"

"Yes."

Moscow asks Sewell about the people he saw in Leroy Street Park and Washington Square on the night of the riot. McLamb is the only one he names.

Repeatedly, Moscow hands Sewell his grand-jury testimony and asks if "that refreshes your recollection." But Sewell says he recognized no one else.

In the first row of spectator seats Murray Kempton, the often acerbic *New York Post* columnist, sighs aloud, "That kid's going to jail."

Thursday, February 23

The standing joke in the Washington Square trial is that Moscow has a surprise witness—his testimony will come as a surprise to the prosecutor. Indeed, Moscow has called a string of neighborhood youths who changed their testimony, developed sudden lapses of memory . . . or simply disappeared.

Today is different. Charles Febee is a thirty-one-year-old, slightly built black. He wears a brown suit, no tie, and speaks in a soft tenor voice. He says he was an Army MP stationed in Bangkok, Thailand, during the Vietnam War. His job was tracking down AWOLs and deserters. His specialty was photo identification—looking at mug shots, then spotting the person.

On the afternoon of September 8, 1976, he says, he registered for a course at a technical school, then went to Washington Square. He played

Frisbee, then "drank some beer and some wine and smoked some"—marijuana.

"All of a sudden I heard this loud roar of noise behind me—'All niggers get out of the park!' " he continues. "I turned around and there was about one hundred white kids with bats and clubs."

He identifies Michael Andriani as the boy who shouted, "All niggers get out of the park!"

"I seen Andriani and this other guy start hitting Carl [Warren] across the head with a club," he continues.

He identifies Rocco Areena as "the other guy." Then he picks out Edward Burns as a boy he saw running with a bat in his hand.

"I started running toward the ramp," he continues. "I ran into two other kids and passed one. Then I got hit."

He identifies the "two other kids" as Michael Doyle and Anthony Paolini.

Febee says he suffered a fractured skull, a broken jaw, and lost the sight of his right eye.

Friday, February 24

Michael Direnzo protests that Moscow failed to turn over *Rosario* and *Brady* material to the defense. Among other things, he says, the prosecutor concealed the fact that Febee had an arrest record.

Moscow explodes. "I find nothing in the fact that Mr. Febee may have struck his wife in June of 1976 that tends to exculpate these defendants or give him back the sight of his right eye."

Undaunted, Direnzo turns to his next point—that Moscow concealed the fact that Febee used an "alias."

As Direnzo addresses Judge Haft, Moscow paces before the empty jury box—whistling. Then he wheels.

"I assume that what counsel means by 'alias' is that at some point in his life the witness changed his name by due process of law," he snaps.

"We do not know that," Direnzo shouts.

Haft observes that the situation is "disintegrating" and calls for "an end to the frivolity and insults."

Then he orders the jury brought in, and Direnzo starts his second day of cross-examining Febee. The defense attorney paces the well of the court, firing questions at the soft-spoken witness. Then he pauses a moment and rests a hand on the prosecution table. Moscow quickly pulls a pile of papers away.

Direnzo snaps at the prosecutor, "You got all folded folders there! What the hell can I see?"

"Gentlemen, please!" Judge Haft admonishes.

"He's acting like a baby!" Direnzo bellows.

When order is finally restored, Direnzo asks Febee how many times he left Washington Square to buy wine or beer. Febee says he can't remember.

"Do you have a bad memory?"

"Yeah."

"Did you have a bad memory on September 8th, 1976?"

"I'll never forget that day."

Monday, February 27

Geoff Abrams strides into Part 32, a cigarette dangling from his lips, and hangs up his battered trench coat. Assistant District Attorney Jessica DeGrazia is discussing her bad back—which kept her out of action on Friday—with Justice Shirley Levitan.

"I could have cured you in five minutes," a court officer interjects.

"How?"

"Hang you up by the thumbs."

"With friends like that, who needs enemies," Judge Levitan quips.

Then a few minutes later, "May we get started, lady and gentleman?"

Abrams rises and informs the court that he has received a letter from his client criticizing his conduct of the case and asking that he be allowed to make his criticisms from the witness stand.

"If they're relevant, I'll permit it. If they're not, I won't permit it," Levitan rules. "Is there anything you wish to say, Mr. Muniz?"

Muniz's reply is incomprehensible.

"I apprehend, Mr. Muniz, that you're getting bad legal advice in the jailhouse." She pauses. "All right, bring in the jurors."

By 12:50 the last of the twelve jurors is chosen and sworn.

It's the first day of the March Term, and the rotation of judges has brought "Turn-'em-Loose Bruce" back to the Criminal Court.

Bruce McM. Wright is a fifty-nine-year-old black judge who earned his nickname and incurred the wrath of the Patrolmen's Benevolent Association, the *Daily News,* and others for his practice of setting little or no bail for persons accused of violent crimes—especially after several of those he released were promptly rearrested for committing other violent crimes. As the protests—including picketing of Wright's home by off-duty cops shouting "Nigger!"—mounted in 1974, Wright was transferred from Criminal to Civil Court. His judicial superiors described the rotation as "routine," but Wright—who on one hand gloried in his new status as "Civil Wright" —denounced it as "racist" and filed suit in federal court "to expose the discriminatory and wrongful motives of those in the judicial administration who . . . must ultimately bear responsibility for my removal from Criminal Court."

Although Wright has been assigned to AP5, a hearing part where he can't set bail, his supporters have called a lunch-hour press conference to hail his return to Criminal Court. Beth Bochnak of the Center for Constitutional Rights, William Kunstler's organization, which represents Wright in his federal suit, stands in the lobby handing out press releases.

> I am very pleased to return to duty in the Criminal Courts today [Wright's statement says]. While I have been pleased as well to serve the people of this city in the Civil Court, I have fought the sinister manner of my assignment there because it was the culmination of a campaign by my judicial colleagues, prosecutorial and police establishments to stop me from administering bail in accordance with legal and constitutional standards, and to silence my criticism

of the daily injustices meted out to poor, Black and Third World defendants in the criminal process.

Kunstler arrives. "You're not outside?"—where the press conference is scheduled—he says to Bochnak.

"We're waiting for Bruce," she explains.

"You sure he knows about it?"

Kunstler talks to the reporters—not about Wright's return but about the Malcolm X case. He says he's seen Thomas Hagan again.

"We got a full affidavit—names, cars used, everything," he continues. "But we can't release it—under terms of our agreement with the judge."

He says he'll move to restore the case to the calendar.

Finally Wright arrives, wearing a brown hat, gray overcoat, and pink shirt. He throws an arm around Kunstler and kisses him on the cheek. Then he greets his other supporters.

At the fringe of the crowd a cop in plain clothes mutters to a companion, "Why's he back on the bench? Why's he back in the Criminal Courts Building? Why? Why? Why?"

By 3:00 P.M. the newsstand, open for the first time since November, is all but cleaned out. All that remains is two copies of the *Wall Street Journal.*

Tuesday, February 28

Geoff Abrams stands in the empty courtroom of Part 32, waiting for the Muniz case to be called, chatting with Richard Occhetti, a colleague in Legal Aid. He explains that he won't make an opening statement.

"There's only two things I'm going to cross on," he adds. "I worked it out with Jimmy [Vinci]. They were friends, he was drunk. Plus the size of the wounds."

"You might get an assault-two," Occhetti says.

"That's all I'm looking for."

"That would be fantastic."

"Next case!" Judge Lang snaps. "Let's call Cortale."

Cortale's case is not on the calendar. But, true to his promise, Richard Kuh informed the court when his case in Brooklyn's federal court "broke." Jim Ryan, ailing with a cold he caught on a Vermont ski trip, was summoned from his sickbed to discuss the rescheduling. As it turns out, he scarcely strains his sore throat.

Lang summons the attorneys to the bench.

Kuh asks Lang to keep the March 27 trial date, even though he is now free.

"I have two pressing problems that have me worried sick," he explains.

First, his father-in-law is seriously ill, his wife is with him in Memphis, and Kuh is "baby-sitting" with their children, ages four and six. "My time available for legal work is cut in half."

Second, he's just joined a new law firm as chief of litigation and has been unable to review any work in the office.

"I expected this case to go in January—" Lang starts.

Kuh protests that the delay is not his fault.

"That's not your fault," Lang agrees. "I intended to move this case in two weeks. I'll move it up to the twentieth."

"I appreciate that concession," Kuh says. "I won't go into my other problems," he adds, lest Lang suspect him of "stalling."

"I didn't say you're stalling, Dick," Lang tells Kuh, a colleague in the D.A.'s office fifteen years ago. "I have a homicide on today. That's a jail case. I intend to move it after yours."

Kuh asks who the judge will be.

Lang says it won't be Leonforte—Supreme Court Justice John C. Leonforte, whom a judicial colleague once described as "the only judge I know who needs an interpreter"—it will be a judge who can handle the case.

"Want to make a record?" Lang asks Kuh.

The attorney nods assent.

"All right!" Lang shouts. "Joseph Cortale."

The lawyers retreat to open court and repeat their remarks for the stenographer.

Moscow's missing witnesses are still missing. He wraps up the prosecution of the Washington Square trial by calling Claudio Navarro and Alex Estrada, two hippie-haired Hispanic youths who say they met Robert McLamb in the West Village a few hours after the riot. Estrada tells the jury, "He said he hit one guy so hard with the bat it flew out of his hands."

Then the jury is excused while the lawyers, wandering aimlessly around the well of the court, argue over how many—if any—of the documents in Febee's damage suit against the city can be introduced in evidence.

It's a disorderly scene. Just as schoolchildren know instinctively what teachers they may terrorize, the lawyers learned that Haft is a judge whose admonitions they could safely ignore. Although his colleagues consider him a good "law man," they feel Haft lacks the heft to control the often chaotic courtroom. As he put it at one point in the trial, he was proceeding with "an abundance of caution."

As Moscow addresses the court, George Kosefas, attorney for Anthony Paolini, interrupts. "You wouldn't talk so much if you were paying for the minutes."

Wednesday, March 1

Charles Febee has been recalled for further cross-examination, but he is excused without being questioned. As soon as he leaves the courtroom, Moscow rises.

"Your Honor, that is the People's direct case."

"The People rest?" Judge Haft asks.

"That is the People's direct case."

In eighteen trial days he has called thirty-eight witnesses and introduced fifty exhibits.

Chain-smoking, Geoff Abrams paces among the spectator seats in the deserted courtroom, muttering to himself, "Keep away from the evidence. Keep away from the evidence. Keep away from the evidence."

In his mind he's going over his closing argument to the jury. He knows there's no hope of acquittal and only a slim shot at a hung jury. He's hoping the jurors will be sympathetic to a pathetic old man and reduce the charge against Muniz to assault in the second degree.

He has finally persuaded Muniz not to take the stand and has called only one witness for the defense—a Legal Aid investigator who said Cintron gave him a different account of the stabbing than he related in court.

When the jury enters the box, Abrams takes his notes—scrawled on sheets of yellow legal paper—places them on the shelf, and, arms folded across his chest, starts to speak.

"There is one question and one question alone to be resolved by you. That is, I submit, what was the intent of Mr. Muniz at the time of the incident? I am not going to submit that Mr. Muniz was in Chicago at the time of the incident. I am not going to submit that serious consequences did not result from that incident . . ."

He speaks so softly that at times his voice can barely be heard above the muted clatter of the stenotype machine.

Abrams says Muniz and Cintron were "drinking buddies," and "I submit to you that there is a reasonable doubt that the defendant intended to cause serious physical injury to Mr. Cintron."

The long day in court is drawing to a close when "Turn-'em-Loose Bruce" strikes again. Judge Wright dismisses the case against Lance Manley, an eighteen-year-old black accused of snatching a wallet from a "decoy cop" who posed as a senior citizen resting on the steps of the Times Square subway station. Although four policemen witnessed the incident, Wright rules there was a lack of "credible evidence."

Transit Authority policeman Jerome Schwartz, who made the arrest, is more than piqued.

"I'm burning up over this," he tells the press. "This guy Wright's unbelievable. We're going to the P.B.A. to ask them to make a formal complaint."

Thursday, March 2

Judge Haft rules on defense motions in the Washington Square trial. He dismisses the conspiracy charges against three of the defendants—Rocco Areena, Edward Burns, and Michael Doyle. "There is, in my view, no evidence . . . that these defendants participated in the conspiracy."

Moscow has already agreed to drop two of the assault charges against all nine defendants because the victim, Manuel Peraza, never showed up in court. There are rumors that he was "bought off" by the father of one of the defendants.

Conrad Ferrigno moves to sever Areena from the other defendants. Harry Hammer joins on behalf of Burns.

"Those motions for a severance are denied," Haft rules. "All right, let's send for the jury."

The jury is brought in and the defense opens. First, Robert Cohen calls two detectives who testify to slight discrepancies in Febee's account of the photo identifications. Then Michael Direnzo calls Michael Andriani to the stand.

Tall and husky—he sometimes works as a mover—Andriani, in sweater and slacks, tells the jury that he joined the crowd in Leroy Street Park "for two minutes."

In even less time he manages to doom his co-defendant, Andres Sanchez. "Andres was going to fight the guy that jumped him in Washington Square Park."

Andriani says he followed the group to Washington Square.

"I seen all these kids running and yelling," he tells the jury. "I said, 'This is crazy. I'm getting out of here.' . . . I ran north out of the park."

He says he ran past the arch and headed north to his girl friend's apartment.

"Did you have any kind of a weapon in your possession?" Direnzo asks.

"No, I didn't."

"Did you strike anyone?"

"No."

Andriani says he was nowhere near the "plateau" where Carl Warren and Charles Febee said they had seen him. He says he never saw either of them until they came to court.

In his cross-examination Moscow asks Andriani about his interrogation by the police two days after the riot.

"I told 'em I had nuttin' to do wit' it," Andriani says. "I was wit' my girl friend."

"Did you lie to them?"

"Yes."

The District Attorney's office announces that it will *not* attempt to reinstate the robbery charges against Lance Manley. It says Wright was "within his right" to dismiss the case because there was a discrepancy between the officers' affidavits and the testimony they gave in court.

After four hours of deliberations the Muniz jury returns at 4:15 P.M. to ask the difference between assault_1 and assault_2. After hearing Justice Levitan's instruction, they retire again.

Geoff Abrams and Jessica DeGrazia repair across the square for a drink at Peggy Doyle's restaurant. They're summoned back to court at 5:00 P.M. to hear the verdict: guilty of assault in the first degree.

Abrams considers it a victory to have kept the jurors talking for nearly five hours.

Friday, March 3

Defense attorney Harry Hammer calls Helen Healy as an alibi witness for Edward Burns, the youth who allegedly kicked the pregnant black woman in the stomach.

Mrs. Healy is a middle-aged woman who works as a clerk for the city's Board of Elections. She speaks with the classic accent of the New York Irish —"woik" and "soitainly." She says she saw Burns at an outdoor musicale at the Fulton Houses on West Seventeenth Street on the night of the riot.

Moscow takes over on cross-examination. "You had no trouble identifying Ed Burns?"

"You could hear him before you seen him," Mrs. Healy explains. "I never hoid a voice like it. . . . He made this noise, like someone was getting strangled."

Then Hammer calls Burns to the stand. He's a short, stocky, blond youth in a pastel blue suit.

"Mr. Burns, where were you on the night of September 8th, 1976?"

"Seventeenth Street."

Burns explains that he was drinking beer—"three or four quarts"—with his buddies when Gerald Botros arrived. "He come up to me and said there's gonna be a fight . . . 'C'mon.' I said, 'I don't want to get involved. I'm having a good time here. I don't know these people.' "

After a few more questions, Hammer asks, "Are you ready? We're all anxious."

Burns lets out a high-pitched shriek that all but shatters the glass in the courtroom windows. Then he repeats it.

"I can't whistle, so I do this to get attention," Burns explains. "They all know me."

"All of Lower Manhattan," Hammer adds.

Following Moscow's cross-examination, the defense rests—all nine defendants.

Monday, March 6

"All right," Justice Burton Roberts orders, "arraign the defendant for sentence."

The Chinese spectators watch silently as Chik Keung Pang, wearing the same white sweater and blue jeans he's worn to every court session, stands as the clerk calls his case.

Roberts asks Assistant District Attorney Nancy Ryan if she has anything to say.

Ryan, a slim, brown-haired woman in a green floral-print dress, asks "this court to impose the maximum it has allowed itself"—four to twelve years.

Unknown to the spectators, she has read the probation report, in which Pang is described as a "disoriented"—no pun intended—alien. Perhaps more important, he apologized to his victim, and Man Bun Lee is not seeking vengeance.

Ryan notes that Lee "was not an ordinary citizen. He was a man who had taken it upon himself to speak out against the youth gangs, which have been terrorizing the community."

"It was not only an assault on Mr. Lee," she says. "It was an assault on all the other Chinese who inhabit Chinatown."

Next, Roberts calls on defense attorney Robert Linzer.

"I have too much respect for this court to think that a five-minute dissertation on my part will change—"

Roberts cuts him off. He says he hopes counsel has "enough respect to know that I have an open mind."

Linzer apologizes. He says, "There's no question that this is a serious crime. There's no question that Mr. Pang will serve a serious period of incarceration."

He says Pang "got in a situation which he wasn't strong enough to handle." Finally, he asks Roberts to consider reducing the "maximum minimum" and let the parole board decide when Pang should be deported.

Roberts turns to court interpreter Laura Ho. "Will you explain to Mr. Pang that the court will hear what he has to say through you, the official interpreter."

After a brief conversation with Pang, she replies, "I have nothing to say, Your Honor."

Roberts launches into an oration—both to the press and to his Chinese audience. His comments are a cascade of contradictions.

First, he notes that Pang "was a tool used by" the Eagles and Ghost Shadows, two Chinese youth gangs. Then he says that his was "a monstrous crime against a most reputable citizen."

But "we do not have different rules for different areas of the city or different rules for different ethnic groups that populate our city."

He calls the gangs "vicious, rotten, antisocial . . . a bunch of parasites." He notes that "ninety-nine percent [of the Chinese community] are hardworking. The sentence of the court can in no way indicate the revulsion and the desire to see that all members of this gang wind up in state prison."

But "the defendant before me does not represent the Ghost Shadows or the Eagles." He says Pang needs an ear operation and suffers from an ulcer. He calls him "a stranger in a strange land."

Yet "the act that he committed was monstrous. . . . A message has to go forth to the Chinese community."

Then he notes that "whatever day he serves in prison will be as five days for anyone else," because Pang will be alone, unable to communicate with others. "For to prison he must go, because the act that he committed was a monstrous act."

Roberts says he's suffered "anguish" over the minimum he must impose. "It is a puzzlement what this court will do with respect to the minimum." He says he considered imposing an indeterminate sentence, but that would be "a cowardly way out." Four to twelve years, he notes, is "not inequitable."

But "an individual must be treated like an individual." He sentences Pang to three to twelve years and recommends deportation on his release. It's an axiom of the courthouse that Roberts rants the loudest . . . and hands out the lightest sentences.

Roberts says Pang has "forever deprived himself of the right to live in these United States. He will never again enter these blessed shores, even as a visitor."

All that's lacking is an orchestra playing "America the Beautiful" softly in the background.

Tuesday, March 7

The courtroom of Part 48 on the thirteenth floor looks like any other in the building. But it is unique. It is the setting for the Extraordinary and Special Term of Supreme Court, presided over by Ernst Rosenberger, a forty-six-year-old, balding, bearded jurist who first made his mark as a civil liberties lawyer. He's the judge designated by Governor Hugh Carey to hear the cases brought by New York's "super-prosecutor."

In 1972 the Knapp Commission, appointed by Mayor John Lindsay in the wake of Frank Serpico's revelations of police corruption, recommended the appointment of a special prosecutor, superseding the five New York City district attorneys, to investigate and prosecute corruption in the criminal justice system. Governor Nelson Rockefeller acquiesced and appointed Maurice Nadjari, a former Hogan assistant who had become chief assistant district attorney in suburban Suffolk County. Nadjari's appointment was heralded as the most momentous development in metropolitan law enforcement since Thomas E. Dewey was named special prosecutor nearly forty years before.

Nadjari took office and came on like, well, like gangbusters. But he quickly went from super-cop to super-flop. Although he successfully prosecuted some corrupt cops, he struck out in attempts to bag bigger game, failing to make charges stick against any major politician, prosecutor, or judge. Of the eleven judges he indicted, the cases against nine were dismissed and two were acquitted. The only case Nadjari personally prosecuted—against former Queens District Attorney Thomas J. Mackell—was reversed on appeal. More ominously, there were increasing complaints about Nadjari's methods—"trial by press release" and "Gestapo-type tactics."

In 1975, Governor Carey started agitating for Nadjari's ouster. The special prosecutor hung on for six months more with an investigation and indictment of Patrick Cunningham, the Bronx Democratic leader, which also was ultimately dismissed. As his successor Carey named John Keenan, chief of the Homicide Bureau under Hogan, chief assistant under Morgenthau, who proceeded far more prudently, if far less flamboyantly.

The case before Rosenberger involves the highest-ranking policeman ever indicted in New York City—Inspector Robert Johnson. A gray-haired, slightly built sixty-two-year-old black, Johnson is the second of three police brass to be brought to trial on charges involving taking bribes from Harlem gamblers. He's accused of perjury for telling a grand jury he "never received any illegal money from anybody in the Police Department, or otherwise." He couldn't be charged with bribery because the payments, allegedly made when Johnson was a sergeant and lieutenant, pre-date the five-year statute of limitations.

After two women alternates are sworn and Justice Rosenberger delivers his preliminary instructions to the jury, Special Assistant Attorney General Robert Simels rises to make his opening address. He's a slim man with dark brown hair coifed in what might be called a "white Afro."

He reads the main sections of the indictment.

"Now, how do we intend to prove these charges?" he asks rhetorically.

He says the grand jury found that "widespread corruption was commonplace" in Harlem police precincts. "The pad" in the Twenty-eighth was $5,000 to $6,000 a month.

"Objection, Your Honor," snaps defense attorney Richard Dienst.

Lifting his chin from his hand, Justice Rosenberger says, "Overruled."

"The grand jury's objective," Simels continues, "was not to target on patrolmen, as has been done in the past, but to reach into the upper limits."

In its case against Inspector Johnson, Simels says, the prosecution will call three corrupt policemen. One will tell how he passed payoff money to Johnson in the female cellblocks of the Twenty-eighth Precinct station house. Another will tell of seeing the transactions. And a third will testify to Johnson's method of taking payoffs when he was in the Bronx—he'd open a desk drawer, then walk out of the room, and the "bagman" would leave the envelope in the open drawer.

Dienst rises in reply. He's a big man with straight, graying hair and thick rimless glasses. His manner is slightly pompous.

In a brilliantly mixed metaphor he tells the jurors, "You have just heard what appears to be a terrible picture painted."

He says Johnson will testify in his own behalf and asks the panel "to keep an open mind."

He stresses two points—that Johnson was transferred out of Manhattan in 1967, before the alleged payments, and that the witnesses against Johnson have "some animosity" against him. Johnson, he explains, "made some decisions that were not very popular," such as integrating radio cars.

Finally he asks the jury to remember his "allegorical witness"—"the presumption of innocence."

Howard Meyer, gray-haired and bearded like Santa Claus, is the third of nine defense lawyers to sum up in the Washington Square trial.

His client, Michael Doyle, sits with his hand bandaged, a finger in a splint. Meyer explained that Doyle slipped on the ice. Beside Doyle sits Andres Sanchez, one eye blackened, a bandage above the other. His attorney said Sanchez was "mugged" in the hallway of his apartment. Thus, the Washington Square case is ending as it began—with Andres Sanchez being beaten bloody by blacks.

"What this case comes down to," Meyer tells the jury, "is Mr. Febee's perceptive credibility."

He notes that Febee observed the man he identified as Doyle for only one or two seconds. In the hours before that, he continues, Febee smoked four marijuana cigarettes and joined his friends in consuming four or five quarts of beer and a quart of wine.

"Mr. Febee described his condition as being 'mellow,' " he says. "I suggest to you that the unfortunate Mr. Febee was stoned."

He reminds the jurors that Febee picked a "stand-in" from the lineup as one of the rioters.

"There is a reason that you can attach a doubt to," he asserts. "I think these are doubts that you can attach a reason to. And that's all you need—is a doubt."

Wednesday, March 8

The chief evidence against James Conyers leans against the wall of Justice Burton Roberts's courtroom—a door on which is scrawled: YOU SENT ME TO JIAL.

The door is from the East Sixty-sixth Street apartment of Lawrence Gerber. Gerber, an eighty-four-year-old lawyer, and his wife, Frances, a seventy-six-year-old invalid, were found strangled to death on November 21, 1976. Conyers, the seventeen-year-old grandson of the Gerbers' maid, is charged with the double slaying. His trial is in its sixth week.

But the testimony has halted. Roberts has sent Assistant District Attorney John Evans out of the courtroom while he confers at the bench with Conyers and his attorney, Otto Fusco. The judge explains that if Conyers pleads guilty to manslaughter, he will impose a sentence of eight and a third to twenty-five years—against the fifteen to life Conyers will receive if he's convicted of murder.

Then Roberts summons the black youth's mother and grandmother and confers with them privately in the robing room. The women emerge in tears.

Evans is called back, and the formal proceedings occur in open court.

Fusco explains that the defendant is ready to plead, but doesn't want to do it with his mother and grandmother present. The women leave the courtroom and Fusco offers the plea.

"The plea is acceptable to the People," Evans says. He explains that there are "certain evidentiary problems" with the prosecution's case—no eyewitness identification or confession. The only strong evidence is the defendant's misspelling of "jial."

Roberts questions Conyers to elicit the facts of the crime.

"Why did you go there? Did you think the Gerbers had done something wrong to your grandma?"

"No."

"Why did you go?" Roberts snaps.

"Yeah," Conyers says, responding to the previous question, "for her to work for white people."

Conyers says he went to the apartment, entered under a ruse, and wrestled Gerber to the floor. Then he took a necktie from the closet and wrapped it around his neck.

"Well, what did you intend to do—to kill him?" Roberts asks.

"To put him to sleep."

"Did you keep pulling it?"

For two or three minutes, Conyers says.

Then he took $300 from Gerber's pocket and entered the next room, where Mrs. Gerber was lying on the bed. He took $2,500 from a dresser drawer and strangled her with the tie. Then he scrawled the message on the door.

"Did you ever think he was a judge?" Roberts asks.

"No."

"Did he ever send you to jail?"

"He never sent me to jail."

Roberts accepts the guilty plea and sets sentencing for April 18—one day after Conyers's eighteenth birthday.

A dozen persons gather around the table in the Legal Aid Society's conference room for the weekly luncheon meeting of Jim Vinci and his bureau chiefs. The table is littered with bags of potato chips, cans of soda, and sandwiches wrapped in wax paper.

Vinci, in shirtsleeves, finishes his kosher salami sandwich, lights a cigarette, and calls the meeting to order.

"Excuse me, I've very important business," Elliott Cook interrupts. "I've half a salami on white—with mustard. Does anybody want it?"

Someone takes the sandwich.

Vinci passes around copies of a memo reporting a grant offer to make up the extra costs of clerical and printing expenses Legal Aid incurred by the crush of blackout cases.

"Do you think we have enough cases on the blackout to get the grant?" he asks.

The answers fly from around the table.

"It's a clerical thing."

"Is this for Manhattan or the whole city?"

"Do you realize this memo could have been written in three sentences?"

The issue is not resolved.

"O.K., one more," Vinci says, passing out another paper. This is a letter from the District Attorney's office asking Legal Aid lawyers to list the name of the assistant district attorney on their motion papers.

"We don't even know who the assistant is," protests Irwin Shaw, "because *they* don't know who the assistant is."

"I, for one, would not assist the D.A. in responding to our motions," Cook says.

"If you want to do it, do it," Vinci rules. "If you don't, don't."

He passes out another memo—this time from Martin Erdman, the attorney-in-charge of Legal Aid's criminal division throughout the city.

For years Erdman, who inherited a fortune from his father, was Legal Aid's leading lawyer in the Criminal Courts Building. Then he was quoted by *Life* as calling judges "whores" and appellate judges "whores who've become madams." For this he was censured by the Appellate Division—later reversed by the Court of Appeals—and the powers that be at Legal Aid deemed it prudent to shift him from in front of the bench to behind a desk. In one of the courthouse's "legal fictions," Legal Aid lawyers don't tell the court they're from Legal Aid; they say, "Office of Martin Erdman."

Erdman's memo asks about a checklist that's being used by Legal Aid lawyers in the Bronx.

"I think he's assuming that we don't do all this," Vinci says.

"Personally, I find this insulting," Cook says.

"Me, too," Vinci agrees.

A voice shouts from the far end of the table: "There any napkins down there?"

Vinci rummages among the trash on the table. But he's not looking for napkins. "Where's the ashtray?" he asks.

Napkins and ashtray are finally found and the meeting resumes.

"I think it's an unwise thing to have a checklist on every case," Cook says.

"Me, too," Vinci adds. "Let's see what happens with the experiment in the Bronx."

Irwin Shaw sifts through the sheets of the checklist. "In a petty larceny I don't think a serology report is necessary," he observes.

Vinci offers the opinion that Erdman wants checklists to provide documentation in case convicted defendants claim they weren't properly represented.

"All this is an admission that our lawyers are incompetent," Cook says.

Carol Halprin, the only woman in the room, tells the group about a decision reported in the morning's *Law Journal:* A Legal Aid lawyer refused to put in a defendant's alibi defense because he wanted to complete the trial quickly and leave on his honeymoon.

"That's not a Legal Aid attorney!" Cook protests. "No way!"

"The case was not affirmed," one lawyer adds.

Another notes that it was a *Brooklyn* case.

And yet another asks the attorney's name.

"There was no name," Halprin says.

"He's now a supervisor," someone quips.

Vinci comes to the defense of the unnamed attorney. "I have gotten hurt in alibi defenses."

Robert Stein changes the topic. "Believe it or not, The Woz has something to raise at this point."

Richard Wajszwillo speaks for the first time in the meeting: "It's been discussed."

So Stein turns to the issue of the letters from the Parole Board asking Legal Aid lawyers for their recommendations. "I think it's shitty that we have to get in the middle of this."

"If we don't reply, it's bad," Vinci observes.

The attorneys think up mock replies:

" 'Let him out? Are you joking?' "

" 'After representing the guy for six months, I know how bad he really is.' "

" 'Send him to Judge Wright—he'll hire him.' "

There's a story in the morning papers about how Judge Bruce Wright had hired a parolee to help with clerical chores and legal research in his old Civil Court chambers. The parolee stole Wright's IBM typewriter, Sony radio, and electric heater.

"The lawyers won't be around," says Robert Kaplan, a pudgy, gray-haired lawyer sitting at Vinci's right. "You know the turnover rate, Jim. . . . Our lawyers don't outlive parole. They leave before the guy gets out of jail."

Stein, balding and mustached, pulls a check from his wallet—a contribution to the Russel Bowman Memorial Fund. Bowman, a senior trial attorney for Legal Aid, was killed in an auto accident on January 25, leaving a widow and three young children.

"The Assistant District Attorney writes 'for deposit only' on the back," Stein observes. "In case I'm going to the track."

"How much was the check?" Vinci asks.

"Ten dollars."

Stein raises another matter. "How come there are two hundred more felony cases in AP1 than in any other AP part?"

"AP1 gets all the fugitives," Vinci explains.

"There're about two hundred fugitives," Kaplan adds.

William Sanneman tosses out a tidbit of gossip. Judge Benjamin Altman is going to the Supreme Court and Milton Williams will become the new administrative judge of the Criminal Court.

Kaplan corrects him. "Williams *thinks* he's going to be the administrative judge."

"I want to discuss tomorrow morning," Vinci announces.

"There's going to be a fire drill," Kaplan quips.

"We're going to meet with Garelik"—Sanford Garelik, chief of the Transit Authority police.

Legal Aid has objected to the T.A. policy of arresting "fare-beats"—youths who jump the turnstiles without paying—instead of serving them summonses. At a previous meeting Garelik defended the practice, saying the T.A. policemen arrested only fare-beats with long records.

"They don't know if he has a long record when they arrest him," Sanneman says. "That's bullshit!"

"What did he run for when he ran for public office?" someone asks about Garelik.

"Mayor."

"He *was* City Council president."

"We'll just be pissing against the wind talking to him," Vinci says. "I don't even want to go to the meeting."

Cook warns Sanneman, "They're launching a new campaign against guys who expose themselves on the subway. So be careful."

"I know," Sanneman quips. "I now take the bus."

"Who's going?" Vinci asks.

"What good is it going to do us to go?"

"We'll go for a little while, then leave," Vinci says. "If you're gonna go to the meeting, for God's sake *get there on time.* I don't want to hear any horseshit—'The Legal Aid attorneys were late.' We'll get there at nine twenty-five and leave at nine thirty-three."

"Who's going to the meeting?"

"Elliott and you and me and who else?" Halprin asks Vinci.

"Where's the meeting?" Sanneman asks.

"Charles Meara's office," Vinci says. Meara is the executive officer of the criminal courts. "Don't be late."

"Meeting over now?" Cook asks.

"Yes," Vinci says.

But Bob Stein raises a new issue—the posting of summer-vacation memos.

Vinci interrupts him. "I don't want to see any of these memos left on the table, 'cause I passed them out to everyone."

"So the vacation thing is tabled till the next meeting?" Stein asks.

"No. Let's talk about it now."

But half the attorneys leave.

John C. Hill, counsel for Robert McLamb, is the eighth attorney to sum up in the Washington Square trial. He's a tub-thumping orator in the tradition of southern black preachers, long on style, short on substance.

"Each of you owe it to yourselves to stand up and be counted," Hill shouts, "be counted for justice . . .

"Come back to this court, if you will, and tell us without restraint what really happened on the evening in question. Tell us, if you will, what part Robert took and what part he did not take, if he took any part at all. And then, as fair men and women, send Robert home. That's where he belongs."

Thursday, March 9

His hands quivering on the shelf in front of the jury box, Michael Direnzo concludes the last of the nine defense summations:

"I implore you. . . . Your vote should be 'Not guilty.' "

His last words are spoken so softly that they cannot be heard beyond the jury box.

Then Moscow rises to sum up for the prosecution.

"No one person could have done what the group was able to do. Get a large enough group together and you can do it with impunity. There's safety in numbers. In this case there's criminal responsibility in numbers."

Seated in the spectator seats are Moscow's parents. His father, Warren, is a craggy-faced former *New York Times* political reporter and author of the classic *Politics in the Empire State.* He sucks an unlit pipe and listens intently as his son speaks.

"We have the men who did the damage—and that includes every one of the defendants. They're all responsible for the death of Marcus Mota."

Friday, March 10

The jury in Inspector Johnson's perjury trial is bussed to Harlem to inspect the women's lockup in the old twenty-eighth Precinct station house on West 123d Street—the place where the payoff money allegedly changed hands.

On their return to the courthouse they're excused for the day. Both prosecutor Simels and defense lawyer Dienst have another matter on their schedules—the sentencing of Adam Butcher, the first of the police brass tried in the gambling-payoff probe. Butcher, a fifty-year-old retired deputy inspector, was convicted of perjury in November for denying that he took money from gamblers.

Simels and Dienst troop across the street to a seventh-floor courtroom in the Civil Court Building, where Supreme Court Justice Fritz Alexander sentences Butcher to nine months in jail.

After hearing Judge Haft charge them for nearly five hours, the jury in the Washington Square trial retires at 5:40 P.M. Harry Hammer immediately starts a pool on when they'll come back with a verdict.

Saturday, March 11

The eleventh-floor hallway, littered with cigarette butts and Styrofoam coffee cups, is deserted as the jury starts its second day of deliberations in the Washington Square trial. And there are no court officers manning the metal detectors.

Judge Haft enters the courtroom, where the defense lawyers are milling.

"I can't talk," he says in a hoarse whisper. The five-hour charge to the jury rendered him speechless.

Haft observes as the court officers set up a microphone and speaker so he can be heard when he addresses the jury.

After he leaves, Michael Andriani, lounging at the prosecution table, asks no one in particular, "Think they'll be in today with a verdict?"

"Never," says John Hill.

"No way," agrees Howard Meyer.

"So why did people pick day two?"—in Hammer's pool—Andriani wonders.

Downstairs, Criminal Court Judge John Brickley presides in AR1. Like the city, the courthouse never sleeps. AR1 is open nights, weekends, and holidays to arraign the newly arrested.

The courtroom is crowded and noisy. Brickley sits on the bench wearing a blue golf jacket, no robe. His horn-rimmed glasses rest on top of his bald head as he conducts the ritual.

"José Vazquez!" the bridgeman shouts.

A stubbly derelict in a shabby overcoat is led to the bridge. There's a hurried conference at the bench among Brickley, the Assistant D.A., and Legal Aid. Then Vazquez pleads guilty to a reduced charge.

"The defendant is discharged," Brickley says wearily.

Inside the rail Assistant District Attorney Stephen Shapiro paces impatiently, waiting for his witnesses to arrive so he can get an arrest warrant signed in a murder case. Robert Fowler, a thirty-one-year-old black, is about to be charged with the February 24 strangling and sexual assault of Christine Coste, a follower of the Reverend Sun Myung Moon.

Shapiro's thoughts, however, are on the case he's trying upstairs. It's a simple robbery case—against Stephen Owen, a black homosexual prostitute who plies his trade in "drag" on West Forty-second Street. He's accused of stealing a watch from a potential "trick." The case is virtually airtight—the victim and two policemen who caught Owen red-handed. But Shapiro isn't happy at the way it's going.

His "opposite number" is Patricia Ferguson, a Legal Aid lawyer trying her first jury case. Throughout the jury selection Justice Burton Roberts badgered her constantly and the fledgling lawyer so discombobulated the judge that he started screaming—not only at her, but at potential jurors and spectators. One venireman told Roberts, "You run your courtroom much too harshly."

"He's crazy," Shapiro tells a companion. "He's going to lose the case for me."

He fears the jury might vote acquittal—out of sympathy for the defense attorney.

Shapiro's witnesses finally arrive, and they huddle with Judge Brickley around the court stenographer at the witness stand. When the whispered conference ends, Brickley signs the warrant and the detective departs to arrest Fowler.

The bridgeman calls the next case.

Jim Ryan spends the Saturday in his sixth-floor office preparing for the Cortale trial. The room has a southern exposure, but the carefully tended plants in the window received little sunlight during the long winter months.

When he thinks about the trial ahead of him, Ryan gets somewhat scared. Everyone in the office considers the case a "loser"—a circumstantial-evidence case with no confession, no eyeball, not even a murder weapon. And Ryan is going up against his former boss—Richard Kuh.

Ryan, a native of Yonkers who attended Holy Cross and Fordham Law School, spent a year in the Attorney General's Consumer Frauds Bureau before joining the D.A.'s staff in 1974—just before Kuh's appointment as district attorney. But he never had any dealings with him until now.

He caught the Cortale case by chance. Each of the senior trial assistants in the D.A.'s office pulls "homicide duty" in rotation. They're on call for twenty-four hours to conduct the investigation in whatever murder case comes along. The first time Ryan pulled homicide duty, he caught the Cortale case. Its complexities caused him to "kiss off the year."

In the eleventh-floor hall some of the Washington Square defendants pass the time by playing catch with a roll of toilet paper. In the courtroom's first row of spectator seats Harry Hammer, impeccable as always in a blue pinstriped suit, passes it by reading the *New York Times.*

Rocco Areena, in leather jacket, jeans, and white sneakers, lounges against the rail and predicts his ultimate acquittal.

"That jury ain't gonna believe Febee," he says. "Seen twenty guys in two seconds. Not even Superman can do that."

"Yeah?" Hammer says. "He went to school."

"Fuck!" Areena replies. "You went to school. You ain't no fucking lawyer. You shoulda been a shoemaker."

"I'm gonna walk," Areena continues. "I'm gonna go tell that fucking Moscow to go fuck himself and I'm walking out of here. And you'll still be arguing with the judge."

At 12:35 P.M. the jury sends out a note.

Nearly an hour passes before all the lawyers and defendants are assembled and the panel is brought back into the courtroom.

"Madam forelady," asks clerk Jimmy Campbell, "has the jury reached a verdict?"

"No, we have not," replies Ruby Wilson, a short, Afro-haired black woman.

Under New York procedure, as the first juror chosen, she automatically became the panel's spokeswoman.

On behalf of the jury, she asks that testimony about Michael Andriani be read back. Out of concern for his voice, Judge Haft assigns the chore to the court stenographer.

In the hours that follow there are more notes—requests for more rereading or questions on the law—but no verdict. Finally, Haft orders the panel sequestered for a second night.

Sunday, March 12

The Washington Square jury resumes its deliberations at 1:00 P.M. The court officers report that none of the jurors went to church. But several of them jogged, and the out-of-condition officers were hard pressed to keep pace during the exercises.

At 1:50 the panel poses another question to Judge Haft: If it finds a defendant guilty of conspiracy, does it have to find him guilty of manslaughter?

It's the first indication that the panel is considering finding any defendant guilty . . . of anything. Needless to say, it has a sobering effect on all nine defendants.

Monday, March 13

While the lawyers conduct the *voir dire* in the case on trial, Judge Peter McQuillan huddles at the side bar for the final formalities in the Miguel Pinero case.

Whispering to the stenographer, Assistant District Attorney Donald Matthews reads from a three-page memorandum: "Absent the evidence suppressed by Justice McQuillan, the People no longer have sufficient proof to warrant submission to a trial jury. An appeal of Justice McQuillan's decision would be fruitless because of the factual findings contained in the decision. Accordingly, the People recommend that the indictment herein be dismissed."

"The motion is granted," McQuillan rules.

In its fourth day of deliberations the jury asks to visit both Washington Square and Leroy Street Park. Judge Haft denies the request. He'd planned to take the jury to the parks at the outset of the trial, but they were then buried under two feet of snow.

Bruce McM. Wright takes the witness stand in Part AP7, down the hall from his own courtroom. He's the complaining witness in the hearing on

Jesse Smitherman, the youth who allegedly stole his typewriter.

In a clear voice he tells Judge Elliott Golden, "Sometime in 1977 he come to the courtroom where I was serving, in Civil Court. . . . He did do some work for me, yes."

"Legal research?"

"Yes."

Wright says he last saw his typewriter, radio, and heater when he left his chambers on February 24. On February 25 they were gone.

"Were those items your property?"

"Yes."

After Smitherman's written confession is introduced in evidence, Judge Golden orders him held for the grand jury. And he observes, "I think the court would take judicial notice of the fact that security in public buildings is almost nonexistent."

Tuesday, March 14

Both sides have made their final arguments in the trial of Inspector Robert Johnson, but Robert Simels remains in court for another matter—the arraignment of James V. Napoli, Sr., a reputed *mafioso* who allegedly controls much of New York's illegal gambling.

The indictment is the culmination of a long investigation by the special prosecutor's office. In 1974, Napoli was given a six-month sentence for contempt of court for refusing to answer questions in a fight-fixing inquiry. While in jail he allegedly arranged for bribes to win special treatment—food from the outside, wine and liquor, special visiting privileges, unsupervised labor in the summons part of Criminal Court, and—the only special privilege not granted—a Christmas leave.

The conduit for the payments allegedly was Mario Gigante, a fellow *mafioso* and brother of Vincent "The Chin" Gigante, the man accused of shooting Mafia kingpin Frank Costello in 1957. Another Gigante brother, Louis, a Roman Catholic priest and former city councilman from the Bronx, faces a ten-day sentence for contempt in the inquiry—for invoking his priestly privilege before the grand jury.

Indicted along with Napoli are his son, James V. Napoli, Jr., a nephew—also named James V. Napoli—Joseph Tuseo, a former correction officer, and a deputy warden, William Luciani.

Wearing a camel's-hair coat, Napoli, Sr., a baggy-eyed man of sixty-eight, sits beside his attorney, Gregory Perrin, waiting for the prints to be processed so he can be arraigned. The wait lasts all afternoon. The joke in the courtroom is that the computer broke down when asked to process the prints of *three* James V. Napolis.

On the fifth day of deliberations Judge Haft orders the Washington Square jury to return to the courthouse after dinner. It's the first time deliberations have lasted into the night.

At 10:00 P.M. the jurors send out a note—asking if they can retire for the night. Judge Haft reluctantly assents.

Wednesday, March 15 After hearing Justice Rosenberger's charge, the Johnson jury retires. Prosecutor Simels immediately checks with the two alternates and learns that they would have voted "guilty." He also learns that several of the jurors saw him on television the night before announcing the Napoli indictment.

Late in the afternoon defense lawyer Ronald Degen sits in Judge Harold Rothwax's courtroom, waiting to answer a calendar call, when a court officer taps him on the shoulder. Degen is wanted immediately in Judge Haft's court.

"Is it a verdict?" Degen asks as they stride rapidly down the hall.

The court officer won't say.

But it's evident that something momentous is in the offing. The court officers have rearranged the seating at the defense table, lining the defendants alphabetically on one side, their attorneys on the other. The first row of spectator seats behind the defendants has been cleared. Finally, eleven court officers form a wall of flesh between the defendants and the spectators.

The jury files in, and Ruby Wilson, verdict sheets in hand, rises.

"Madam forelady," asks clerk Jimmy Campbell, "has the jury agreed on a verdict?"

"Yes, we have."

Michael Andriani is ordered to stand.

"Has the jury agreed upon a verdict as to the defendant Michael Andriani?"

"Yes, we have."

"As to count one, how do you find the defendant Michael Andriani to the charge of conspiracy in the second degree?"

"Not guilty."

There's a gasp of expectation in the house.

"And as to conspiracy in the third degree?"

"Guilty."

This time an ominous hush.

"Count number three, manslaughter in the first degree?"

"Not guilty."

"Count number four, riot in the third"—Campbell corrects himself—"in the first degree?"

"Guilty."

"Count number five, assault in the first degree?"—against Febee, with intent to do serious bodily harm.

"Not guilty."

"Count number six, assault in the first degree?"—against Febee, during the commission of a felony, to wit, riot.

"Guilty."

"Count number nine, assault in the second degree?"—against Carl Warren.

"Guilty."

"Count number ten, assault in the second degree?"—also against Warren.
"Guilty."

Then Rocco Areena stands as Wilson reads the verdict: as Areena predicted to Harry Hammer, not guilty on all counts.

The court officers pull Areena out of the well and direct him to a place in the cleared row of spectator seats.

Next Carlos Boutureira—guilty of the same counts as Andriani.

His mother starts to sob as the verdict is read.

Then Edward Burns. Again, not guilty on all counts.

Burns is led to a seat beside Areena and bursts into tears.

It's beginning to appear as if all nine defendants will escape conviction on the manslaughter charge. Then the verdict on Joseph Chiapetti is read: guilty on all counts.

Robert Brown, Chiapetti's attorney, leans across the table and sarcastically tells his client, "Congratulations."

Michael Doyle—guilty of four assaults.

Robert McLamb—guilty on all counts.

Anthony Paolini—not guilty on all counts.

He too takes a place in the spectator seats. Behind him his mother starts to sob.

Andres Sanchez—guilty on all counts.

His voice choked with emotion, Judge Haft addresses the jury:

"It has been said that someone really shouldn't thank a jury when it brings in a verdict, because that's a civic responsibility that we all have and a duty that we all have and therefore thanks are not in order. But it seems to me that this case is one where that saying has no application.

"You have been jurors in this case for over nine weeks. You have sat here during that period of time with the most incredible record for attendance that I think has ever been compiled. Not one of you has been late. Not one of you has been absent. . . . You have given this case every bit of your attention and your consideration. . . . You have suffered through it all with unfailing patience and good spirits. . . .

"Now, the law permits no comment by a judge on a jury's verdict, and that's as it should be. . . . So I'm not going to comment at all on the verdict. I will say how diligently you've gone about this job during this period of deliberations as well as through the entire trial. . . .

"Among other things, I will miss seeing all of you and I've at least enjoyed that experience during this trial. So again, thank you very much."

The jurors file out of the courtroom for the last time.

Moscow immediately moves to remand the convicted defendants, indicating he will ask for prison sentences for all six. After vociferous defense objections, Judge Haft rules:

"Upon due consideration, I am going to remand each of the six defendants until the sentence date on April nineteenth."

Thursday, March 16 At 6:30 P.M. on its second day of deliberations the Johnson jury returns with its verdict: not guilty. Afterward, several of the jurors tell Justice Rosenberger that they believe Johnson lied—both before the grand jury and on the witness stand. But they could not accept the account of Michael McShane, a cop convicted of corruption, that he saw the money change hands in the women's lockup. Therefore, the legal corroboration needed to prove perjury was lacking.

Rosenberger is pleasantly surprised to find the panel hewed so closely to the letter of the law.

Friday, March 17 St. Patrick's Day. A semi-holiday in the courthouse. Only a handful of cases are on the calendars. Many of the court officers and police witnesses are marching in the parade up Fifth Avenue. Many of the judges are sitting in the reviewing stand.

In Justice Burton Roberts's courtroom the jury returns with a verdict: As Stephen Shapiro feared, the panel acquits Stephen Owen.

Monday, March 20 Outside the courthouse about 125 persons—mostly Italian Americans from Greenwich Village—picket, protesting the conviction in the Washington Square case. They form a circle chanting, "We want justice for the six!" Their placards read:

> 6 OUT OF 100
> MOSCOW IS NOT A HERO
> STOP ANTI-ITALIAN PRESS COVERAGE

One flier passed out by an outfit called the Greenwich Village Youth Council says, "We feel that the press has been attacking the Italian-American community and . . . we want local kids saved from further injustice by the press and the judicial process."

Another by Peter Copani, who describes himself as "an investigative writer of street plays," says, "The community was clearly at war . . . against the criminal element which made it impossible for neighborhood people to use not only Washington Square park but many of the parks. . . . The crime is that innocent people were hit. A tragedy not uncommon in Vietnam."

Judge Lang sends the Cortale case to Part 33, the courtroom of Acting Supreme Court Justice Dennis Edwards, Jr. Lang checked and learned that neither Ryan nor Kuh had appeared previously before Edwards. Harold Rothwax calls the choice "inspired."

The Supreme Court Office of Probation is dark and gloomy. Laid out like a figure eight, it fills the entire south wing of the tenth floor. Tiny offices sealed in translucent glass line the walls, blocking any sunlight that might stream through the windows. In the center of each loop is a latticework of cubicle offices, divided by six-foot-high translucent-glass panels.

One loop is occupied by Probation's investigative staff, which prepares pre-sentence reports on defendants; the other, by the supervisory staff, which keeps tabs on prisoners on probation.

Robert LaSado sits in his eight-by-eight-foot cubicle in the investigative wing when the receptionist calls: There's a delegation of about a dozen persons who want to talk to him about the Washington Square case.

LaSado is a short, stocky man of forty-one with long brown hair and thick glasses. A probation officer for seven years, a welfare worker before that, he has an academic air about him. Among other things, he reads Rilke for relaxation. He dons his jacket and goes out to meet the delegation.

By the time he walks the few feet to the reception room, the delegation swells to more than twenty. LaSado looks for a place where he can sit down with them.

After a few minutes he finds it—an empty office in the center wing of the tenth floor, a rare bit of unoccupied space in the building.

By now the delegation has swelled to more than fifty. As LaSado leads them down the hall, more protesters pile off the elevators.

"Look, I know how the system works," one man tells LaSado. "They gave you this case because you're Italian."

"Non è vero," LaSado replies in Italian. *"Non sono italiano, sono spagnòlo."* ("That's not true. I'm not Italian, I'm Spanish.")

So many persons crowd into the tiny office that they overflow into the anteroom outside.

"I cannot help but be impressed by the number of people here," LaSado says. "It's very unusual."

But there are too many of them and too many try to speak at once. LaSado suggests that they draft a statement, which he'll consider.

A petition is drawn up on the spot. By the time the group leaves, it contains 116 signatures.

As the group departs, Anthony Paolini—one of the three acquitted defendants—tells LaSado, "If things had gone a little differently, you'd be writing a probation report on me."

Jim Ryan is in the waiting room of Part 33 conferring with the witnesses he'll present in the *Wade* hearing for the Cortale case when the clerk approaches counsel in the courtroom.

"Good morning. Both sides ready."

"We have an application to make," Richard Kuh replies.

"The People are ready," says Roger Frydrychowski. It's his first day on the job and his first official action as an assistant district attorney.

"All right," the clerk replies. "You can get the A.D.A., if you don't mind. The judge is going to come out."

Frydrychowski fetches Ryan, and the clerk intones his announcement as Judge Edwards mounts the bench. Edwards is a soft-spoken man—"unflappable," according to his judicial colleagues. At fifty-six he has chocolate skin and black hair that lies so close to the scalp it appears painted on. He went to Harvard Law School long before it became fashionable for blacks to do so and spent most of his career in the courts, thirteen years as a Criminal Court judge, a dozen years before that as law secretary to a Supreme Court justice. He quickly makes it known that he's a no-nonsense jurist.

"The People against Joseph Cortale, on bail," the clerk intones, eliding the final *e* to pronounce the name "Cortal."

"The People are ready," Ryan announces.

"We're ready for a hearing today," Kuh says. "I would ask that jury selection start next Monday, Your Honor."

Without lifting his chin from his hand, Edwards suggests that Kuh make his motions.

"We're not here for discovery, Your Honor," Kuh starts.

"I'm trying to find out what we're here for," Edwards replies.

Kuh takes up the running issue of the erased tape, but Edwards cuts him off.

"Once it's labeled 'reargument,' I cannot hear it."

Kuh starts again, and again Edwards cuts him off.

"I say to you, that motion must respectfully be referred to Mr. Justice Lang."

A third time Kuh starts. A third time Edwards cuts him off.

"I'm not going to listen to you."

It's obvious that Kuh has started off on the wrong foot with Edwards.

The judge suggests that they call Lang.

Kuh suggests that they go to see him.

"You want to enjoy the exercise?" Edwards says.

Kuh suggests that they take up his other motions first.

"I'll leave it up to you, sir," Edwards replies.

Kuh asks for a "brief hearing" regarding some notes that were destroyed by Detective Sergeant Gerald McQueen after he prepared a report in the case. He starts citing cases on the issue.

"I will accept no cases on argument," Edwards says. "If you're going to give me law, submit a memo."

Ryan protests that Kuh had plenty of time to make the motion, but kept it in his "back pocket." "I think a hearing would be inappropriate."

Kuh says a hearing will take only an hour, while the trial will last three weeks.

"I'll ask you a simple question," Edwards says. "What relevance is the length of the trial to your motion?"

He suggests that Kuh put his motion in writing.

Kuh asks that the defense be provided with a trial transcript at state expense.

"This is the type of motion that should be put in writing," Edwards rules.

Kuh asks for a list of prosecution witnesses and delivery of *Rosario* material.

Ryan replies that he'll present the list at the start of the trial and turn over *Rosario* material the day before the witness is scheduled to testify.

"I don't think a trial should be a game," Kuh says. "I particularly don't think a murder trial should be a game."

"I don't believe that we are participating in gamesmanship at all," Ryan says.

Kuh continues to argue. Edwards cuts him off, saying he must think the court is "naïve."

"As far as *Rosario* material is concerned, the application is denied," Edwards rules. But he grants Kuh leave to renew the motion once the trial starts.

The judge asks how long the trial will last.

"Four to five weeks," Ryan replies.

"From what I've listened to this morning, five weeks is more likely," Edwards says. "Conservatively, we'll think in terms of six weeks. . . . Any other applications?"

"Yes, Your Honor," Kuh says.

He asks for police reports on other suspects in the case and for any medical and psychiatric reports on prosecution witnesses.

Ryan starts to argue against it.

Edwards cuts him off. "I don't see what relevance it has. I'll deny the application as I did the *Rosario* material."

Kuh starts to argue the point again.

Edwards raises his palm and carefully accents a single word: *"Period."*

Kuh asks that jury selection be deferred.

"At the moment, you have the rowing oar," Edwards says. "The longer you talk, the further away the jury selection will be."

Kuh asks for any charts the prosecution will present. He says Ryan agreed to turn them over at the start of the trial.

"The trial starts with the selection of the jury," Edwards rules.

Kuh says he has other "discovery" points. "I take it Your Honor's ruling would be the same."

"Absolutely."

Kuh asks for any prosecution dossiers on potential jurors.

"I don't understand the application," Edwards says. "Therefore, I will not honor it."

Ryan says there are no dossiers.

"Any other applications?"

"Not at this time, Your Honor."

The attorneys leave to reargue before Lang.

"Oh, no!" Irving Lang groans as Ryan, Kuh, and Cortale return to his courtroom.

Ryan takes a seat in the jury box beside John Moscow, who is waiting to learn the trial date on his next case—an obscenity prosecution for "kiddie porn."

"While we're waiting," Lang rules, "recall on Cortale."

Kuh asks for a hearing on the missing tape. Ryan tries to interrupt.

"Mr. Ryan is not the judge in this case," Kuh snaps.

Lang says he's letting them argue in hopes that their anger will "dissipate" in *his* courtroom.

Kuh says Ryan is acting with "great discourtesy" and demands that he sit down.

"I prefer to stand."

Lang directs him to sit.

Kuh starts to argue. Ryan starts to rise. With a wave of his hand Lang motions him back to his seat.

But the prosecutor soon pops up again.

"That's not why we're here," he protests. He says Judge Edwards sent the matter back to Lang to see if he'd entertain a motion for reargument, but Kuh is already rearguing it.

Kuh snaps that Ryan has been "too busy jumping up and down" to understand what he's been saying.

Lang suggests that they both "cool down." He grants the motion for reargument, then denies the request for a hearing.

The stenotypist cuts him off. She's run out of paper.

"Off the record," Kuh says. He asks that the stenotypist read back Lang's remarks. "We may want the minutes."

The stenotypist reads back Lang's remarks.

"The motion for a hearing is denied," Lang rules. "That's my ruling. Please return to Judge Edwards."

Kuh reports Lang's ruling to Judge Edwards.

"May we now proceed to something else?" Edwards says.

But Kuh returns to the missing tape.

Again Edwards cuts him off. "Obviously, at this point I would not even allow you to make a record."

Kuh asks for an adjournment to allow him time to prepare the written memos.

"The People would object to that, Your Honor," Ryan says, noting that his witnesses are on hand.

Kuh asks that Ryan deliver *Rosario* materials on the witnesses at the *Wade* hearing. Ryan says he intends to call only the detective to testify to the fairness of the identification. He gives Kuh Xerox copies of several sheets from the detective's memo book.

Kuh protests that his copy is not identical with the prosecutor's. It seems that after the Xeroxes were made, the detective indexed his memo book with tabs. Edwards directs that Ryan produce a Xerox with the tabs.

Kuh makes several other requests. Each time Ryan objects.

"I never get to finish a sentence before I'm interrupted," Kuh protests.

"The interrupting this time will be by the court," Edwards says.

Kuh asks for a hearing on the eyewitness's "alcoholism."

"That application will be denied," Edwards rules. "Proceed without further delay. Call the first witness."

"The People call Christopher Riggan."

Riggan, his gold detective's shield pinned over his jacket pocket, is a solidly built man of about fifty with straight reddish hair and metal-rimmed glasses. Under Ryan's questioning he says that on June 11, 1976—the morning of the murders—he spoke with Florence Benfield, a receptionist in an office on the fifteenth floor of 2 Penn Plaza down the hall from the death scene. She told him that she had seen a man in the hallway when she came to work. She described him as "male, white, about thirty-seven, about five foot ten, stocky build, wearing a light blue suit."

Later that day, Riggan continues, he spoke with Mrs. Benfield again and showed her a photograph from Applied Systematics' annual report. The photograph depicted the company's three top officers—Cortale, Acca, and Galietta. Mrs. Benfield identified Cortale as the man she had seen.

Then Kuh takes over for a cross-examination that lasts the rest of the day.

Two floors below, where the five blacks stand accused of murder during the Harlem supermarket robbery, the pre-trial hearings finally come to an end. Justice Clifford Scott orders the jury selection to start on April 3, the first day of the April Term, when a fresh panel of prospective jurors will be available.

Tuesday, March 21

Room 546 is a clerk's office converted into the courtroom of Jury 4. Air-conditioning vents run along the ceiling. A safe, once used to store court records, fills one wall. Against the other is the jury box—a low platform with eight desk chairs. The judge's bench is jerry-built of plywood. The spectator seats look as if they were bought at a rummage sale.

The tiny courtroom is the scene of a relatively rare event in the Criminal Courts Building—a misdemeanor trial before a six-man jury. In 1977, of the 83,348 cases heard in the Criminal Court, only 153 went to trial—seventy convictions, eighty-three acquittals.

The trial may be rare, but it's not going to be unique. Throughout the courthouse the assault case against Anthony Stone has become known as "the videotape trial"—the first use of videotaped testimony in a New York court. But Assistant District Attorney Gary Black has informed Judge Eugene Schwartzwald that Leonard Richardson will testify in person and therefore the tape will not be played.

Defense attorney Mel Sachs, a dapper dresser who favors flashy suits and big bow ties, cross-examines Anthony Jenkins, the man Stone allegedly assaulted in the Port Authority bus terminal. Jenkins is a stocky black with horn-rimmed glasses. He claims to be a college-educated accountant, but his speech is semi-literate. He "axed" questions and ends almost every sentence with "you know?"

Sachs determines that Jenkins is a resident of Philadelphia who came to New York the weekend of the incident for "leisure." At the time he was a merchandising coordinator in Gimbel's Philadelphia store—it isn't clear if he worked there two months or longer. By the time he testified before the grand jury he was unemployed. He subsequently worked "for about two months" for Diamond Security as a guard. He says he's now a self-employed accountant with a clientele of about twenty-five, but keeps no records of his own finances.

Suddenly Sachs switches the subject. "Isn't it true that you were charged with assaulting a police officer in Philadelphia?"

Gary Black jumps to his feet shouting, "Objection!"

"Sustained," Judge Schwartzwald rules.

Sachs brings out that Jenkins told the court he'd planned to catch a bus back to Philadelphia at 2:30 A.M., but missed it. He told one grand jury the departure time was 2:00 and another 1:45.

While he waited, Jenkins says, he dozed off—as he puts it, "making *z*'s." He wasn't wearing his glasses, he explains, because he was afraid they'd be "ripped off."

Jenkins says he was accosted by Stone—in uniform—who "axed" him, "Do you have a ticket?"

Sachs brings out that Jenkins argued with Stone and refused to show it.

"Mr. Jenkins, didn't you say to him . . . 'Don't Bogart me!'?"

"I said something like that."

"So you did say it?"

Judge Schwartzwald, a short, balding man with a walrus mustache, brings the session to a close, telling the jurors they'll pick up with Bogart after lunch.

Justice James J. Leff is presiding in "Part 30." At fifty-seven he's a Falstaffian figure, round and jolly, with a high forehead and horn-rimmed glasses. Before ascending the bench nine years ago, he was an acknowledged expert on New York's complex election law, handling cases for appellants as disparate as Tammany's Carmine DeSapio and the Conservative Party. He's also a judicial iconoclast who presides without a robe and who told an interviewer that judges—including himself—are overpaid. Aside from a one-day headline, the only result of Leff's lament was that his fellow justices stopped holding their weekly lunches in his chambers. He has his own idea of how to clear the courthouse calendars: At arraignment each defendant would be given $2,500; if he pleads guilty immediately, he'll have that much to spend on "goodies" from the prison commissary; if he goes to trial, he must use all or part of the cash for attorney's fees. In 1973, Leff ran for chief judge of the Court of Appeals. He likes to joke that Judge Charles Breitel and Jacob Fuchsberg "spoiled" his chance of winning—by garnering five million votes between them.

Joanne Chesimard is brought before the bar. She's a slightly built black woman with an Afro hairdo, wearing round tinted glasses and a bright orange *khanga.* She now calls herself Assata Shakur.

In the early 1970s she was one of the nation's most-wanted women, a founder of the Black Liberation Army and later a defendant in a series of celebrated trials—for kidnaping, bank robbery, and murder. One trial had to be postponed because she was pregnant—from a conception that occurred while she and a male co-defendant were locked in a witnesses' waiting room during a ten-minute recess. She is now serving a life sentence for the murder of a state trooper during a shoot-out on the New Jersey Turnpike.

Somehow the onetime leader of the Black Liberation Army, notoriously heterosexual, has become a heroine to radical lesbians. About three dozen of them sit in the courtroom—tough-looking white women with duck-tail haircuts, almost all clad in leather or denim. They rise and give a clenched-fist salute as Chesimard is brought to the bar.

Her present case dates from 1971, when she allegedly tried to rob a Michigan man at gunpoint in his room at the Statler-Hilton Hotel. During a struggle for the gun, she was shot in the stomach, but managed to escape and flee through the lobby. She was captured on the street outside.

Assistant District Attorney Philip Russotti submits an eight-page memorandum to Justice Leff and paraphrases the key passages:

> The defendant has claimed that she has been denied a speedy trial. Faced with circumstances similar to those existing in the instant case a Supreme Court justice in Brooklyn dismissed a murder indictment against this defendant on speedy trial grounds. . . . Even if the People were successful in defeating the claim, the People would then be faced with trying a 7-year-old case in which the victim suffered bites and the defendant a bullet through her stomach.
>
> However, there is no realistic possibility that the defendant would serve any substantial additional incarceration as a result of this conviction, if there were one. The defendant . . . is serving a life sentence and is not eligible for parole in New Jersey until 1997. New Jersey authorities responsible for prosecuting the case have informed this office that they are virtually certain the conviction will not be overturned. . . .
>
> Therefore, considering all of these circumstances, it would be a waste of precious resources to pursue this prosecution.
>
> For the reasons set forth above the People respectfully recommend that the indictment be dismissed.

"The defendant wholeheartedly concurs," says Chesimard's counsel, Evelyn Williams.

"The motion of the People—" Justice Leff starts.

Williams interrupts him. She has obtained an order in federal court barring Chesimard's removal to New Jersey pending a hearing on where she'll be incarcerated.

"I'm sure they'll respect the order," Leff says. "Remand the defendant."

As Chesimard is led away, the radical lesbians stand and applaud. While court officers try vainly to quiet them, Leff rises and bows, first to the left, then to the right.

After the two-day *Wade* hearing Judge Edwards rules that Mrs. Benfield can make an in-court identification of Joseph Cortale.

Then he turns to the prosecutor. "I was wondering if you wanted to give more thought to the length of the trial, in view of the length of the hearing. Perhaps you want to sleep on that."

"I will, Your Honor," Jim Ryan replies.

Wednesday, March 22

Judge Edwards has set a two-stage process for jury selection in the Cortale case. Today and tomorrow will be spent culling out potential jurors who can sit through the protracted trial; the actual *voir dire* won't start until next week. By 11:15 A.M. the first panel of prospects is exhausted. Out of fifty potential jurors, thirteen are able to serve.

Thursday, March 23

Seated in the last row of spectator seats, Murray Weinstein leans forward and taps Michael Sage on the shoulder.

"At the rate this is going," he whispers, "this case'll go to July—July fifteenth."

Weinstein, an eighty-one-year-old retired cabdriver, and Sage, a seventy-four-year-old former television production assistant, are "thirteenth jurors" —courtroom buffs, members of the small army of retired men who spend their days watching the free show of a criminal trial. They keep book on the lawyers like boys with baseball stars.

They're watching Richard Kuh in the Cortale case—Sage remembers him as the ferocious prosecutor of Lenny Bruce fourteen years ago—because he promises the best show in the building. But come Monday they'll be in Justice Rosenberger's courtroom watching Jack Evseroff. A Brooklyn lawyer whose courtroom antics are as colorful as his custom-made suits, Evseroff will be defending Leon Port, a lawyer charged with bribing the arresting officers in a gun case.

"You're not going to fall asleep in his courtroom," Sage tells Weinstein.

As prospective juror after prospective juror parades to the bench to tell Judge Edwards why he can't serve, Sage finally rises.

"This is going to be a tedious thing," he says, "too tedious."

He leaves the courtroom to look elsewhere for legal fireworks.

Friday, March 24

Good Friday. A half-holiday in the courthouse. In Supreme Court only the calendar parts are functioning.

Judge Harold Rothwax rules on motions in the case of Arsenio Favor, a twenty-nine-year-old Filipino physician accused of murdering his wife, Nenita, also a doctor, with an injection of succinylcholine, a powerful muscle relaxant that breaks down in the body.

Rothwax summons the attorneys to the bench—Michael Davidson, the thirty-seven-year-old prosecutor, and Murray Cutler, a sixty-one-year-old street-wise defense lawyer—and tells them that he has reviewed the grand-jury minutes.

"They find no natural cause of death," he says. "They find no unnatural cause of death."

But he will not dismiss the indictment.

"This is a circumstantial-evidence case," he explains. "The totality of evidence must exclude every other hypothesis."

As the argument continues, Favor, a handsome man with sculpted hair and a mod-style light blue suit, sits at the defense table, his dark face obviously reddening.

Finally Rothwax cuts off Cutler. "Counsel, I have spent just about all the time I can spend on this."

In open court he repeats his ruling and orders the trial to start May 1.

Cutler, a New York City detective before becoming a defense lawyer, expected no less. To him, judges are policemen in black robes.

Monday, March 27

Standing in the drizzle outside the courthouse, William Depperman passes out a new leaflet:

LARRY FLYNT SHOOTING IS
LATEST CIA PUBLICITY STUNT

Richard Kuh starts his *voir dire* of prospective jurors in the Cortale case. Both he and Ryan seem to be seeking the same type of juror—older, business-oriented white men.

"Mr. Lazarus," Kuh asks one venireman, "do you have any doubt that I'm not Perry Mason?"

He explains that the fictional defense lawyer always solves his cases by pointing out the real murderer sitting in the courtroom. But in this case, he says, there will still be a "mystery" at the end of the trial.

Judge Edwards interjects, "That's up to the jury."

Mel Sachs cross-examines policeman John Karkut, Anthony Stone's partner on the morning of the Jenkins incident.

"Did Officer Stone ever hand you his hat and nightstick?"

"No."

Then Sachs turns to a conversation Karkut had with Deputy Inspector Cox.

"He said Stone was through," Karkut says. "He read me my rights and said if I lied they'd have my job."

He adds that the prosecutor, Gary Black, asked him to change his testimony and warned him of the penalties for perjury. He quotes Black as saying, "You witnessed more than you're telling us."

In the afternoon the perjury trial of Lawrence DeLucia opens. He's the second of three former assistant attorneys general to be brought to trial in the Bernard Landers investigation.

"I understand that Mr. DeLucia wishes to waive trial by jury," Judge Aloysius Melia says.

"That's correct, Your Honor," replies defense attorney Patrick Wall.

DeLucia, an obese man of forty-six with curly gray hair, signs the waiver of his right to trial by jury. Then Melia questions him to make sure that he understands what he's doing. Finally he rules:

"So ordered."

Assistant District Attorney Peter Benitez, tanned after a week's vacation in Martinique, rises to make his opening statement.

"The People will prove, . . ." he says—prove that DeLucia perjured himself when he denied that Bernard Landers had told him that he'd made loans to two assistant attorneys general and threatened to divulge this information to Robert Abrams, the Democratic candidate for attorney general in 1976, unless the state settled Landers's claim for $89,000. And they will prove it through the testimony of Landers and his tape recording of the telephone conversation.

Then Wall—tall, stout, and blond. He admits that DeLucia's answers "were false, objectively false. But Your Honor will find there was no attempt to cover up." He says DeLucia received the same information from Peter Wells, Landers's attorney, and immediately passed it on to the Attorney General.

"Where in the world is there any motive for falsehood on the part of Mr. DeLucia?"

Tuesday, March 28 In the hallway outside Part 33, where jury selection in the Cortale case is in its fourth day, Avon Gresham and Pablo Torres supervise as a plumber starts repairs on the water fountain—the first step in a project to restore all the building's drinking fountains.

Leonard Richardson, denied the opportunity to be the first videotaped witness in New York history, testifies in person at Anthony Stone's assault trial.

Mel Sachs questions him closely about his psychiatric history. Gary Black objects to his "boundless and unlimited inquiry."

"Overruled," Judge Schwartzwald rules. "But don't make a career of it," he tells Sachs.

Rolling his eyes and rubbing them frequently, Richardson reiterates his account of the beating. At one point he presses his forefingers against his temples.

"Are you all right?" Sachs asks.

Richardson nods yes.

Sachs confronts Richardson with some of the Q. and A. from the videotape session and asks if he remembers it.

"You was yellin' at me," the witness snarls. "You di'n't ask me anything."

Sachs repeats the question and answer. "You remember that, don't you?"

"No," Richardson says. "I don't remember that day."

The cross-examination continues. Sachs asks if Jenkins tried to block the blows.

"No."

"No, not at all?"

"No."

"And you're sure about that?"

"I'm sure about that."

"And if the man you're talking about said he was blocking the blows, he'd be a liar?"

"Objection!"

"Sustained."

In the narrow corridor outside Jury 4, Legal Aid's John Zirinsky confers with William Depperman.

"You know what I do to people I don't like?" Depperman asks.

"What?"

"I call up the phone company and pretend I'm them. I say I'm going to Europe for four weeks and please shut off my phone."

Then they enter the adjoining courtroom of Jury 3, where Zirinsky tells Judge Anita Florio that because of the things Depperman printed about him—among other things he called the lawyer part of "the frame-up system"—Legal Aid feels it can no longer represent him. The case is adjourned again until an 18B lawyer can be appointed to represent the "assassination researcher."

Wednesday, March 29

Sergeant Richard Canale of the Port Authority police tells the six-man jury in the Anthony Stone case about the ten-inch kitchen knife that was found in Anthony Jenkins's back pocket.

"Could you tell the jury—in your own words—what happened to that knife?" Mel Sachs asks.

"In my own words, I don't know."

"Is the knife missing?"

"Yes."

The first row of Judge Melia's courtroom is filled with reporters as Peter Benitez rises.

"Call Louis Lefkowitz."

A few seconds later a court officer opens a side door of the courtroom and Lefkowitz enters, walking jauntily to the witness box. He's a bald, bouncy man of seventy-three who's been New York state's attorney general since 1957. A Republican whose speech is still tinged with the "dese" and "dose" accents of the Lower East Side, Lefkowitz introduced Nelson Rockefeller to the technique of stumping by stomach—munching hot dogs in Coney Island and pizza in Little Italy—and he glories in his campaign appellation, "The People's Lawyer." Unlike his federal counterpart, the New York Attorney General has only limited jurisdiction in criminal matters. In fact, this is the first time that Lefkowitz has ever appeared in a criminal courtroom.

He nods to Judge Melia, takes the oath, and spells his name for the stenographer.

Benitez quickly brings him to the meeting in his New York City office on September 20, 1974.

"I had no idea what was coming up at that meeting," Lefkowitz says.

He says he was told that Peter Wells had called DeLucia and told him that Bernard Landers had diaries that showed loans to two members of the Department of Law—Joseph Hopkins and Martin Geruso—and contributions to the political campaigns of Lefkowitz and others and that if Landers didn't get the $89,000 he was owed, he'd go to the District Attorney.

Lefkowitz says he asked Hopkins about it. Hopkins replied, "As far as I'm concerned, I got a counsel fee. I never got a loan."

"I was a little upset and angry," Lefkowitz continues. He notes that it's against the practice of his office for assistants to take outside legal work.

He says he told Hopkins, "The proper thing is to give the money back." He adds that he ordered Hopkins to tell the same thing to Geruso, who by then had left the Attorney General's office for the Office of General Services.

"As far as I'm concerned, it looked like blackmail," Lefkowitz says. "It looked like a shakedown against the state."

He says he ordered his aides to defend against Landers's lawsuit "to the hilt."

He has no recollection that Robert Abrams's name was mentioned at the meeting.

Pat Wall's cross-examination is brief, eliciting only that Lefkowitz assumed at the meeting that DeLucia's receipt of the information was "recent."

Lefkowitz steps down, shakes hands with both Benitez and Wall, and walks rapidly out of the courtroom. In the hall outside he perches on a windowsill and holds an impromptu press conference, defending the action he took in the case.

Thursday, March 30

Anthony Stone takes the stand in his own defense. Under Mel Sachs's questioning he recapitulates his career and the events that led up to the encounter with Jenkins. At about 4:00 A.M. he and Officer Karkut started making a "sweep" of the bus terminal to rout out the drifters and derelicts. He approached Jenkins and tapped him on the leg with his nightstick.

"Do you have a ticket, sir?" he asked.

"Look, man, I had enough for one night, so please leave me the fuck alone and don't bother me," Jenkins replied.

Sachs ascertains that Stone was in uniform and asks him to continue.

Stone says he again asked Jenkins for his ticket.

"Hey! Didn't I tell you to leave me the fuck alone?"

Stone asked for some identification.

"I ain't showing you nothing!"

Stone told him he was under arrest.

"What for?"

"Disorderly conduct. Stand up!"

"I ain't gonna do nothing!"

Stone says he pulled out his walkie-talkie and told the station that he was returning with a prisoner.

"Stand up!" he again ordered.

"You're not taking me nowhere!"

Jenkins, he continues, then threw down the newspaper he was holding "and sprang at me," hitting his chest. Stone says he threw a "cowboy punch" with his right hand, then a left, and Jenkins fell back in his seat. He sprang forward again and grabbed for Stone's gun belt. Stone kicked him in the body and Jenkins fell to the floor.

"I never had any other contact with Mr. Jenkins."

Sachs asks if he injured his hands.

"To make it short, he had a hard head."

Shlomo Tal and Pini Balabin are being arraigned for murder before Judge Harold Rothwax. Tal, thirty-one, is short and bearded; Balabin, twenty-nine, tall, thin, and hawk-nosed. Both are gem cutters on West Forty-seventh Street's "Diamond Row," both Israeli nationals.

They've been indicted after a six-month investigation of one of the most sensational crimes of recent years—the robbery-murder of diamond broker Pinchos Jaroslawicz, who disappeared on September 20, 1977, along with more than $500,000 worth of diamonds. He was last seen knocking on the door to Tal's office.

At the time, Tal said he knew nothing about Jaroslawicz's disappearance. For five days he went about his business. Then he too disappeared, only to be found three days later sleeping in his car. He then told the police a fantastic story of how two men had burst in and robbed them, killing Jaroslawicz and threatening Tal with death if he went to the authorities. He said the men returned five days later, abducted him, and left him drugged in the car. Tal then led the police to Jaroslawicz's body, wrapped in plastic and stuffed in a two-by-two-by-three-foot wooden box in his office. The box was so small that the police had not examined it in their previous search.

Processing the prisoners took longer than usual, and the joke in the courtroom was that the prints had to be sent to Tel Aviv . . . and the rap sheets came back reading right-to-left!

Once started, however, the proceedings go quickly.

Balabin's lawyer, Abraham Brodsky, an aging veteran of New York's criminal bar, points out that his client's real first name is Pinhas—"Pini" is only a nickname.

The indictment is amended and the two defendants plead not guilty.

Assistant District Attorney Peter Stevens asks that they be remanded. He cites the severity of the sentence they face if convicted, the fact that they have a half million dollars' worth of diamonds to finance their escape, and the fact that they are not American citizens. Then he adds something that indicates that the authorities indeed may have sent the prints to Tel Aviv—both defendants have criminal records in Israel, Tal for auto theft, Balabin for drugs and theft.

Rothwax remands the defendants until Monday, when he'll hold a bail hearing.

"And tell Corrections!" he instructs the clerk, "so we don't have to send out Indian scouts to look for them."

After six days the twelfth juror is sworn in the Cortale case. The attorneys start the task of choosing four alternates.

Friday, March 31 Pat Wall presents the defense in the DeLucia trial. First, J. Edward Murray, an assistant attorney general, relates how DeLucia told him of Wells's call on September 18, and confirms Lefkowitz's account of the September 20 meeting. Then DeLucia tells substantially the same story.

Wall, hands thrust in his pants pockets as he paces the well of the empty courtroom, asks him about the call from Landers.

"When you testified before the grand jury, did you have any recollection of that conversation?"

"None whatsoever."

The defense rests, the attorneys sum up, and Judge Melia announces, "I will reserve decision until two o'clock."

After forty-five minutes of deliberations, the six-man jury in Anthony Stone's assault trial returns with its verdict: not guilty.

Mel Sachs joins Stone and Dominick Evangelista, president of the Port Authority Patrolmen's Benevolent Association, for a celebration drink at Maruffi's, a bar in back of the courthouse that is the hangout for cops and court officers.

While Stone pours dime after dime in the pay phone to tell the good news to his family and friends, Sachs, a professional magician in his off-duty hours, entertains Evangelista and his buddies with sleight-of-hand tricks and regales them with choice tidbits of his summation:

" 'He said he was in New York "partying." And he had a ten-inch knife in his back pocket. What kind of party was he going to—a luau?' "

At precisely 2:00 P.M., Judge Melia starts reading his decision.

"The basic facts do not appear to be in dispute," he says.

After recapitulating the testimony, he notes that DeLucia did not have reason to lie about the call, but Wells did. The attorney could be accused of a breach of fiduciary relationship or even blackmail for making such a call. Melia calls Wells's account "incredible."

On the other hand, "it does not appear to matter one iota" whether the information DeLucia relayed came from Landers or Wells. The "ultimate source" was still the same.

He notes that at the September 20 meeting DeLucia identified both Hopkins and Geruso as the assistants who had received money from Landers, but Landers never mentioned their names in his call.

"Whence came those names?" Melia asks. "The only logical conclusion from the testimony is that he got it from Wells."

But he adds, "I find it difficult to explain the defendant's total lack of recall" of Landers's call.

He goes on to criticize the D.A.'s office, noting that DeLucia's alleged perjury occupies only three out of 175 pages of testimony. If the D.A.'s office was intent on eliciting information, he says, it should have refreshed

DeLucia's recollection of Landers's call or even played the tape for him.

The judge concludes, "Both based on the evidence and the lack of evidence, the court has a reasonable doubt. Accordingly, the court finds the defendant guilty. The defendant is discharged."

Pat Wall jumps to his feet. "The court may have misspoken itself," he says, saying "guilty" instead of "not guilty."

Judge Melia bends toward the stenographer. "Amend the record." Then he walks off the bench.

Mary DeBourbon asks a visitor to her eighth-floor office if there's a verdict in the DeLucia case.

"Not guilty."

She walks over and yanks a half-finished press release from her secretary's typewriter.

"Huh?" exclaims a surprised Madeline Soto.

"He was acquitted," DeBourbon explains.

"All you have to do is change one word," the visitor suggests.

"We don't announce acquittals."

Three alternates have been chosen in the Cortale case, but the fourth proves elusive. By midafternoon the last panel of March jurors is exhausted. Except for some already seated in other trials, there isn't a potential juror in the building who hasn't been questioned in the Cortale case. The selection process will have to go over until Monday.

Jim Ryan's thoughts are not on the jury box, but on the transit talks at the Americana Hotel. If there's no settlement by midnight, the city's subways and buses will be struck, perhaps for weeks. Ryan has arranged to get a lift to work from his brother, but many of the jurors may not be able to get to the courthouse. In addition, many of his witnesses come from Long Island —and negotiations on the Long Island Rail Road are racing the same midnight deadline.

After a long day in the courts John Zirinsky returns to his West Side apartment . . . and finds the phone has been disconnected.

Monday, April 3

There was no transit strike. Subways, buses, and the Long Island Rail Road continue to run and the courthouse continues to function.

A new panel of prospective jurors is brought into Part 33, and the search for the elusive fourth alternate in the Cortale case continues.

Two dozen Orthodox Jews, bearded and wearing *yarmulkes,* sit in Harold Rothwax's courtroom. They are friends of the slain diamond dealer Pinchos Jaroslawicz, in court to see that justice is meted out to his killers.

But there is nothing to see. Judge Rothwax announces, "By consent of all the parties . . . these proceedings will be held in chambers."

While Shlomo Tal and Pini Balabin sit at the defense table, judge and counsel retire to Rothwax's robing room. An hour later Rothwax returns to the bench and announces that the two defendants will remain remanded.

At 3:09 P.M. the fourth alternate is sworn in the Cortale case. Over eight days of jury selection Judge Edwards and the lawyers questioned 347 veniremen. The final panel is composed of ten men—one of them black—and two women.

Following Edwards's preliminary instructions, Jim Ryan rises to deliver his opening address to the jury. He lays a sheaf of white legal papers on the shelf.

"Good afternoon, everyone."

Only a handful of people are in the courtroom. In the second row, behind the defense table, sit Cortale's wife, Rosemary, and their son, a mustached man in his twenties. In the first row on the prosecution side of the aisle is the press contingent and, several rows behind them, the widows of Eugene Acca and Enrico Galietta. The "thirteenth jurors" have all departed to watch the Leon Port trial.

His left hand in his pants pocket, gesturing with his right, Ryan reads the indictment charging Cortale with the June 11, 1976, murders of Acca and Galietta.

He describes Cortale as a "self-made man" with only a high-school education "who built the company from an idea to a company that did over two million dollars' worth of business." It was a one-man show. "When you dealt with Applied Systematics, you dealt with Joseph Cortale."

But in 1975, he continues, Cortale started borrowing money from the company, at first $5,000 a month, then $50,000 in September.

Kuh rises to object.

"He's setting forth what he intends to prove," Judge Edwards rules. "The court will allow it."

When Acca and Galietta found out about the loans, Ryan says, they forced Cortale out of the business and made him sell his shares to the corporation, repaying the loans with the money he received.

Soon afterward, Ryan continues, Cortale approached Acca and Galietta with a deal that would "set him up for life"—$500,000. But Acca and Galietta found out that the deal was in the works when Cortale was still president of Applied Systematics and drastically reduced his share. After that their relations with Cortale "continued to deteriorate."

The prosecutor tells the panel that on June 11 Cortale lured Acca and Galietta to Applied Systematics' New York City office in Suite 1535 at 2 Penn Plaza "on the pretext of meeting a supposed business client." Acca was shot once in the head, Galietta three or four times "in a desperate attempt to flee."

Cortale, Ryan claims, then came to the police "and told them the tale of Sidney Greene. . . . That story is nothing but an intricate web of lies."

While Kuh smiles angelically at the jury, Ryan says he will produce witnesses "who will shatter and tear apart for you the tale of Sidney Greene."

"In broad strokes that is the essence of what the People intend to prove," he concludes.

After a brief recess it's Kuh's turn. His notes are typed on white legal paper. He sips water from a paper cup and thanks the jurors for their patience. He says he will "analyze" Ryan's remarks and "anticipate" his evidence.

Within two hours after the murders, he says, "a high-ranking police officer . . . made the charge with absolutely no proof that Joseph Cortale was responsible." The police, he charges, then set out to generate "nonexistent proof."

He admits that Cortale was in the hall outside the death scene, but long before the murders occurred. His presence might be proof if the murders occurred in an isolated Alaskan hunting lodge, but "this was no Alaskan hunting lodge. This was probably one of the busiest office buildings in New York."

He tells the panel there *was* a Sidney Greene. "What that man's real name is, who he is—the police haven't yet found out," he says. "The police haven't yet found Judge Crater."

Kuh says one witness described the man in the corridor as five foot nine. He asks Cortale to stand.

Cortale, appearing about twenty pounds heavier than he did in January, rises.

"How reliable is anyone who thinks this big guy there is less than six feet tall?" Kuh asks.

The defense lawyer continues, peppering his remarks with "I suggest to you" and "Wouldn't you think?" Ryan realizes that Kuh is arguing to the jury, which is improper on opening. But he doesn't object. The more Kuh goes out on a limb, the better he likes it. He's convinced that Edwards will not admit a lot of the material Kuh mentions.

"It is not unheard of for law enforcement to make a mistake," Kuh concludes. "Mr. Cortale is not only presumed innocent, but *is* innocent of these crimes."

Once the jury is excused, Kuh rises and asks Judge Edwards to dismiss the indictment. He says Ryan presented "no evidence" in his opening showing Cortale was guilty.

"Motion denied," Edwards rules.

Kuh submits written memoranda on motions he made previously. Edwards asks Ryan to respond to them by noon tomorrow.

"We'll see you in the morning, then," he says, rising and starting off the bench.

"If Your Honor please," Kuh says, "we have other motions."

Edwards, obviously impatient to get off the bench, simply responds, "We'll hear them in the morning."

Tuesday, April 4

Before the Cortale jury is brought in, Kuh offers to stipulate to the identification of the victims and the cause of death. This is a frequent defense ploy in murder cases, to preclude the jury from hearing grieving relatives or the gory details of the autopsy findings.

"Your Honor," Ryan replies, "at this time I'm not willing to stipulate."

Kuh says he'll object to any such testimony.

"Sometimes a little anticipation can be beneficial," Judge Edwards observes. "Sometimes it can be needless." Then he nods to Ryan. "All right?"

"The People are ready, Your Honor."

The jury is brought in and Ryan calls his first witness—a draftsman in the D.A.'s office who made maps of the fifteenth floor of 2 Penn Plaza and of the street outside. Ryan finishes in five minutes. Kuh's cross-examination lasts the rest of the morning. He seems determined to leave no nit unpicked.

Weeping, Frances Stapleton is led into Part 109 on the seventh floor of the Civil Court Building. She's a stocky black woman of twenty-nine who wears a rolled-up nylon stocking for a cap and a suede coat over a blue sweater and slacks. She's weeping because she knows she's about to receive a sentence stiffer than those meted out to many murderers.

Stapleton and her sister, Rosella McFarland, were charged with selling 1⅝ ounces of heroin for $1,350 to an undercover policeman. They were tried separately. McFarland was acquitted, Stapleton convicted. She now faces a *minimum* sentence of fifteen years to life.

In 1973, at the behest of Governor Nelson Rockefeller, the New York legislature enacted the toughest narcotics law in the nation. "Draconian" is one of the milder adjectives that have been applied to it. Under the measure, persons convicted of dealing in or possessing hard drugs are considered A felons and face minimum sentences of one year to life up to fifteen to life. The law was an admission that Rockefeller's drug-rehabilitation program, launched with election-year fanfare in 1966, was a $6 billion failure.

The new law proved almost equally costly. Because persons accused of A_1 and A_2 felonies are allowed to plead to nothing less than A_3, there is little point to pleading. Virtually every narcotics defendant goes to trial. As a result, the legislature had to create one hundred new judgeships to handle the increased case load, at a cost of $100 million.

Needless to say, the tough new law made as much of a dent in New York's narcotics problem as Rockefeller's rehabilitation program. Because the police lack the money and manpower for the lengthy and far-reaching investigations needed to nab major drug traffickers, most of those hit with the severe sentences have been street-level dealers like Frances Stapleton.

Stapleton's Legal Aid lawyer, Jonathan Jacobs, has only one hope of averting the harsh sentence. By some fluke, the jury convicted Stapleton of sale, but not of possession. Jacobs submitted a motion arguing that it is a "repugnant verdict"—contrary to common sense.

But Justice Fritz Alexander quickly disposes of it. "The motion must be and is in all respects denied." The reasons, he adds, are set forth in his written opinion.

"We're ready to proceed," Jacobs says.

Holding a handkerchief to her face, Stapleton rises as the clerk arraigns her for sentence.

Alexander asks the Assistant District Attorney if she has anything to say.

"The People have no recommendation," replies Priscilla Hall.

She's an assistant under New York City's special narcotics prosecutor, Stirling Johnson, Jr. Each of the city's five district attorneys has assigned assistants to the centralized, federally funded agency set up to prosecute narcotics cases.

Then it's Jacobs's turn. The probation report, he says, is "of very little help to any of us in this case." He notes the "mandatory incarceration" required by law and adds, "It really leaves me very little to say." He asks for the minimum sentence.

Alexander turns to the defendant.

"Your Honor—" she starts. But she cannot control her convulsive weeping and collapses in her chair.

After a few seconds, only slightly more composed, she stands and says through her sobs, "I axed my lawyer to put me on the stand, so I could tell you what happened and he di'n' put me on the stand. I di'n' sell no stuff."

Alexander, a rotund black with a high-domed forehead fringed by kinky black hair, is unmoved. He notes that she doesn't understand what "sale" means under the law, but she knew what she was doing. It was "rank, unbridled trafficking in narcotics." He adds that there would have been "little benefit in her taking the stand" and says Jacobs "did all that he could for you."

"I have no choice in regard to the minimum sentence to be imposed," he continues. "If I had a choice, I would not impose a sentence as long as fifteen years. I have no choice."

He sentences her to state prison "for a period not in excess of your natural life and not less than fifteen years."

Stapleton, still weeping, is led from the courtroom.

Kenneth Laifang, a draftsman who works on the fifteenth floor of 2 Penn Plaza, takes the stand in the Cortale case. He tells the jury that he arrived at work at about 8:45 A.M. on the fatal June 11.

"I came off the elevator and I heard noises."

"Can you describe the noises?" Ryan asks.

"Crack, crack, crack. Something like that."

Laifang says he saw an acquaintance in the hall and raised his hands in mock surrender and said, "Don't shoot me."

Wednesday, April 5

Patrolman Frank Galgano of the Crime Scenes Unit tells the Cortale jury what he found in Suite 1535 on the morning of the murders—fingerprints, bullet holes in the wall, and a pad with the name "Sidney Green" written on it.

Harry Hammer and Greg Perrin compare notes in the courthouse lobby. Colleagues in the District Attorney's office fifteen years ago, they now represent several of six psychiatrists arrested this morning on charges of falsifying $131,000 in Medicaid claims.

"They ought to have made some arrangement to notify counsel," Perrin says.

Normally, when a man under investigation—especially for a white-collar crime—has retained counsel, the District Attorney's office notifies the lawyer that there's an indictment and he surrenders his client. In this case, however, D.A.'s detectives routed the defendants out of bed at 7:00 A.M. and they've been sitting in the lockup all day waiting for their prints to be processed in Albany. Judge Irving Lang quipped that they could pass the time preparing "730 forms"—the psychiatric reports on defendants' mental capacity to stand trial.

"I had a specific understanding with the guy," Hammer says sadly, "but they treat him like every other black murderer."

Wearing the same green sweater he wore throughout his trial, Peter Muniz is led into Part 32 for sentencing.

First the clerk arraigns him as a predicate felon—for having committed an assault with a knife in 1972.

"Do you admit that you were so convicted?"

"Yes, I was," Muniz replies.

"Was that conviction obtained in violation of your constitutional rights?"

Muniz gapes incredulously. "No."

Then Jessica DeGrazia addresses the judge. She says Muniz has "a long history of assaultive conduct. . . . He has a capacity to commit homicide one of these days." At his age, she adds, there's "no prospect of rehabilitation." She asks for "substantially more" than the minimum of three to six years.

In reply Geoff Abrams observes that Muniz has "a drinking problem." "I would ask Your Honor—all things considered—to be as lenient as possible."

Justice Shirley Levitan says it's a "difficult decision." "Apparently, *any* drinking by Mr. Muniz is too much," she adds, noting that his latest assault is "an almost exact duplicate" of the 1972 case. "The community is entitled to some protection."

She sentences Muniz to four to eight years in prison.

Geoff Abrams is pleased. He expected five to ten or six to twelve.

"I won the trial," DeGrazia tells him in the hall, "you won the sentence."

Sal Salerno, a securities adviser whose offices were then on the fifteenth floor of 2 Penn Plaza, tells the Cortale jury what he saw on the morning of June 11, 1976.

He was on his way to the men's room at about 9:00 A.M. when Kenneth McDonald approached hurriedly and said, "Come with me!" McDonald explained that a man was lying on the floor in a suite down the hall.

He opened the door for Salerno, who stepped inside and bent over the body of Enrico Galietta. He started to feel for a pulse, then realized that the man was dead. They started out of the office.

"He said, 'Oh, my God!' and we looked in and I saw another body," Salerno says. "It was obvious there was nothing I could do for him. At that point I said, 'Let's get out of here!' We didn't even go into that room."

They returned to Salerno's office and told the receptionist to call the police.

Thursday, April 6

Kenneth McDonald tells the Cortale jury how he discovered the bodies of Eugene Acca and Enrico Galietta. He's a stocky man of twenty-seven with straight brown hair, a shaggy mustache, and metal-rimmed glasses. He's president of the Star Messenger Service, which does 90 percent of its business for Applied Systematics.

He says he arrived at Applied Systematics' New York office at about 8:53 A.M. on June 11 and unlocked the door.

"I noticed Mr. Galietta laying on the floor near my feet," he says. "There was no glasses and his face was covered with blood."

McDonald says he ran down the hall to another office and asked a switchboard operator to call the police.

Jim Ryan shows him a photograph of the dead Galietta and asks him to identify it. McDonald's hands shake visibly as he holds the picture and identifies it.

McDonald says he returned to the office with Sal Salerno. Salerno bent over the body and tried to take his pulse, then remarked that the man was dead and that he'd been shot.

"Let's get out of here!" Salerno said.

As they started to leave, McDonald continues, he noticed an arm on a table in an adjoining room. He switched on the light "and realized it had been Mr. Acca."

Friday, April 7

His head propped on his hand, Joseph Cortale gazes intently at the witness—Dr. Millard Hyland, New York City's deputy chief medical examiner.

Dr. Hyland tells the jury that Eugene Acca was shot once in the left forehead. "The cause of death was certified as a gunshot wound in the head and brain."

He tells the jury that there were four bullet tracks in Galietta's body—one in the left forehead with powder burns around it, one through the back and into the stomach, an "in-and-out" track through the right shoulder, and another where the back of Galietta's head was sheared off. He speculates that the shoulder and back-of-head tracks were caused by the same bullet.

"The cause of death was certified as multiple gunshot wounds."

Jim Ryan has one further question about Acca. "Could an individual with that type of wound be able to write anything?"

"Handwrite?" Dr. Hyland asks. "With a pencil?"

"Yes."

"No, sir."

Ryan has demonstrated that the pad with the name "Sidney Green" was not Acca's dying declaration.

Monday, April 10

Rocco Areena, acquitted in the Washington Square riot case, stands before the bench in Jury 1 on another assault charge. He's accused of slugging William Smith with a plaster cast on his arm. The fight started when Smith, who had been shopping in Greenwich Village, tried to shoo away youths who were sitting on his car.

The Washington Square trial lasted nearly two months. The formalities in Areena's assault case are completed much more quickly. After a brief bench conference, Conrad Ferrigno enters Areena's guilty plea to a charge of harassment, and Judge Milton Williams imposes a sentence of thirty days in jail or a $250 fine.

Across the street, on the seventh floor of the Civil Court Building, John Moscow is about to exhibit the chief evidence in his obscenity trial. On his desk are two cardboard cartons, each containing hundreds of reels of eight-millimeter film. Beside them is a projector, in the back of the courtroom a screen. The four defendants are charged with selling 3,971 reels of two films to undercover detectives.

Supreme Court Justice Jerome Marks enters the stipulation "that there's in excess of fifteen hundred of one, in excess of fifteen hundred of the other."

"So we don't have to watch three thousand films," he explains to the jury.

Just before the lights are flicked out, Geoff Abrams and Bob Stein of Legal Aid—Stein appropriately wearing a raincoat—slip into a front-row seat to catch the show.

The films are grainy, often out of focus, and badly lit. In the first, a red-haired freckle-faced boy and a brown-haired girl, both about eleven, undress, kiss, caress, and eventually copulate . . . after a fashion. In the second, a long-haired prepubescent boy and an even younger curly-haired blond girl go through the same gyrations.

Then the lights are turned on. Abrams and Stein have left, bored beyond belief. The jurors show no emotion.

Tuesday, April 11

Bored by the second day of testimony about Joseph Cortale's business dealings, Michael Sage—shod in sneakers—slips out of the courtroom and stands in the hall talking with another "thirteenth juror." Their conversation is not about the Cortale case but about Jack Evseroff's conduct in the Leon Port bribery trial, which has just gone to the jury.

"Were you there when he called the witness a Nazi?" Sage asks.

"No."

"I thought he was going to hit the roof, he was so loud."

"Oh, he can be loud. He's got some very big clients in Brooklyn, a lot of the Mafia guys."

Wednesday, April 12 Raymond Marquez—"Spanish Raymond"—stands before Judge Harold Rothwax for arraignment. He and Robert Ramirez were arrested more than a year before and charged with promoting gambling and possession of gambling records. The District Attorney's office has finally got around to indicting them.

Marquez is a short, stocky man with a scruffy mustache. He is casually clad in a suede jacket and jeans. He looks more like a Hispanic handyman whose gambling is confined to dominoes on the front stoop than the reputed numbers king of Harlem.

"Raymond Marquez," asks court clerk Frank Lanotte, "how do you plead?"

"Not guilty."

"Robert Ramirez, how do you plead?"

"Not guilty."

Rothwax notes that the lawyers have asked for time to prepare motions. "If you want forty-five days—"

"I'd appreciate it, Judge," says Paul Goldberger.

Rothwax sets the case down for May 24. "Parole is continued."

Spanish Raymond, Ramirez, Goldberger, and his co-counsel, Paul Feldman, ride downstairs in the elevators.

"I read through the first paragraph"—of the indictment. "Zippo," Goldberger tells Feldman. "The second paragraph. Zippo."

"It's another phony case again," Feldman says.

"Incredible!"

"With anybody else, they would have thrown it out."

"Don't worry, the judge will throw it out."

Martin Geruso is on for sentence, but the session is postponed because Stephen Shiffrin can't attend. Instead, he sits primly in District Attorney Morgenthau's office listening intently as the boss announces the result of his year-long investigation—the indictment of a man who's legally dead!

It's a tale of financial finagling and international intrigue that spans three continents and nine nations. Five officials of the defunct American Bank and Trust Company—which closed in September 1976, the fourth largest bank failure in American history—are charged with multimillion-dollar violations of New York State's banking laws. The indictments, totaling 170 pages, allege a single count of conspiracy, plus fifty-five counts of misappropriation of bank funds and twenty-five counts of falsification of bank records to conceal the illegal transactions. In the main, the five defendants are charged with making millions of dollars in illegal loans to companies controlled by David Graiver, a director of the bank, and the funds allegedly were then channeled to the Banque pour l'Amérique du Sud, a Belgian bank controlled by the Graiver family.

Graiver is an Argentine national and the alleged mastermind of the plot. His family is reputed to be the money managers for Argentina's leftist

Montanero terrorists, and several members of the family were jailed by the South American nation's military junta. David Graiver reportedly was killed in a plane crash near Acapulco, Mexico, five weeks before the American Bank and Trust Company failed. Relatives identified fragments of a charred body as Graiver's and immediately had the remains cremated. Tomorrow would have been his thirty-eighth birthday.

"The grand jury apparently believed they were not indicting a dead man," Morgenthau says.

But he will not say what evidence there is that Graiver is still alive. The suspicion—voiced privately—is that he fled behind the Iron Curtain to Czechoslovakia. Interpol has been notified.

Morgenthau says the life of the grand jury has been extended into 1979 and that the crimes it is investigating include homicide—on the theory that if Graiver faked his own death, he may have been responsible for those of the two pilots who died in the crash.

The reporters have one question. How does the D.A. press charges against a dead man?

Chief Assistant District Attorney Peter Zimroth supplies an answer. "We're arraigning an urn?"

Detective Christopher Riggan relates Joseph Cortale's account of his movements on the morning of the murders: He arranged a meeting of Sidney Greene, a potential client of Applied Systematics, with Acca and Galietta at the 2 Penn Plaza office. He said Greene had identified himself as the comptroller of Bobbie Brooks, a leading manufacturer of ladies' sportswear. Cortale arrived at the office at about 8:20 A.M. and found he'd forgotten his key. So he crossed Seventh Avenue to the cafeteria in the basement of the Montgomery Ward Building for a bite of breakfast. He called the office several times from pay phones in the lobby of the Montgomery Ward Building and the Statler-Hilton Hotel across the street, but there was no answer. Finally, he phoned Greene to explain the situation and Greene said the deal was off. Then he went home, took a shower, and sent his suit to the cleaners.

Next Riggan produces a series of handwritten notes in which Cortale recorded his dealings with Sidney Greene. Ryan asks him to read the memos to the jury.

Kuh suggests that Ryan do it.

Judge Edwards suggests the "best voice." He turns to the jury. "Do you have any preference who you'd like to hear?"

There's a flash of laughter.

But the jury doesn't vote. Edwards suggests that Ryan read the memos.

"Dusty" Ryan, a petite schoolteacher in suburban Westchester County, in court to see the people her husband has been talking about for two years, listens as Ryan reads:

" 'Five-slash-eighteen. Nine-thirty A.M. Sidney Greene, comptroller Bobbie Brooks, fourteen-o-seven Broadway'—I think—'Private line six-nine-seven nine-eight-nine-seven . . . If interest by A.S.I. Greene wants meeting' —abbreviation 'as soon as possible'—'after Memorial Day at A.S.I. office in Manhattan. He's emphatic that we are not to come to his office until agreement reached. Feels union would find out. All hell to pay.

" 'Five-slash-twenty-five. Spoke to Gene Acca ref. F. M. appointment. He indicated interest if no problem with union. . . . Gene asked me to check with Rick [Galietta] for his schedule. . . .

" 'Five slash-twenty-eight. Spoke to Rick for confirm on above schedule. Next week hard. Available only on Monday six-slash-seven, Friday six-slash-eleven. . . .

" 'Six-slash-three. Called Sidney Greene at twelve-thirty. Sec. advised stuck at factory, South Carolina. Should be back Friday A.M. . . .

" 'Six-slash-seven. Eleven A.M. Greene called. Apologized for last week. O.K.'d Friday appointment. . . .

" 'Six-slash-eight. Greene arrives at Two Penn Plaza about ten-forty-five. Sorry to hear I was no longer C.E.O. [chief executive officer] at A.S.I. Passed amenities. . . .

" 'Six-slash-eight. E.A.A. [Eugene A. Acca] called to confirm meeting on Friday morning. I said it was on.

" 'Six-slash-ten. Three-fifteen. Spoke with Bobbie Robbins. Confirmed appointment for tomorrow A.M.' "

Despite Jack Evseroff's histrionics, the Leon Port jury hangs, eleven to one for conviction.

Thursday, April 13

Big and rumpled, William Kunstler sits in the first row of Part 35, talking with members of the Butler and Johnson families in the row behind him. The Malcolm X murder case has been restored to the calendar.

"I flew all morning to get here," Kunstler tells them. "I stayed with Rap Brown last night. He runs a Muslim food store in Atlanta. He has a mosque in his house. It was good to see him. I haven't seen him in a long time."

In the late 1960s, H. Rap Brown was one of the most controversial figures in the Black Revolution. The chairman of SNCC, the Student Nonviolent Coordinating Committee, he was anything but nonviolent. He disappeared in 1970, when he was wanted on charges of riot and arson in Maryland and a gun charge in Louisiana. In 1971 he was wounded and captured in a shoot-out with police on a West Side rooftop after sticking up a bar. He was convicted, imprisoned, and very shortly paroled.

When the Malcolm X case is called, Judge Harold Rothwax briefly reviews the history of Kunstler's motion.

"I'll hear you, Mr. Kunstler, and then I'll hear you, Mr. Alpert, in response."

Kunstler notes that he has submitted to the court a sealed affidavit in which Thomas Hagan named his confederates in the crime and supplied the details of how it was done.

In addition, he says, under the Freedom of Information Act he has received FBI files on the case "which identify the killers as coming from Newark, New Jersey."

"I just got them this morning," he adds.

He quotes from a February 22, 1965, telegram to J. Edgar Hoover. " 'The theory of the case . . . is that the killers were imported to New York City. . . . One of them was recognized as a member of the Newark temple.' "

"The names are blacked out, of course," he adds.

Kunstler quotes another FBI report naming the suspect as "one of the Nation of Islam's strongmen from Newark."

"That's what I've got from just a preliminary reading of this handful of documents."

He cites another report saying that Hagan met at a New York hotel a few days before the slaying with a person on the payroll of the FBI.

Kunstler notes that the D.A.'s office called his claim "preposterous," but "I think current events have shown that nothing is preposterous as far as the FBI is concerned. . . . There's no claim that the FBI killed Malcolm X, only that they instigated it."

"Judge," he continues, "I don't know what more you could really show. You will have a shocking story unfolding in this courtroom."

He likens it to Judge Sirica and the Watergate case.

His head propped on his fist, Rothwax interrupts to ask when he can get copies of the FBI reports.

Kunstler says he'll have them Xeroxed today.

"All we're asking, Judge, is a chance to prove this. If we get a chance, we'll prove it."

In reply, Assistant District Attorney Allen Alpert says Kunstler "implied" that law enforcement was involved in the murder, but "that would have nothing at all to do with the criminal responsibility of Butler and Johnson."

"It's all in essence"—he pauses—"smoke to get a hearing."

Rothwax asks if Alpert checked out the names in Hagan's affidavit.

"No, I've not."

If the names in the FBI reports are the same as those in Hagan's affidavit, Rothwax observes, "then the probabilities are somewhat affected."

Alpert says the only thing before the court is Hagan's statement.

Rothwax asks him to check it out.

Alpert replies that it's "*their* obligation."

"It's not their obligation to ask them to do things they can't do," the judge snaps. "Apparently, you're not making any inquiry. Why don't you try? . . . If you seek, maybe you shall find. . . . I'd like to see those FBI reports without the blanks. Hagan may be lying or he may be telling the truth."

He says the matter is not yet ready for a hearing, but "let's see where it goes."

Alpert protests that Kunstler moves by "dribs and drabs" and asks that a bottom line be drawn. He asks the court to decide on the basis of the papers before it.

"Judge, we're prepared to rest on this," Kunstler says, waving the sheaf of FBI reports.

Alpert protests that the court is "asking me to go on a fishing expedition."

"It doesn't seem to me you can say simply, 'Bosh! That's not enough,' " Rothwax replies. "I'd like to see what that report says."

He asks the lawyers to decide between themselves when they'll be ready to come back to court.

"That's fair enough, Judge," Kunstler says.

In the hall outside, he gleefully tells members of the Butler and Johnson families, "We're on the road now! We're on the road! The judge has changed totally."

Norman Fells takes the stand in the Cortale case. He's a bushy-haired, mustached management consultant whose office adjoins Applied Systematics'. Under Ryan's questioning he says he arrived at work on June 11 at about 8:00 or 8:05 A.M. He set up his schedule for the day, then about 8:30 walked down the hall to Suite 1500 to pick up his mail, but the room was still locked. He returned to his office.

"As I was opening my door, I saw someone next door"—at Applied Systematics. "He appeared to be opening the door next to mine with a key."

But Fells could not identify the man.

About five or ten minutes later, Fells continues, "I heard what sounded like someone hammering on a pipe."

How many times?

"Four or five or maybe six times."

Friday, April 14

Like other calendar judges, from time to time James Leff presides over a jury trial, taking testimony in the afternoon when the rest of the day's docket has been cleared. For the past week he's heard the case of Donald Wright, a twenty-year-old black accused of robbing a McDonald's hamburger shop.

Before the calendar is called, Leff charges the jury. The panel retires at 10:38 A.M.

At 10:41 the foreman sends out a note: They've reached a verdict.

It takes a few minutes more before the lawyers can be brought back to court. Then Wright rises to learn he's been found guilty. No one is sure—there are no statistics on such things—but it may have set a courthouse record for speediest verdict.

Leff thanks the jurors and offers to treat them all to Big Macs for lunch.

Herald Fahringer and Stephen Shiffrin confer at the bench with Judge Melia.

Fahringer tells them that his habit of staying in court and working through the lunch hour when he's on trial "probably saved my life." He was in the courthouse in Lawrenceville, Georgia, when an unknown sniper shot his client, *Hustler*'s Larry Flynt, and Flynt's local lawyer, Gene Reeves, Jr., as they were returning from lunch.

The lawyers, back in court for the sentencing of Martin Geruso, work out an unusual procedure with Judge Melia: Fahringer will speak first. The defense lawyer has already submitted a fifty-page sentencing memorandum.

Geruso, his beard shaved off to reveal a double chin, listens as Fahringer launches into a half-hour plea for mercy.

"What social utility is achieved by placing Mr. Geruso in jail?" he asks.

He says Geruso faces automatic disbarment—"about as severe punishment as anyone can possibly suffer."

Geruso, he continues, has a heart condition and he cites a doctor's report that "confinement . . . would seriously imperil Mr. Geruso's life." He says he was "scarred" by the experience of another client who died when he was sent to prison.

Geruso's wife, Patricia, and two of his four children sit in the first row along with Geruso's father. Fahringer asks the father to rise and tells Judge Melia that he is legally blind and dependent on his son.

"When we look at the bookkeeping of a man's life, we open the ledger," Fahringer says, listing the assets on one side, the liabilities on the other. He says Geruso's assets are many. The liabilities: "He has made one mistake."

"He says to this day, he believes to this day . . . 'I never felt my judgment was influenced, I never did anything wrong.' . . . He was more a fool than he was a felon."

Fahringer cites the precedent of the Dolkart case for placing a white-collar criminal on probation. "To do anything more to him, it seems to me, is uncivilized."

Judge Melia turns to the defendant. "Mr. Geruso, do you wish to add anything?"

"Just one thing, Your Honor," Geruso says, barely rising from his chair, his voice croaking with emotion. "Please don't hurt the innocent. Please."

Then Shiffrin: "He was motivated by the meanest, grossest aspects of greed." He says Geruso took money for a prostitute, to gamble, to replenish his bank account.

He notes that Geruso originally agreed to cooperate with the D.A.'s office, then changed his mind. "He refused to mitigate in any way his evil."

The prosecutor argues against what he calls "the one-bite-of-the-apple theory—the defendant is entitled to one bite of the crooked apple."

He also argues against "cardiac immunity," saying Geruso suffered from his heart condition when he committed his crimes. He adds that there are excellent medical facilities in the state's prisons.

Sipping water from a cup embossed with a patriotic red-white-and-blue motif, Melia listens as Shiffrin delineates the differences from the Dolkart case: Dolkart pleaded guilty; he restored the money he stole; and he cooperated with the authorities. Shiffrin cites a series of precedents for sending bribe takers to prison and says the legislature, in its wisdom, provided for a sentence of up to seven years.

"If this upper limit of seven years has any meaning at all, this is the case where it should be applied."

He asks Melia to impose a sentence of two to six years.

Fahringer rises quickly to add one point. Geruso agreed to cooperate, but refused to wear a "wire" to amass evidence against others.

Measuring his words, Judge Melia says he has considered all the factors in the case. He calls Geruso's acts "crimes of greed and self-indulgence." He says they were premeditated, repeated, and persistent.

"Confinement is not required merely for the sake of meting out punishment," he says. "I think it important to tell the white-collar community that it does not have one automatic free pass at criminal activity."

As Geruso slumps in his seat, Melia imposes a one-year sentence.

The long day of testimony in the Cortale case is drawing to a close when the defense offers an exhibit in evidence. Judge Edwards denies the motion.

"I suggest Your Honor's ruling is as outrageous as any ruling I've seen in any court," Kuh says.

Unflappable as always, Edwards replies, "I was going to say I'm flattered, but you're entitled to your opinion. Again, as I suggested to you many, many times, I'm not here to function to incur your approbation or approval. If you agree with my ruling, fine. If you disagree with my ruling, you have an exception for the record. And you're experienced enough to protect your rights.

"With that happy note, we'll conclude today."

Monday, April 17

Henry Stein, showroom manager for Bobbie Brooks, tells the Cortale jury that there's no Sidney Greene employed by the company, certainly not as comptroller. Besides, he says, Bobbie Brooks's comptroller works at the company's main office in Cleveland.

Tuesday, April 18

Detective Richard Nohan testifies that 697–9897 (the number Cortale gave as that of Sidney Greene's office) is a pay phone in the lobby of the Grace Building on West Forty-second Street.

Then Ryan calls Mrs. Roberta Robbins—Bobbie Robbins—administrative assistant first to Cortale, then to Eugene Acca. She's a petite woman who looks a little like Shirley MacLaine. She wears a sharply tailored pants suit with a crimson blouse. Her brown hair is trimmed in a Vidal Sassoon cut. She speaks very softly.

After all the pre-trial brouhaha—Kuh's harping about the "willful destruction" of her concealed tape recording, Ryan's description of her evidence as "damaging"—her testimony turns out to be an anticlimax, a tying up of loose ends.

She says she helped arrange Cortale's June 11 meeting with Acca and Galietta, but did not know what it was about. Cortale never told her the name "Sidney Greene."

She identifies the name "Sidney Green"—without the final *e*—on the pad found in the office as written in Acca's hand.

She describes Cortale as "frustrated or upset because they [Acca and Galietta] were going to lower the percentage he was going to get."

She identifies a list of employees who had keys to the Penn Plaza office and says that, at the request of the police, she circulated a memo to Applied Systematics' employees asking if any of them knew Sidney Greene.

Finally Ryan asks her about a conversation she had with Cortale on the night before the murders.

Cortale said, "If I get into trouble, will you—"
She cut him off. "Don't be silly. How would you get into trouble?"

Wednesday, April 19

Cold rain falls in torrents outdoors, but the court officers outside Part 106—moved back to the Civil Court Building after the Washington Square trial—wear summer uniforms of short-sleeved white shirts. With hand-held metal detectors they carefully screen the seventy-five spectators who have come to hear the post-conviction arguments in the case. There's even talk of making them leave their umbrellas outside the courtroom, but it's finally decided that that would create too much confusion afterwards.

The crowd, mostly Italians from Greenwich Village, includes two of the acquitted defendants—Edward Burns and Anthony Paolini—parents of several of the convicted defendants, and Anthony Costanza, a barrel-chested athlete, his red hair shaved to the scalp, who was observed during the trial sitting in the back of the courtroom, signaling answers to witnesses from the neighborhood.

At 11:15 A.M. the six convicted defendants are led from the bullpen to the jury box. During his month in jail Joseph Chiapetti has grown a beard.

Six court officers sit behind the defendants. Nine others are stationed around the courtroom.

Judge Haft opens the proceeding. "I have reviewed the charge and found a few errors which I think ought to be corrected."

"It's a little late," mumbles an assistant district attorney in the first row.

John Moscow, fresh from a conviction the day before in his obscenity trial, chuckles.

The attorneys cluster around the bench as Haft goes over the transcript with them.

In the spectator seats Mrs. McLamb weeps. Burns smiles at his former co-defendants.

When the bench conference ends, Haft reads the results into the record: "Counsel have stipulated to the following corrections of the transcript."

The changes turn out to be minor corrections of stenographers' errors: "Dif" instead of "Dave"; "Resto" instead of "Rizzo"; "with" instead of "where"; and so on.

Then Haft asks, "Are there any applications or motions?"

Robert Cohen rises. "I have a motion, Your Honor." He moves to set aside the conviction of Andres Sanchez.

And the long day of legal arguments begins.

Florence Benfield repeats the testimony she gave at Cortale's *Wade* hearing—of seeing Cortale in the hall at about 8:50 A.M.

Her account is corroborated by Stratton Lee, Jr., who rode up on the elevator with her. Lee is a thin black youth, neatly dressed, studious-looking in horn-rimmed glasses. A freshman at Harvard Business School, he worked during the summer of 1976 at his father's real-estate office on the fifteenth floor of 2 Penn Plaza.

Lee didn't observe Cortale, but he fixes the time of their arrival at 8:50 A.M.—because he looked at his watch and had to wait until his father arrived and unlocked the office.

While he waited, Lee says, "a man came in about nine o'clock saying someone had been shot."

Thursday, April 20

Nonchalantly chewing gum, James Conyers stands before the court for sentence.

Few sentences in the courthouse come off on schedule. Either the lawyers are tied up on other trials—often in other counties—or the probation reports are not ready. Conyers's case is no exception. His sentencing comes two days behind the date set by Justice Burton Roberts.

Assistant District Attorney John Evans explains the exigencies that induced him to accept Conyers's plea of manslaughter, then goes on to attack the juvenile justice system. It "almost encourages kids under sixteen to rob and steal with virtually no fear of punishment."

He starts reciting Conyers's juvenile record: assault—A.C.D.'d; robbery and assault—probation; robbery and assault—probation; robbery and assault—A.C.D.'d.

There's more, but Justice Roberts interrupts. "That is one of the deficiencies of the so-called juvenile reform act. . . . That is why the act is a sham and why the act should be amended."

"The Family Court is totally ineffective in this state," Evans asserts. "It is a waste of time and money."

Roberts, noting that Conyers is eligible for "youthful offender" treatment, turns to Arthur Hendrickson, who is filling in for defense attorney Otto Fusco. "Do you make such an application, Counsel?"

For the record, Hendrickson makes the application.

"The court states that because of the horrendous nature of this crime and the background of the defendant, he is not worthy of it," Roberts rules.

Evans asks the court to impose "the maximum sentence it could impose."

By contrast, Hendrickson asks Roberts to "extend to himself the full measure of his compassion."

He too attacks the juvenile justice system. "I don't think he got lenient treatment. He didn't get any treatment. He became a digit. He became less than human."

Roberts turns to the slightly built defendant in a black sports shirt and blue jeans. "Do you wish to say anything before I impose sentence on you?"

Hands clasped behind his back, Conyers answers, "No."

"This is one of the most horrendous homicides that I have ever had before me," Roberts shouts.

He notes that the victims were an eighty-four-year-old man, partially blind, and his seventy-six-year-old wife, an invalid unable to walk, weighing only fifty-six pounds.

"They never did you any harm," Roberts says. "They probably never did anybody any harm."

He notes that Conyers has a long record of delinquency. At the age of three he set fire to an apartment. At the age of fourteen he sodomized his half sister.

"Society was aware of where you were going a long time ago," Roberts shouts, his face flushed with anger. "But society characteristically gives lip service to treatment."

He observes that New York State lacks the facilities to treat juvenile offenders.

"This man—for he is a man now—was led to believe that crime is a way of life for which he would never really be punished. . . . I'm sick and tired of seeing sixteen- and seventeen-year-olds in this courtroom charged with homicide."

He calls Conyers a "wild animal" and says it would have been "horrible" if he had been acquitted.

"I don't know what's going to happen to you, Mr. Conyers, but it's the recommendation of this court that you stay in jail as long as the law permits."

He imposes concurrent sentences of eight and a third to twenty-five years in prison.

Conyers shows no emotion. His mother and grandmother weep.

Richard Michalski of the New York Telephone Company produces computer printouts called "MUD lists" (for message-unit detail) showing that Cortale never made the calls he claimed to have made from his home in suburban Glen Cove to the number listed for Sidney Greene.

Friday, April 21

John Palica, assistant manager of the cafeteria in the basement of the Montgomery Ward Building, testifies that Joseph Cortale was in the restaurant from about 8:40 to 9:20 on the morning of the murders. It's a key point, since it shows that Cortale couldn't have made the telephone calls he claimed to have made from the building lobby or the Statler-Hilton Hotel. But it also contradicts Mrs. Benfield's account of seeing Cortale on the fifteenth floor at 8:50 A.M.

The day's testimony ends at 11:10 A.M.

Once the jury leaves, Kuh rises to protest against the short sessions, saying he doesn't know when he should subpoena his witnesses.

"May I interrupt?" Judge Edwards says. "[Ryan] has said he is on schedule. He intends to finish by next Tuesday or Wednesday."

"Each day we come in here and leave early," Kuh complains.

"I should say you have made your record. Period," Edwards says softly. "Do you have any other applications?"

"Yes, I have other applications," Kuh replies. "If I may restate one I made before."

"If you made it before, I will not entertain it," Edwards rules.

Jim Ryan notes, "It's possible we may conclude the People's case on Monday."

"It won't trouble anyone if you do," Edwards observes.

Monday, April 24

Jim Ryan calls Angelo DiTaranto, director of operations at Applied Systematics. A slim, dark-complexioned man with a trace of silver in his black hair, DiTaranto tells of a meeting Cortale held with Applied Systematics' middle-management men thirteen days after the murders.

"He stated that we could help ourselves," DiTaranto says, "by asking Harold Gottfried to step down as head of the company [and] ask Cortale to come back as head of the company."

"If [Gottfried] refused to step down," DiTaranto continues, "we would tell him that we would go on strike, so to speak, not do any work, stop production."

AP18 is a makeshift courtroom converted from the robing room of AP17 on the second floor. It's a tiny room with eight wooden chairs for spectator seats. The judge's bench is a wooden table.

The defendant in the non-jury trial is Toby James Wilkins, a thirty-year-old traffic-patrol agent (male meter maid) who's charged with official misconduct and attempted coercion.

Mrs. Gail Baxter, a thirty-two-year-old secretary from Yonkers, claimed that when Wilkins was ticketing her car on East Fifty-ninth Street he offered to "forget about it" if she kissed him. She said he had "a look of perversion" in his eyes.

Defense attorney Ira Rabb calls Wilkins's partner, James Braddy, to the stand. Like Wilkins, he's a tall, mustached black in a brown uniform.

It's a scene straight out of Perry Mason: Braddy says *he*—not Wilkins—told Mrs. Baxter, "Why don't you give me a little kiss and let's forget about it?"

Assistant District Attorney Michael Diner jumps to his feet. "I must interrupt to warn you that you may be making an admission that could leave you open to prosecution. It is my duty to advise you of your rights against self-incrimination. You have the right to consult with a lawyer. What you are saying amounts to a confession."

Judge John Brickley adjourns the trial for a month to give Braddy time to consult with counsel.

Jim Ryan calls what turns out to be the final prosecution witness in the Cortale case—Detective Thomas Ryne, who tells of the futile efforts he and his partner made in the search for Sidney Greene. No one they interviewed had heard of him.

Kuh pops up. "If Your Honor please, I object. This is clear hearsay."

"Yes?" Judge Edwards says softly. "Do you want to modify that? Do you have an objection?"

"Objection. Hearsay. I think it is appropriate to state the basis, Your Honor. If Your Honor doesn't want to hear it, objection."

"Since we've been at this for nearly three weeks," Edwards lectures him,

"I've clearly asked that the objection be framed simply 'Objection.' It certainly cannot come as a surprise, the request that the objection be voiced as a simple 'objection.' "

"Your Honor," Kuh protests, "if the proper basis is not shown, it may not be properly preserved."

"Are you aware of the court's ruling as to that?"

"I'm aware of what the law has been in this jurisdiction ever since I've been practicing, Your Honor, in many, many courts."

"Again, without a speech, are you aware that's the practice that we've been following?" Edwards continues. "Why can't you simply say 'Objection'? What's the problem?"

"Because, Your Honor, . . . there are instances when the proper basis has to be stated, and I don't think the word 'hearsay' is that burdensome, Your Honor, to say the least."

"If the objection is on the basis of hearsay, objection overruled," Edwards rules. "If you want to rise and voice an 'objection'—period—I'll be glad to entertain it."

"I further object, Your Honor."

"Further objection sustained. . . . Thank you kindly. Next question."

Tuesday, April 25

Jim Ryan has a problem: His final witness is spending the day on a kidney-dialysis machine. With the jury absent, he asks Judge Edwards for a one-day adjournment or permission to call the witness on rebuttal.

Kuh protests. "The prosecutor either puts on his witness or rests his case." He says he will not consent to calling a non-rebuttal witness on rebuttal.

"What would be the nature of the testimony?" Edwards asks Ryan.

The prosecutor says the witness works for a firm called Compass Data and had business dealings with Cortale. And Compass Data is in the same building as Bobbie Brooks's New York office.

"That was the source of the idea which the defendant used to come up with the alibi or story of Sidney Greene," Ryan says.

Kuh says it's "scraping of tag ends to piece together the mosaic." "I suggest . . . the proof is irrelevant."

"Mr. Ryan, anything further?" Edwards asks.

"We can put Mr. Cortale in that building shortly before the crimes," Ryan says. He calls this "significant."

Cortale beckons to Kuh and whispers in his ear. Then Kuh tells the court that Bobbie Brooks is "an extremely well-known name in the dress industry" and that Cortale spent ten years in the garment business."

"Anything further?"

Ryan shakes his head.

"The motion, I guess, for a continuance is denied."

Ryan bows to the inevitable. "The People rest."

Kuh moves for a dismissal on grounds that the People have failed to prove a *prima facie* case.

"It's your prerogative to say whatever you wish to," Edwards says.

So the attorneys argue—a preview of their summations to the jury.

Kuh says there is "no direct proof" against Cortale. Even the existence of Sidney Greene has not been disproved. He dismisses the MUD lists.

"All that does is muddy the water. It doesn't clarify anything. It does not eliminate every reasonable possibility of innocence."

He says Palica and Mrs. Benfield contradict each other as to Cortale's whereabouts at 8:50 A.M.

"The burden is on the prosecution. As a matter of law no circumstantial case has been made out. . . . Incidentally, the prosecution has never shown that Mr. Cortale had a gun."

"All of Mr. Ryan's proof still leaves one hypothesis consistent with innocence," he says, noting that a half-smoked Kent cigarette was found at the death scene, as well as an unidentified fingerprint on a Styrofoam coffee cup. Thus, "we have an indication of someone else in the suite."

He says the prosecution "threw this garbage can—and I use that word advisedly—into the grand jury" and came up with the indictment.

Ryan, in rebuttal, insists, "The People have proven a *prima facie* circumstantial case."

First, it established motive. Then it showed that "the defendant brought the two deceased to the place where they were executed." Finally, Cortale told "a very elaborate story . . . about a person who the People would submit was put forward as a fall guy. . . . Mr. Greene did not exist but in the mind of Joseph Cortale."

He notes that Cortale never disclosed the name of the purported client to Acca or Galietta, yet the name "Sidney Green" was found on the pad in Acca's handwriting. That, he says, "places Joseph Cortale within the doors of that suite."

He insists that the prosecution proved that Cortale "knowingly brought Mr. Acca and Mr. Galietta to that suite with the intention of causing their deaths."

Kuh says Ryan "had all kinds of drivel in this record." He notes that Ryan didn't address himself to the unidentified fingerprint or the cigarette butt.

Ryan replies that the only thing he forgot to mention was Cortale's statement to Mrs. Robbins: "If I get into trouble, will you—"

Kuh calls that "a little bit ridiculous on its face," saying it's absurd that Cortale would work out such an elaborate plot, then admit it on the eve of execution.

"The court's conclusion is that sufficient credible proof at the conclusion of the People's case has been demonstrated," Edwards rules. "The motion to dismiss . . . is denied by the court."

After a brief recess and further colloquy, Edwards suggests, "Shall we call the jury in?"

The attorneys agree, and a court officer fetches the panel.

Edwards reminds Ryan to rest his case.

Once the jurors are seated, Ryan rises and says, "Your Honor, at this time the People rest."

Several of the jurors seem shocked.

Kuh calls the first defense witness—Detective Riggan. He wants to get on the record several points he couldn't make on cross-examination.

"Detective Riggan," he starts, "have any guns been recovered in this case?"

"I don't think there's any question," Edwards says.

"I just want to make it crystal clear," Kuh explains.

He asks if Riggan inventoried the dead men's effects.

"Objection."

"Sustained."

He asks if the detective conferred with Rosalie George at 393 Seventh Avenue.

"Objection."

"Sustained."

Kuh asks if Rosalie George has moved to Florida.

"Objection."

"Sustained."

"I respectfully submit that Your Honor is barring the defense from effectively presenting its case," Kuh says.

He asks Riggan about the half-smoked Kent cigarette and calls upon the prosecutor to produce the cigarette.

"If Mr. Kuh wants to look at the cigarette, I will gladly show it to him," Ryan says.

"Why not let the jury see?" He asks that Ryan be ordered to produce the cigarette.

"Objection."

"Sustained."

"I have nothing further of this witness."

Wednesday, April 26

Richard Kuh calls Janet Gallo to the stand. She's a petite brunette in a Navy pea jacket who works as a secretary in another office on the fifteenth floor of 2 Penn Plaza. She says that on the morning of the murders she got off the elevator at about 8:35 A.M. and saw two men standing there.

"Normally, at that hour," she explains, "there's no one hanging around."

She didn't see their faces.

Howard Meyer is defending another Washington Square assault case.

On trial in Jury 4 before Judge Anita Florio and a six-man misdemeanor jury is Diego Tolosa, the twenty-six-year-old son of a Colombian diplomat. Although he wears a pin-striped suit and tie, with his shoulder-length black hair and cheeks as smooth as his attorney's are hairy, it's hard to tell at a glance if he's a man or a woman.

Tolosa was arrested for smoking a "joint" in Washington Square. Several witnesses to the incident filed complaints of police brutality, and the cops, as is their custom, upped the ante against Tolosa to assault and resisting arrest.

Meyer asks Tolosa what happened at the station house. Tolosa says he was beaten in the lockup and told that if the police-brutality complaints weren't withdrawn, "I'd be taken to the Tombs and I'd be fucked in the ass by niggers."

With two black men on the jury, it's a point Meyer is anxious to bring out.

Tolosa starts to sob on the witness stand.

"I was ready to kill myself," he continues. "The last thing in the world that I wanted was to be fucked in the ass by niggers."

Even Meyer is taken by surprise. He wonders how the two black jurors feel.

Thursday, April 27

Kuh calls four character witnesses for Cortale, then informs Judge Edwards at the bench that he has no more witnesses. Edwards excuses the jury until Monday—tomorrow is a Jewish holiday—and tells them that the trial will conclude early next week.

Once the panel leaves the courtroom, Kuh asks for time—and funds—to bring Rosalie George from Florida. She's a woman Cortale was seen talking with in the cafeteria across the street from 2 Penn Plaza.

"The People have been forced to rest," Edwards rules. "I'm sorry, but I'll have to take the same attitude with respect to the defense."

Kuh also is forced to rest his case.

At 11:00 P.M. the jury reports that it has acquitted Diego Tolosa of assault, but is hopelessly deadlocked on resisting arrest. Judge Florio excuses the panel and declares a mistrial. Howard Meyer learns that they split four to two for conviction. The holdouts for acquittal were the two black jurors.

Friday, April 28

Abe Brodsky paces the eleventh-floor hallway waiting until Judge Harold Rothwax charges the jury in a gun-possession case and the courtroom doors are unlocked.

Like most defense lawyers, he prefers to represent men he *knows* are guilty. If he wins, he can take pride in a job well done. If he loses, he can say that justice was done. Either way, he can sleep nights. But if he defends an innocent man and he's convicted . . .

Once the jury retires, Brodsky enters the courtroom and learns that his case—the murder case of Shlomo Tal and Pini Balabin—is not on the calendar.

Rothwax spies him sitting in the first row of spectator seats and calls, "Mr. Brodsky!"

The defense attorney steps inside the rail and informs the judge that he filed motions for discovery, returnable today.

"Well," Rothwax says, "we'll have to get Mr. Stevens up here."

"I've spoken to Mr. Stevens," Brodsky says. " 'Give us what we want. Voluntary disclosure.' 'Tomorrow. Tomorrow.' *Mañana. Mañana. Mañana.*"

"Second call," Rothwax orders.

Two hours later, as Brodsky and Assistant District Attorney Peter Stevens approach the bench, a court officer hands Rothwax a note. The jury asks that portions of the testimony be reread.

"Talk to you later," Rothwax tells the lawyers. "Ten or fifteen minutes."
"Monday?" Brodsky suggests.
"O.K."
"Nine-thirty?" Brodsky has a case in federal court scheduled to start at 10:00 A.M.
"I'm sorry," Rothwax tells him. "My son has to go to school and I'm the only one who can take him. There's no way I can be here by nine-thirty."

Monday, May 1

Richard Kuh sits at the defense table scrawling notes for his summation. Cortale, in shirtsleeves, sits at a blackboard making a list under the heading: SOURCES OF NUMEROUS REASONABLE DOUBTS. He looks up and notices reporters copying the points.

"That's plagiarism," he quips.

To Kuh it's no joke. He jumps up and turns the blackboard around so the newsmen can't read it.

Judge Edwards mounts the bench and announces the trial schedule: Kuh's summation today, Ryan's tomorrow; he'll charge the jury and they'll start deliberations Wednesday.

Kuh protests that Ryan will have overnight to prepare a reply to his remarks. "Your Honor's present ruling is grossly unfair."

The clerk reports that juror No. 9 is ill. Edwards orders him replaced with the first alternate, Judith Ahlborg.

The jurors—now nine men and three women—take their places.

"May I proceed, Your Honor?" Kuh asks.

"Do you want to rest?" Edwards suggests.

"The defense rests."

Then Kuh walks to the jury box and sets his papers on top of a fat briefcase. He immediately addresses himself to the question, "Why didn't Joe Cortale take the witness stand?"

He cites several reasons: First, the prosecution's case was "so patently full of holes, big enough to drive a Mack truck through," there was no need. Second, Cortale suffers from a heart condition and Kuh didn't want to subject him to the strain. Third, Ryan read Cortale's statement into the record so the jurors know what he has to say. Finally, he didn't want to expose Cortale to Ryan's cross-examination.

"Jurors don't want to see a bearbait, a torture before them," he explains.

He accuses Ryan of "horse-shedding" his witnesses. He says the term derives from the old-time practice of lawyers' preparing witnesses in the horse shed adjoining the courthouse, but it's a thinly veiled obscenity.

He accuses Ryan of "misleading" the jury in an "effort to convict an innocent man."

He notes the conflict between the accounts of Palica and Mrs. Benfield. "Mr. Cortale could not be at two places at the same time. Isn't it reasonable at the very least to have a reasonable doubt?"

Juror No. 2—Helen Mandell, a plump, red-haired copywriter for Sears—nods her head in agreement. Cortale sits impassively, his chin resting on his hand. Ryan scribbles furiously on a yellow legal pad.

Kuh says there are three basic elements to the prosecution's case: Mrs. Benfield, Sidney Greene, and Bobbie Robbins.

He calls Mrs. Benfield "a walking reasonable doubt" and insists that her identification cannot be credited.

Then he turns to Sidney Greene. "I don't suggest to you that there was a person whose name is Sidney Greene. [But] that doesn't mean that there wasn't somebody who said, 'I am Sidney Greene.' "

As a group of future legal secretaries studying at the Katharine Gibbs School fill the spectator seats to watch a real live murder trial, Kuh calls for a ten-minute recess. The women emit a collective groan.

When the recess ends, Kuh resumes, "Ladies and gentlemen, I left you with a cliff-hanger: 'What would the police have done if they had been interested in finding out if there really was a Sidney Greene?' "

But he digresses. He notes that the MUD lists don't show the calls Cortale says he made to Sidney Greene, and "I can't tell you why that's so." But "it defies common sense to convict someone of murder because calls don't appear on a MUD list."

As for the police insistence that they uncovered no trace of Sidney Greene: "Where is Aldo Moro? . . . Where is or what has happened to Jimmy Hoffa? . . . Where indeed is Judge Crater?"

"That," Kuh says, "leads us to Bobbie Robbins or lunch."

They break for lunch.

During the luncheon recess the Supreme Court officers celebrate Law Day by staging a rally in the park across the street from the courthouse. They're protesting the pending reclassification of their job assignments by Richard J. Bartlett, the state administrative judge. One carries a sign: BARTLETT SLOT US NOT. And a dummy in a black robe is strung from a tree—Bartlett hanged in effigy.

Charles Meara, the executive officer in charge of the courts' non-judicial personnel, watches the rally from across the street and wonders which judge lent them the robe.

After lunch Kuh turns to Bobbie Robbins's testimony, calling it "highly inconsistent" with the prosecution's picture of Cortale as a calculating killer.

Then he runs through a list of other matters. There's "not an iota of proof that Mr. Cortale ever had a handgun." There's the half-smoked cigarette and the unidentified fingerprint on the coffee cup.

"I suggest to you that the same person who left his fingerprint on the Styrofoam cup left that cigarette," he says.

"What really happened?" he asks rhetorically. "It was a rub-out, it was a hit-killing, it was a professional job."

And "who might have hired the hit-man?" Perhaps those who took over Applied Systematics, Kuh suggests. Perhaps organized crime.

Launching into his peroration, he quotes from *Othello:* " 'Who steals my purse steals trash; 'tis something, nothing;/ 'Twas mine, 'tis his, and has been slave to thousands;/ But he that filches from me my good name' "—he turns toward the prosecutor—"Mr. Ryan, 'Robs me of that which not enriches him/ And makes me poor indeed.' "

He asks the jury to "give Joseph Cortale back his good name."

Then, pointing at the prosecutor with his glasses, "They haven't found nothing. You are asked to pull their ashes out of the fire. I think this case is riddled with holes, riddled with improbabilities, riddled with doubts. . . . You have the power to restore Mr. Cortale to a full life."

Tuesday, May 2

For once the sun is shining brightly as William Depperman stands at the courthouse entrance, passing out yet another leaflet:

JOHN ZIRINSKY EXPOSED AS
GOV'T PLANT IN J.F.K. CASE

Fifteen floors above, Jim Ryan starts his summation. He says that circumstantial evidence is often stronger than direct evidence.

Of Kuh's summation, he notes that "the best defense is a good offense." He calls the defense attorney's arguments "nit picking, misquotation of evidence, arguing nonexistent issues, and putting up a smoke screen."

As an example, he cites the unidentified fingerprint, which he calls "of no significance whatsoever."

"Objection," Kuh snaps. "Speculative."

"Try not to interrupt," Judge Edwards tells him. He says Ryan did not interrupt Kuh's summation and calls the prosecutor's statement "classically fair comment."

Kuh replies that he'll object when he feels he has a right to.

"If it goes beyond the direction of the court, I'll have to take other action," Edwards warns him.

The judge is obviously nearing the "flapping" point.

Kuh smiles angelically with his arms folded as Ryan resumes.

"Finally, the issue is not me. The real issue in this case is Joseph Cortale and the absolutely incredible tale of lies that Joseph Cortale told the police."

He reviews how Acca and Galietta forced Cortale out of Applied Systematics. "Was he sore? You better believe it."

Then he notes that Cortale's first action was an attempt to swindle his former partners.

Finally he turns to the double murder. "Joseph Cortale and nobody else brought Gene Acca and Rick Galietta to Suite 1535 that day."

He says the killer was familiar with the suite. He knew how to put a brad in the lock so the door couldn't be opened from the outside and how to disconnect the telephone switchboard. "The killer had been there before."

Then there was the name "Sidney Green" on the pad. How did it get there? "From the mouth of Joseph Cortale to the hand of Gene Acca."

Ryan postulates what happened next. "When Gene Acca looked up, there was one well-placed shot." Next, Cortale shot at Galietta. One hit, one miss. Galietta ran past Cortale toward the door. There was another miss, another hit, and Galietta fell. Finally, there was a shot at close range into his skull.

"That certainly doesn't sound like a professional job to me."

Ryan looks at the clock and observes that the morning session has reached the midway mark. If he keeps going, he says, he'll be able to finish before lunch. Or would the jurors prefer a recess?

Juror No. 5—John Jahling, a blond bank vice-president—raises his hand. "I'd like a recess."

Court is recessed for the usual ten-minute break that stretches to thirty.

When the session resumes, Dusty Ryan takes a front-row seat to hear her husband. Ryan says Kuh tried to confuse the jury as to the time of the murders, but three different witnesses placed the shots at between 8:30 and 8:45 A.M. He calls Kuh "a very artful defense attorney doing what he does best—making issues out of non-issues."

He turns to Florence Benfield. "Florence Benfield, if believed, totally destroys the foundation of Joe Cortale's story."

Finally, he takes up Sidney Greene. He calls Cortale's account "obviously absurd on its face."

"All the blame and all the suspicion is cast upon a nonexistent person," Ryan says. "Mr. Cortale would have you believe, number one, that Sidney Greene is the killer."

But, according to Cortale's account, he spoke with Greene on the telephone a few minutes after the murders. That meant that Greene went from the death scene to the one place where he could be traced. "It's absurd. It makes absolutely no sense."

As for the notes that Cortale made of his conversations with Greene, "They do not have the ring of truth. That's not the way business people operate."

At 1:00 P.M., Ryan tells the jury that he has about a half hour more. He asks them if they want to break for lunch or let him continue. This time they tell him to continue.

Ryan turns to the MUD lists and says, "The simple, inescapable conclusion is that those calls were not made. . . . This means that Mr. Cortale's story is a lie. Sidney Greene does not exist, never did exist."

But the name "Sidney Green" on the pad puts Cortale in the room. "Joseph Cortale was in that room on that date, and he is responsible under the law for what happened in that room."

"Objection."

"Overruled."

Finally, Ryan turns to the testimony of Mrs. Robbins and DiTaranto's account of Cortale's meeting with the middle-management men to attempt to regain control of the company. "It makes sense of everything else in the case."

He concludes by asking the jury to return a verdict of guilty.

Judge Edwards excuses the jury. Then he starts off the bench.

But Richard Kuh has one more matter. He notes that Edwards forbade counsel to talk to the jurors or even nod hello to them should they pass in the hall.

"This morning, Your Honor, before court opened, Your Honor was walking down the hall in active conversation with juror number ten, Mr. Kent," he continues. "I certainly assume that that had absolutely nothing to do with this case. . . . I don't know what to say—"

"If that's what you wish to call to the court's attention, denied," Edwards rules.

"I ask that Mr. Kent be disqualified and removed from the jury in light of Your Honor having conversation with him during the trial," Kuh shouts.

"I said I won't entertain it," Edwards replies tartly. "I won't even dignify it."

He walks off the bench toward the door that leads to the jury room and his robing room.

"I suggest the door be closed," Kuh calls.

Edwards's patience finally snaps. "I suggest you leave the court and remember you're a member of the bar."

He walks out the door.

"I will leave the record reflect Your Honor said that with the door open," Kuh calls after him.

Through the open door Edwards can be heard applauding.

Wednesday, May 3

After hearing Judge Edwards's charge, the Cortale jury retires at 11:50 A.M. to start its deliberations.

Harvey Rosen, a bearded assistant district attorney, drops by the courtroom to congratulate Jim Ryan on his summation.

"My wife says I convinced her," Ryan replies.

For the first time in nearly two years the prosecutor feels there's a possibility he might win the case. The feeling started a few days before, when Kuh rested without putting Cortale on the stand, and increased after the summations.

Were Ryan to see—and hear—inside the jury room, he might feel differently. The first vote is seven to five for acquittal. Favoring conviction are juror No. 3, Steve Abatis, a postal clerk who worked nine years as a policeman in his native Greece; No. 5, Jahling, the blond banker; and Nos. 10, 11, and 12, three older men—Arthur Kent, the retired auditor whom Kuh tried to dismiss; Ernest Babulak, a record keeper for Citibank; and Jens Vadstrup, a retired cashier.

As the jury continues its deliberations, a minor dispute arises about who said what at the post-murder meeting of Cortale and Applied Systematics' middle-management men. So at 3:15 they return to the courtroom to have the testimony reread.

The request baffles Ryan. Angelo DiTaranto's account of the meeting was uncontroverted.

The testimony is reread—far more than the jurors need. It changes no one's mind. The second vote also is seven to five to acquit.

Two of Cortale's children pass the time in the courtroom by playing backgammon. A court officer fetches a pile of old magazines for other members of the family to read during the agonizing wait.

At 6:30 the jury is taken to dinner.

Jim Ryan is too nervous to eat. Unlike the defendant, who bloated under stress, during the course of the trial Ryan has lost ten pounds.

In Part AR1, Judge Louis Neco presides over night court. There's one headline case on his calendar—the arraignment of Anthony Ferino, a forty-three-year-old Long Island cabby, who's accused of the gunpoint robbery of a diamond necklace from Mrs. Henry Kaiser, widow of the late shipbuilder and automobile manufacturer.

Assistant District Attorney Peter Stevens points out a minor error in the complaint: The necklace, still not recovered, is worth $500,000, not, as it's written, "$500.00."

The prosecutor asks for bail of $250,000, saying Ferino was identified as one of two men who accosted Mrs. Kaiser when she returned to her plush East Side apartment after a party at Studio 54, the city's newest "in" discotheque.

Judge Neco sets bail at $50,000 bond or $20,000 cash.

In the first row of spectator seats defense attorney Henry Schnitzer looks around impatiently. He's handling a case for an absent colleague, defending his first prostitution arrest in fifteen years. The papers have been processed, the defendant is in the bullpen—but the arresting officer has disappeared. Schnitzer is sore, suspecting that while he waits, the cop is probably boozing in some saloon, making $13.50 an hour in overtime.

The Cortale jury returns at 8:30 P.M. and takes another vote. This time it's eleven to one to acquit. Only Abatis holds out for conviction. He was convinced by the MUD lists that Cortale never made the calls to Sidney Greene and therefore his whole story was a lie. But the others argue that the prosecution did not draw the net of circumstantial evidence tight enough: There's still the possibility that someone else slipped into the suite and shot Acca and Galietta.

Abatis can't hold out alone. At 9:45 the jury reports that it has reached a verdict.

As the jurors file past the defense table, Abatis flashes a smile at Cortale.

"Will the defendant please rise," the clerk intones. "Will the foreman please rise."

Foreman David Beard, manager of New York University's computer operations and the lone black on the jury, stands and faces Cortale.

The clerk asks for the verdict on count No. 1—the murder of Eugene Acca.

"Not guilty."

Mrs. Rosemary Cortale screams with joy and starts to sob.

The clerk asks for the verdict on the second count—the murder of Enrico Galietta.

"Not guilty."

Mrs. Cortale jumps up and rushes into the well of the court to embrace her husband. A court officer gently pushes her back.

"Plenty of time," he says.

The formalities must be completed. Judge Edwards discharges the defendant. Then he thanks the jurors, saying he'd be happy to have any of them serve in his courtroom again. Kuh adds his thanks. And even Ryan: "I appreciate the effort."

Edwards sends the jurors home, admonishing them to travel in groups if possible because of the late hour.

Cortale's daughter rushes to a pay phone in the hall. "Grandma, accept the charges," she screams. "Everything's OK. He's not guilty. We're coming home."

Inside the courtroom reporters crowd around Cortale.

"It's hard to say what I'm going to do next," the acquitted defendant tells them. "Two years of my life have been virtually wrecked. My family has stuck by me through all of this and I'm going to make it up to them."

He adds that he's "financially wiped out."

Was he worried?

"I never had any doubts because I didn't do anything," Cortale replies. "Someone up above was taking care of me. Now the strain is over."

Bob Crane of the *Daily News* asks what he'd do if he were walking down the street and saw Sidney Greene.

"I'd like to see Sidney Greene," Cortale replies. "I'm a reasonable man, but big as he is I'd like to take him."

Clutching the charts that were on display throughout the trial, Jim Ryan leaves the courtroom and crowds into an elevator with several of the jurors.

"I was very happy that you arrived at a verdict," he tells them.

His greatest fear throughout the trial was a hung jury, and the prospect of having to go through the whole ordeal again.

Helen Mandell tries to console him. "It was a tough case.

Thursday, May 4

Cigar in hand, District Attorney Morgenthau strolls through the lobby, checking out a new system designed to speed the processing of fingerprints.

Fishing for an angle for a second-day story on the Cortale case, Mike Pearl corners him and asks if the D.A.'s office is going to renew the search for Sidney Greene.

"As far as we're concerned, Sidney Greene doesn't exist," Morgenthau tells him. "We feel that we had the right man."

"So a guilty man was set free?" Pearl asks.

"That sometimes happens."

And he predicts that it will happen again in the case of Dr. Arsenio Favor.

Friday, May 5

"The defendant is ready for sentence," Lawrence Hochheiser tells Justice Hortense Gabel.

"I would think that we can defer sentence," Justice Gabel replies from the bench.

The mechanics were discussed in a robing-room conference, but the judge still wants to hear what Philip Carlo has to say. After the inevitable delay, he is finally arraigned for sentencing for grand larceny by forged check.

Hochheiser notes that Carlo's wife is in the courtroom, and his father, too upset to attend the proceedings, is outside in the hall.

"I think you'd better call him back," Judge Gabel says.

Carlo runs out and fetches his father. Except for his clean-shaven upper lip, Carlo is a carbon copy of the old man.

"I'd like to hear from you," Justice Gabel tells Carlo, "what you feel you ought to do to pay back your family and society."

Carlo starts to thank the judge.

"Don't thank me!" she snaps.

Carlo says he's "more than grateful" to be given the opportunity to pay back the money he stole. He adds that he's been seeing a psychiatrist.

At the prosecution table Jim Ryan taps his foot in frustration while Justice Gabel spells out the three things Carlo must do to win probation: First, he must make restitution of $3,684.74. Second, he must pay a fine of $6,315.26 over eighteen months—he, not his father. (Fine and restitution together come to exactly $10,000.) And "the most important thing you can do is give some time to society."

She warns Carlo that if there's any violation of those terms, he'll go to prison.

"If I didn't think there was a little hope for you, I wouldn't be doing this," she says.

Ryan rises—to "put on the record that the People are going to speak against a probationary type of sentence." Then he packs up his papers and stalks angrily from the courtroom. It has not been his week.

Monday, May 8

Monday's court calendars are always the heaviest of the week, but Judge Irving Lang's is exceptional. Seven dittoed docket sheets taped to the marble wall outside Part 44 list a total of fifty-one cases. Yet he spends his first two hours hearing only one.

Nine lawyers cluster around the defense table, and others, unable to find chairs, sit in the jury box. They are heavy hitters of corporate litigation, counsel who command five-figure fees for arguing multimillion-dollar lawsuits.

There's Saul Streit, tanned and white-haired, the retired administrative justice of the Supreme Court. He was a judge of the old Court of General Sessions when the courthouse was built, and his name adorns the bronze dedication in the lobby.

There's Milton Gould, high-domed and wearing metal-rimmed glasses, the litigation specialist of the politically potent firm of Shea, Gould, Climenko & Casey. The Mets' Shea Stadium is named for the firm's senior partner and the city's premier power broker, William Shea.

And more . . .

They represent nine American Stock Exchange specialists charged in a massive indictment—one thousand counts—with entering fictitious transactions on the AmEx ticker in order to keep the prices of lightly traded options in line with the underlying stock prices on the New York Stock Exchange.

The nine are among thirty-six specialists who were censured by the exchange, fined a total of $195,000, and suspended from trading for one to four weeks for their actions. They were also censured by the Securities and Exchange Commission and enjoined from repeating the practice.

They were subsequently indicted for violating both New York State's Penal Law and Martin Act, which governs securities sales. The action is one of the few criminal cases brought by the Attorney General's office, which has limited criminal jurisdiction in such matters as securities, theater syndication, and charitable solicitation.

The defendants are not in court for the legal arguments.

Gould argued that the indictments should be dismissed "in the interest of justice": The defendants have been punished enough. Now Stanley Arkin—thin, balding, and bespectacled—argues technical points of law. Lang has dismissed two of his motions.

"One more and I have three strikes," Arkin quips.

He swings anyway, arguing that the defendants had no intent to defraud, but entered the fictitious sales in an effort to avoid losing the option market to the Chicago exchange.

Is he suggesting that the defendants "should get a medal"? Lang asks.

"We'll settle for a dismissal," Arkin replies.

Other lawyers rise, urging that the Penal Law counts be dropped because there was no intent to defraud, and Lang indicates a willingness to accept their arguments. Then Jerome Londin steps out of the jury box. He barely opens his mouth when Lang cuts him off.

"I'm quite upset with you and with all the other counsel in the case."

In his motion papers Londin argued that the prosecutor, Special Assistant Attorney General Stephen Lapidus, has a personal interest in protracting the litigation because he left the Attorney General's office during the course of the case and is now being paid *per diem* to continue it.

Lang calls the charge "shocking, outrageous, and scurrilous."

"There's a former special prosecutor who's a master at that type of pleading," he adds—a reference to Maurice Nadjari.

Londin makes his point, then Lang says, "All right, I'd like to hear from the People next."

Lapidus rises—a young man with a cherubic face and brown curly hair. A pipe projects from his breast pocket.

"These defendants—" he starts, with a wave of his hand.

"Don't point at us," Gould snaps. "We're not the defendants. We're lawyers."

Lang asks Lapidus about a colloquy reported in the grand-jury minutes. The foreman of the panel that returned the indictments said the defendants had been punished enough and shouldn't be punished further.

Lapidus's reply is lengthy and convoluted.

"I never thought I'd get such a Talmudic explanation," Lang says.

"Not Talmudic," Gould says. "Byzantine."

Lang finally cuts off the arguments, saying he'll rule on the motions on May 31.

"I want all the defendants here on the adjourn day," he adds.

Tuesday, May 9

"With regard to Arsenio Favor, previously marked ready," Judge Harold Rothwax rules, "that matter is transferred forthwith to Mr. Justice Melia."

Prosecutor Michael Davidson, defense counsel Murray Cutler, and the defendant troop upstairs to Part 37. Dr. Favor wears a beige jacket, brown slacks, and tinted airplane glasses.

Judge Aloysius Melia is not a man who wastes time. The first order of business is a *Huntley* hearing on the admissibility of Dr. Favor's statements to the police, and he directs Davidson to call his first witness immediately.

Detective John Janeczko takes the stand. Davidson asks him about the material-witness order he obtained from Justice Burton Roberts on February 12, 1977. "What had Judge Roberts directed you to do?"

"Objection," Cutler says. "The warrant speaks for itself."

"Sustained."

Janeczko says he went to Kennedy Airport and found Dr. Favor waiting to board a Manila-bound plane. He took him aside and told him that he'd obtained a court order barring him from leaving the country.

"O.K., fine," Favor replied.

Janeczko says he advised Dr. Favor of his rights and repeated the *Miranda* warning again in the police car, reading it from a card he carries.

Davidson offers the card in evidence.

"Let's have some testimony," Melia says impatiently.

In the car, Janeczko says, Dr. Favor told them he was taking his children home to the Philippines and was not sure of his future plans. He admitted having an affair six months before, but said he no longer saw the girl.

They stopped to pick up sandwiches, Janeczko continues, then went to the police station.

Cutler objects that Janeczko is reading from notes.

"Mr. Cutler," Judge Melia snaps, "you've been around these courts many years, thirty or better."

"Yes, Your Honor."

"This is a purely technical objection without any merit."

"Exception."

"You have your objection. *Period*," Melia rules.

Janeczko says Dr. Favor was questioned again at the station. He said he had no theories as to his wife's death. At first he thought the cause was a pulmonary embolism, but it could have been a drug reaction.

He said his wife had complained about a problem with her left breast, Janeczko continues, so he took her to the hospital for a biopsy on February 1. The tests indicated that her condition was benign, and she was sent home. On February 8, when she complained of pain, he took her back to the hospital. They got there about noon.

Dr. Richard was busy, so Dr. Favor "took it upon himself to examine his wife." He took a blood sample and prescribed an "I.V."—intravenous solution—and Demerol, a sedative.

He stayed with her all day, then went to dinner. He returned to the hospital, visited his wife again, then went to his room and watched a basketball game on television. At 11:30 he left a wake-up call for 6:30 A.M. and went to bed.

He was awakened about midnight and told his wife was ill. He went to the emergency room and "saw the efforts of the doctors trying to revive his wife."

Janeczko says he asked Dr. Favor about his love affairs. Favor replied that he had one six months before—it was "in the open." Janeczko asked the name of the girl, and Favor told him—Dorca Jorean, a clerk at Columbia Presbyterian Hospital.

He then asked about succinylcholine. Dr. Favor replied that he knew it was a muscle relaxant, administered by an anesthesiologist, but didn't know the dosage. Janeczko says he asked if 10 cc. was fatal. "He stated to me that he had no idea."

Dr. Favor, Janeczko continues, said he would feel responsible if his wife died of a drug reaction, because he had prescribed an antibiotic. If a person is allergic, Dr. Favor said, 10 mg. is fatal. He had prescribed 200.

He says Favor claimed he had no knowledge of how the succinylcholine that was found in his home got there.

Then, Janeczko continues, he told Favor that the police were aware of his girl friends and knew he wanted a divorce. At this point Favor said he wanted to tell the truth and started crying.

"He said he was in love with Dorca and she was in love with him."

Dr. Favor, according to Janeczko, also admitted that he was "completely familiar with usages and dosages" of succinylcholine.

Under further questioning, Dr. Favor said that he'd applied at two hospitals for future employment. It was one way he could stay in the United States. The other was by marrying an American citizen.

Janeczko says he concluded by asking Dr. Favor if he knew how his wife died. "He said no." If he'd injected her with succinylcholine? "He said no." If he'd lied to them? "He said no."

Cutler's cross-examination is brief and perfunctory, eliciting only that the detective "cursed once" at Favor.

"I'll hear you, Mr. Cutler," Judge Melia says.

The defense lawyer argues that there's no proof that Dr. Favor understood his rights.

"Dr. Favor is a highly educated man," Melia rules. "He gave every evidence of understanding the situation. . . . The motion to suppress these statements is denied."

Cutler never expected to win the point—he only wanted an advance look at part of the prosecution's case.

"Are we ready to proceed with the next step, which is jury selection?" the judge asks.

Davidson says, "Yes"—and a panel of sixty is brought into court.

At lunchtime Cutler and Dr. Favor walk out the Baxter Street entrance—opened the day before for the first time in months—and stroll to Chinatown. There the ex-cop from Brooklyn introduces his oriental client to moo shu pork.

Wednesday, May 10

About thirty persons—most of them women, some mothers with infant children—march in a circle on the Centre Street sidewalk outside the courthouse protesting the Washington Square verdict. They carry homemade signs:

> FREE THE SIX!!! FREE THE SIX!!!
> THE GUILTY TALKED AND THEY WALKED
> HELP US HELP THE 6 INNOCENT MEN
> LET OUR BOYS GO FREE
> THE SIX ARE JUST SCAPEGOATS
> A JAIL SENTENCE WILL BE A DEATH SENTENCE

One woman picket gets into an argument with a black bystander.

"It wasn't a racial thing?" he snaps at her.

"No."

"What about that dead boy who was minding his own business?"

"The ones that did it are walking the street."

A male picket cautions her, "Don't start anything."

Then Greg Gully, the baby-faced organizer of the protests, comes over to calm the confrontation.

The pickets continue to circle, reversing every few laps because some women complain they get dizzy. They start a feeble chant:

"Justice for the six! Justice for the six!"

A black walking past into the building shouts at them, "They ought to lock those kids up for ninety-nine years!"

Thursday, May 11

Paule Ransay, the alleged kidnaper of eleven-year-old Marci Klein, testifies at her *Huntley* hearing. She's a short, pudgy woman with curly brown hair and a puffy face. She speaks softly with the slight French accent of her native Martinique.

She claims that Calvin Klein, the fashion designer, engineered the kidnapping of his own daughter. It's a variant of the Bronfman defense, successfully employed the year before by the men accused of snatching liquor heir Samuel Bronfman II. They claimed that Bronfman hatched the plot himself to get money from his father.

Assistant District Attorney Thomas Demakis—balding, bespectacled, and mustached—brings out that she told a different story after her arrest. He asks the Kleins' onetime baby-sitter about the Saturday session at FBI headquarters when she confessed.

"Did you tell the detectives that the reason you lied Friday night was to give Dominique [her half brother and co-defendant] a chance to get out of the country?"

"Yes."

Did she tell them that the reason they committed the crime was "to get money for Dominique to go to school?"

"Yes."

The courtroom is hushed. The only sound besides the two voices is the clatter of the stenotype machine. Judge Harold Rothwax pulls his chair close to the witness box, his incredulity showing on his furrowed brow.

"Do you remember you told the detective the reason you wanted to speak to Calvin Klein was to tell him you never would hurt Marci?"

"I don't think I did."

Defense attorney Alan Seidler takes over on re-direct: "When you said no one else was involved, was that false?"

"Yes, it was."

Seidler asks why she lied.

"I still had hope that Mr. Klein was going to do certain things for me, give me certain things."

Judge Rothwax interrupts. "You were ready to implicate your brother, but not ready to implicate Mr. Klein—is that what you're telling me?"

"He could talk for himself."

Seidler asks why she implicated Dominique.

"The only reason I talked about him is I thought he was gone."

Demakis jumps up to note that Dominique was already in custody—and she knew it.

"Miss Ransay," Rothwax interrupts, "how well did you know Mr. Klein?"

There is a long silence.

His voice rising, Rothwax asks again, "What was the nature of your relationship with Mr. Klein from beginning to end?"

Another pause. Then: "It's not something I want to say because . . ." Her last words are inaudible.

"Well, tell me about it now!" Rothwax snaps.

Another long pause. Then: "We were friends and then we became intimate friends."

"What does that mean, Miss Ransay?"

There is yet another long silence.

"Were you lovers?"

"Yes," she whispers.

Rothwax continues the questioning, eliciting that she and Klein met only three times. The first time, she says, was in the lobby of her apartment house. She borrowed $1,300, which she in turn lent to her boy friend. The second time he came to her apartment and they made love. The third time they met on the street outside her apartment and discussed the kidnaping. Klein, she says, gave her $300.

The judge presses for further details.

"Your Honor, I object," Seidler says. He says the question goes beyond the scope of the hearing.

"It goes to credibility," Rothwax rules.

Miss Ransay resumes: "He told me that he would like me to kidnap his daughter in the summertime and asked me to find two other people." She adds that he promised her $100,000, plus the $100,000 ransom.

Seidler, a tall, cadaverous man, sprawls in his seat, eyes closed, his hands folded with forefingers pointing toward the ceiling.

Rothwax tries to pinpoint the time of her meetings and telephone conversations with Klein. Her replies are so soft that even the stenographer, seated two feet away, has difficulty hearing her.

At one point Seidler jumps to his feet to object.

Rothwax turns angrily on him, saying the attorney's comments suggested an answer to the witness. He carefully accents each word of his warning: *"Don't let it happen again."*

Finally, the judge asks why she hadn't implicated Klein before.

"I knew he was a powerful man," she replies. "I knew he had money, . . . so I felt secure."

The hearing recesses.

Mike Pearl of the *Post* jumps out of the jury box and dashes to the center aisle, where Demakis is conferring with Chief Assistant District Attorney Peter Zimroth. He asks why the prosecutor did not inquire into *why* Klein would want to kidnap his own daughter.

"That's because you think like a newspaperman and I think like a lawyer," Zimroth replies.

"Aren't you curious?"

"Yes. But this is not the time or place to bring it out."

Friday, May 12

Four court officers flank a table outside the entrance to Part 106 on the seventh floor of the Civil Court Building. With hand-held metal detectors they screen the eighty spectators who have turned out for the Washington Square sentencing.

There are familiar faces from the two months of trial and two months of protest rallies—Greg Gully, who dropped out of St. John's University to organize the demonstrations; Perry Knowlton, the gray-haired literary agent who is Michael Doyle's guardian; Carlos Boutureira's mother, dark like her son, but as short and plump as he is tall and lean; the barrel-chested Anthony Costanzo, his red hair growing back since he shaved his head after losing a New Year's bet; and Anthony Paolini, one of the three acquitted defendants, hobbling on a crutch, having sprained his ankle playing basketball.

By 10:00 A.M. the courtroom is filled. It's a wide, shallow room, with only four rows of benches for spectators—who sit closer to the judge than the jurors in the box against the right wall. The first row is filled with reporters and attorneys. The room is windowless and dimly lit. Although the walls are lined with marble paneling, it has the acoustical resonance of a half-filled clothes hamper.

Not until 10:55 does the short-sleeved court officer call the session to order, for once giving the full spiel:

"All rise! Come to order! Hear ye! Hear ye! All persons having business before Part 106 of the Supreme Court of the State of New York, held in and for the County of New York, draw near, give your attention and ye shall be heard! The Honorable Robert M. Haft presiding. His Honor, the justice of this court!"

Haft mounts the bench. "Gentlemen, the reason for the delay . . ."

He explains that Robert McLamb's counsel, John C. Hill, called to say he was detained in the Bronx on another case. He should arrive by 11:30. In the interim Haft hears the other cases on his calendar.

Hill arrives at 11:40. There's another wait until Ronald Degen is fetched from the courtroom where he's on trial. Then at 11:52 the doors are locked and the six defendants are led into the courtroom, each escorted by a court officer.

They are seated in the first row of the jury box, arrayed from left to right, obviously according to the severity of the sentences Haft will impose—Joseph Chiapetti, Carlos Boutureira, Robert McLamb, Michael Andriani, Michael Doyle, and Andres Sanchez. The six court officers take seats behind them. Eleven others patrol the courtroom.

Counsel put their names on the record. Hill apologizes for being late.

Judge Haft officially denies the defense motions to set aside the verdict, then states that he has not yet received a reply to Robert Cohen's motions on behalf of Sanchez.

Prosecutor John Moscow asks that Sanchez's sentencing be deferred until June 12, because Cohen's motions entail "extensive memorandums." Haft agrees.

The five other defendants are arraigned for sentence.

Then Moscow rises. "Sentences of imprisonment must be required," he says. "There appears to be a feeling among youths in the area that such attacks can be carried out with impunity."

He devotes most of his comments to Michael Doyle, the only defendant for whom Robert LaSado recommended probation. He recites Doyle's extensive record of juvenile arrests and observes that he was placed on probation under Knowlton's guardianship and removed to upstate New York. On his first day back in the city, Moscow says, he participated in the Washington Square riot, striking one man with a baseball bat while he lay on the ground pleading, "Oh, my God! Don't hit me!" and going on to wield the blow that blinded Charles Febee.

Moscow notes that the probation report says Doyle has a "good opportunity to make a new life for himself." But he had that chance before, the prosecutor says, and then "committed one of the most heinous acts."

Then, one by one, the defense lawyers rise to plead for mercy.

First, Conrad Ferrigno, who succeeded Robert Brown as Chiapetti's counsel.

"Nobody is happy when a person dies," he says. "Nobody is happy when a person is maimed." But he insists that the result was never intended.

He says Chiapetti is an Air Force veteran who received a medical discharge and is neither "malicious" nor "cruel."

"This incident may have reflected a sense of frustration by people in general," he continues. "To select six individuals and make them the scapegoats for all the evil in New York is totally unfair."

He asks Haft to be "as lenient as possible."

Haft asks Chiapetti if he has anything to say.

"No, sir."

Then Degen on behalf of Boutureira.

He notes that the defendants are only six out of seventy-five or eighty who participated in the attack and that the prosecutor gave immunity to many witnesses. "These people are walking away," he says. "They're going unpunished."

He calls Boutureira an "immature youth" and notes that he has two prior convictions—a gun charge as a youthful offender and the gas-station burglary during the blackout. He too asks Haft to be "as lenient as possible."

When Haft asks Boutureira if he has anything to say, he shakes his head.

Next Hill on behalf of McLamb.

The attorney notes that McLamb was sixteen at the time of the incident and asks for youthful-offender treatment.

As he speaks, Haft wipes a tear first from his left eye, then from his right, then rises and pours a glass of water from a carafe at the edge of the bench.

Hill calls the case "an indictment of society." He acknowledges that McLamb must be punished, but "punishment for what, Your Honor?" he shouts. He says the only thing the judge should consider is what will make McLamb "a better person." He says McLamb "has never encountered a kind situation in his life."

McLamb too has nothing to say.

Then Michael Direnzo on behalf of Andriani.

"He was nothing more than a curious bystander," the attorney insists. "Mr. Andriani stands here today. He says, 'I did not do it. I am innocent.' "

Direnzo turns to Andriani's previous arrest for a 1975 robbery. He says the victim was a man who sold pills to neighborhood youngsters.

"He wasn't robbed," Direnzo insists. "He was chased. He was chased because Mr. Andriani didn't want to see any harm befalling children. It was a compassionate act."

The probation report, he notes, says that Carl Warren—the man Andriani allegedly struck—suffers "narcolepsy" as a result of the attack.

"I'm not so sure that he didn't suffer from this prior to this incident."

He notes also that Warren has to take an amphetamine derivative for his ailment.

"He will have a license to use this narcotic for the rest of his life."

The attorney quotes from a letter Warren sent to Judge Haft: " 'If those guys don't get the maximum sentence, the judge will have one more guy to sentence—me, for contempt of court.' "

Direnzo calls Andriani "a decent guy, probably the most decent guy in the bunch," and asks Haft to "have mercy."

Andriani is the only defendant who speaks in his own behalf: "I'm innocent. I didn't do this. I didn't do anything. . . . If I'm guilty of anything, I'm guilty of being stupid enough to follow."

Finally, Howard Meyer for Doyle.

He opens by challenging Moscow's account of Doyle's juvenile arrest record. He says the perpetrator in one incident was not Doyle but Timothy DeVito, who would have been a defendant in this case "but for his pervasive ineptitude." DeVito overslept and missed the riot by five minutes.

"From the beginning Mr. Doyle has asserted his innocence—from day one," Meyer says. "He continues to assert his innocence, realizes it jeopardizes his freedom, but will continue to do so."

Meyer notes that the probation report describes Doyle as "maturing and growing" and calls him "responsive to guidance and supervision." "Michael Doyle is not a recidivist," he asserts. "He is a young man with promise."

He asks Haft to follow the recommendation of the report and place Doyle on probation.

Haft changes his glasses to read his prepared remarks. They're directed not to the attorneys' pleas for mercy but to the community protests—an indication that all the demonstrations were counterproductive.

"Some of the community—not the majority, I am sure—seek to excuse the defendants' actions," Haft says. "There can never be justification for vigilantes."

He calls claims that the youths were trying to rid the park of drug dealers "absurd," noting that the attackers not only patronized the dealers, but forewarned them.

The victims, he says, were not dope dealers, but a college student playing volleyball, a disabled Vietnam veteran playing Frisbee, a bicyclist known as "Laughing Mario," a man walking home from work.

"Those who claim this incident was not racial . . . are totally naïve or don't wish to see the truth," he asserts. "All who were struck were black or Hispanic. . . . The sole reason that anyone was struck was the color of his skin."

Others may have participated, but that "doesn't expiate" the guilt of these defendants.

"They are not scapegoats," he says. "They are not martyrs. They were part of a raging mob."

Then he turns to the defendants.

Joseph Chiapetti, he says, was "unquestionably the leader" and "deserves the severest sanction." He sentences him to four to twelve years in prison.

Carlos Boutureira, he continues, was Chiapetti's "most enthusiastic follower." He has an "established pattern of violent behavior," Haft says, and "is certainly a danger to the community." Haft notes that he suppressed Boutureira's confession. He denies youthful-offender treatment and sentences him to three and a third to ten years in prison.

Boutureira slumps in his seat and starts to sob. In the spectator seats his mother weeps.

Robert McLamb, according to Haft, was a "most active supporter" who warned the gamblers and dope dealers. His confession also was suppressed. He calls McLamb "a vicious street fighter" who "is clearly a menace to the community." Again he denies Y.O. treatment and sentences McLamb to three and a third to ten years.

McLamb smiles. At the end of the row Sanchez, aware of what awaits him, hangs his head.

Michael Andriani, Haft says, "ran with the crowd." He describes him as "friendly, outgoing, and generally cooperative," but he committed "truly despicable acts." Haft sentences him to six years in prison.

Michael Doyle, the judge concludes, is "intelligent, inquisitive, and well liked," but he "reverted to run with the pack." Since then he has made rapid progress. He declares Doyle a youthful offender: the conviction will not appear on his record.

The judge observes that Doyle has "potential for rehabilitation," but that cannot be his only consideration. There is also deterrence and punishment. A prison sentence will serve to deter both Doyle and others. And "punishment *per se* must be imposed here. . . . That act cannot go unpunished." He sentences Doyle to four years in prison. Like Andriani, he'll be eligible for parole after serving one year; the others will have to serve at least the minimum.

The six defendants are led away, the doors are unlocked, and the spectators are released from their two hours' custody.

An hour later Boutureira is brought back before Judge Haft, who imposes a "zip-three" sentence—to run concurrently with the Washington Square term—for the blackout burglary.

Monday, May 15

AR1 and AR2 are all but deserted. It's the slowest day of the year. A record total of 3.38 inches of rain fell on Sunday—Mother's Day—and the police logged only sixty-one arrests in all of Manhattan.

One of those arrested is arraigned before Family Court Judge Rose McBrien, sitting by designation in AR1. He's listed as "John Doe." He's a disheveled, barefoot black who refused to tell his name either to the police or R.O.R. officer, and there's no record of his fingerprints. His face is battered and bruised. His tattered overcoat is stained with blood and urine. He's charged with theft of services—for jumping a subway turnstile—and assaulting the arresting officer. He obviously got the worst of the encounter.

The Assistant District Attorney asks for five hundred dollars bail.

"He doesn't have a place to live," Legal Aid protests. "Obviously, he's indigent."

The lawyer says Legal Aid will provide him with funds to go to a shelter.

"All right, I'll parole him," says Judge McBrien.

On other floors, it's business as usual in the courthouse.

In Part 37, where the trial of Dr. Arsenio Favor is in its second day of testimony, Michael Davidson introduces the "murder weapon" into evidence—a stainless-steel stand for intravenous injections with two bottles of yellow glucose solution hooked up to the plastic tubing.

Down the hall in Part 72 the attorneys await the arrival of a fresh panel of prospective jurors so they can continue the *voir dire* for juror No. 9 in the murder trial of the five blacks accused of killing a customer during the robbery of a Harlem supermarket.

Two floors below, Geoff Abrams, wearing his battered trench coat, sits on the front bench of Part 35, waiting for his case to be called and listening as Abe Brodsky argues motions in the case of Shlomo Tal and Pini Balabin. Brodsky asks that the prosecution be ordered to divulge the names of its witnesses.

Judge Harold Rothwax denies the motion. "To do so would jeopardize the safety of those witnesses. . . . I will not endanger them."

"All I can say, Judge," Brodsky replies, "is I am disappointed."

In AP5 on the fourth floor the clerk runs out of ready cases, so "Turn-'em-

Loose Bruce" Wright turns himself loose and walks off the bench for a brief recess.

In the first-floor coffee shop David Hackel, proprietor for twenty-five years, waits on two blacks and a stubbly Hispanic, calling out the orders to the cook.

"Scramble two medium, takes bacon and French!"

"Butter roll to stay!"

He pours a cup of coffee and a cup of tea and takes the order of a cigar-smoking attorney.

The coffee shop, officially "Rand's Food Shop," looks like a thousand other greasy spoons—three U-shaped Formica counters, a grill, a Coke machine, and two tanks for coffee. Cakes and pastries—"Home-baked by Beatrice," Hackel's wife—fill glass cases. A poster-sized photograph of the building greets customers at the take-out counter, and the walls are adorned with hand-lettered signs illustrated with pictures clipped from magazines:

HOT PASTRAMI MAKES A PERSON FEEL SEXY
NUDE BURGER AND COTTAGE CHEESE
GET SOME "SOUL" WITH OUR LOCAL GRITS

Hackel caters to a growth industry. In 1953 he served fifty to sixty cups of coffee a day. Today, despite the proliferation of electric coffee makers throughout the building, he serves seven hundred.

In those twenty-five years he's seen them come and go. He's seen the clientele change from the neighborhood boys he grew up with—hauled in on gambling charges—to black and Hispanic addicts who nod out over their coffee cups and burn their noses. He's seen assistant district attorneys so green they couldn't find their way to the courtrooms return to preside over them.

He's catered to attorneys and arsonists, prostitutes and pimps, judges and jurors, muggers and murderers, religious fanatics and political protesters—all sitting shoulder to shoulder, every race and creed, every kind of criminal, and every variety of nut.

He's seen them come and go. And he knows that they'll keep coming.

Tuesday, May 16

Like Al Capp's Joe Btfsplk, William Depperman brings rain. Having been arrested again in Washington Square, he stands in the drizzle distributing yet another leaflet. No screaming headlines this time, just a mass of mimeographed words.

> The real estate interests reaped the benefits of the 1976 racist attacks in Washington Square Park, in which local white thugs . . . were sent on a rampage through the park with baseball bats, broken bottles, and other weapons, seriously wounding many—all of oppressed nationality—and killing one pregnant Puerto Rican woman and one black Olympic athlete. The police complied with the crime by making themselves scarce during the attacks, in conformity to the green light that their capitalist masters had given the murderous attack. New York Mayor Edward "Capital Punishment" Koch . . . lives right across the street from Washington Square Park and undoubtedly played a pivotal role in organizing the attack.

Postscript

The log ends, but the life of the courthouse continues. During the weeks and months since May 15, the following events occurred:

Andres Sanchez was sentenced to two and a half to seven and a half years in prison for his part in the Washington Square riot. He and four co-defendants—all but Carlos Boutureira, who was serving a sentence for burglary—were freed on bail pending appeal. Anthony "Dif" DeFranco, who disappeared on the day he was scheduled to testify, was arrested for attempted robbery in Greenwich Village. At his arraignment he was hit with an additional charge of contempt of court in the Washington Square case.

Dr. Arsenio Favor was tried for the murder of his wife. After twenty-five hours of deliberation, the jury was hung, eight to four for conviction. The District Attorney's office planned to retry him.

Cecil Wiggins pleaded guilty to his part in the Marci Klein kidnapping. Paule and Dominique Ransay stood trial, but a mistrial was declared when the lone juror holding out for acquittal became ill. At the outset of their retrial, they pleaded guilty and exonerated Calvin Klein of any part in the plot.

Former Surrogate S. Samuel DiFalco died of a heart attack before he could be brought to trial in the Supreme Court corruption case. The case of Charles Fisher, the first of his co-defendants to be tried, also ended with a hung jury, nine to three for conviction. A second co-defendant, Howard Roseman, was convicted of contempt of the grand jury.

After deliberating for two days, a jury convicted Shlomo Tal and Pini Balabin of second-degree murder in the death of diamond dealer Pinchos Jaroslawicz. They were sentenced to twenty-five years to life in prison.

Bernard Bergman was paroled from Rikers Island after serving eight months of his one-year sentence.

Justice Burton Roberts was reassigned to the Civil Term of the Supreme Court.

Judge Benjamin Altman was reassigned to the Supreme Court and, despite Robert Kaplan's prediction, Milton Williams was named to succeed him as administrative judge of the Criminal Court.

Judges Peter McQuillan and Dennis Edwards were elected to the Supreme Court bench.

Martin Erdman of Legal Aid was named by Mayor Koch to join the "whores" on the Criminal Court bench.

"Turn-'em-Loose Bruce" tried to become truly "Civil Wright." Fearing he would not be reappointed to the Criminal Court when his term expired, he ran for election to the Civil Court from a Harlem district, but lost, 7,833 to 6,341.

Louis J. Lefkowitz retired after serving twenty-two years as New York's attorney general.

J. Wallace LaPrade was removed as chief of the FBI's New York office for conducting unauthorized surveillance of political dissidents and was subsequently ousted from the bureau for refusing to cooperate in the investigation.

Mike Pearl got a new sign on his desk:

MIKE PEARL
DAILY SUN
AND BEFORE THAT:
NEW YORK POST
WORLD JOURNAL TRIBUNE
JOURNAL-AMERICAN
DAILY MIRROR

But the *Sun* didn't rise and Pearl returned to the *Post.* Among his colleagues, Leslie Maitland switched to general assignment for the *Times,* while John Mulligan left the AP to become deputy commissioner of the Fire Department.

By the end of October, thirty-eight prosecution witnesses had testified in the trial of the five blacks charged with killing a customer during the Harlem supermarket robbery. As many as eighty remained to be called. The trial seemed likely to eclipse the fifteen-month record of the 1970–71 Panther 21 case as the longest trial in New York State history.

And William Depperman was finally brought to trial for defacing the Washington Square arch and New York University library. That trial, too, ended with a hung jury. By then, Depperman had been hit with other charges—of assaulting rival assassination theorists. And by then he'd acquired a new cause—charging that Kung Fu actor Bruce Lee was murdered by the Hong Kong movie director Run Run Shaw.

Glossary: Courthouse Jargon and Nomenclature

A felony (B felony, etc.) Under New York State's revised Penal Law, enacted in 1967, felonies are divided into categories from A through E according to severity of sentence. A felonies (murder$_2$, kidnaping) carry fifteen or twenty-five years to life. B (manslaughter$_1$, robbery$_1$, rape, arson) zero to twenty-five years. C (assault$_1$, robbery$_2$, etc.) zero to fifteen years. D (assault$_2$, grand larceny$_1$, etc.) zero to seven years. E (grand larceny$_2$, etc.) zero to four.

A misdemeanors (assault$_3$, petit larceny, etc.) carry zero to one year. B misdemeanors, zero to three months. Violations (disorderly conduct, loitering, etc.) zero to fifteen days.

An attempt to commit a crime—used primarily for pleading purposes—reduces the charge one grade.

In 1973, at Governor Rockefeller's behest, most narcotics crimes were made A felonies, the sentence varying with the amount: A_1, fifteen to life; A_2, six to life; A_3, one to life. Under the statute persons accused of A_1 and A_2 felonies can plead to nothing lower than A_3.

During the period of this book New York's murder$_1$ statute, providing the death penalty for killing a policeman or prison guard, was declared unconstitutional.

Under legislation that took effect September 1, 1978, juveniles aged thirteen to sixteen may be prosecuted as adults for A felonies, and those fourteen to sixteen may be prosecuted as adults for B felonies.

A.C.D. Adjourn in contemplation of dismissal. The case is adjourned indefinitely, and the charge is automatically dismissed if the defendant stays "clean" for six months. Used primarily for first offenders facing minor charges.

A.D.A. Assistant district attorney.

A.O. (or A/O) Shorthand for arresting officer.

AP All-purpose part of Criminal Court.

AR Arraignment part of Criminal Court.

Appellate Division —of Supreme Court. The intermediate appellate court. There are four Appellate Divisions, in Manhattan, Brooklyn, Albany, and Buffalo. The Appellate Division–First Department hears appeals from Manhattan and the Bronx. Appellate Division justices are designated by the governor from among the Supreme Court justices. He also designates the presiding justice (P.J.), who is administrator of all the courts in his jurisdiction. The Manhattan and Brooklyn P.J.s jointly designate an administrative judge for all the courts in New York City.

Appellate Term —of Supreme Court. Three-judge panels that hear appeals from the Civil and Criminal courts.

Baxter Street lawyer A lawyer with offices near the courthouse, who usually represents petty criminals (gamblers, prostitutes, etc.) in Criminal Court.

***Brady* material** In *Brady* v. *Maryland,* 373 U.S. 83 (1963), the U.S. Supreme Court required the prosecution to turn over to the defense any material tending to exculpate the defendant.

Bridgeman The court officer in Criminal Court who stands between the judge and the parties to the case, calling the calendar and processing the papers.

Bullet A one-year sentence.

Bullpen The cells adjoining the courtrooms.

CPCS Criminal possession of a controlled substance, i.e., narcotics.

CPSP Criminal possession of stolen property.

CPW Criminal possession of a weapon.

Court of Appeals New York State's highest court. Its seven members are called "judges." During the period of this book they were elected for fourteen-year terms. Under terms of a constitutional amendment approved in 1977, future judges will be appointed by the governor. The chief judge of the Court of Appeals designates a state administrative judge.

Criminal Court —of the City of New York. Created under the court reorganization of 1962 from a merger of the old Court of Special Sessions and the Magistrates Courts. It holds arraignments and preliminary hearings on felonies and tries violations and misdemeanors. Trials may be held before a judge or six-man jury. Its judges are appointed by the mayor for a ten-year term.

DD5 A detective's report on his investigation—from the number of the Detective Division form.

18B lawyer Under Article 35, §18(b) of New York State's County Law, private lawyers are appointed to represent indigent defendants when Legal Aid cannot. They are paid fifteen dollars an hour for courtroom time, ten dollars an hour for office work. Because the lists are kept by the Appellate Division, some defendants call them "pelican lawyers."

Eyeball Eyewitness identification.

Family Court —of the State of New York. Hears domestic disputes and juvenile-delinquency cases. Its judges are appointed by the mayor for a ten-year term.

G.L. Grand larceny.

GTC General trial and conference part of Supreme Court, the calendar parts.

***Gannett* motion** To bar the press from a preliminary hearing on grounds that the publicity will prejudice potential jurors—from the Court of Appeals' ruling in *Gannett* v. *DePasquale,* 43 N.Y.2d 370 (1977).

General Sessions From November 1, 1683, until August 30, 1962, the Court of General Sessions was the trial court for felonies in Manhattan. Under the court reorganization of 1962 it was merged with the Supreme Court.

Hold A demand from another jurisdiction not to release a prisoner pending his transfer or extradition.

***Huntley* hearing** A pre-trial hearing, mandated by the Court of Appeals in *People* v. *Huntley,* 15 N.Y.2d 72 (1965), to determine the admissibility of a defendant's statements to police or prosecutors.

Jury —Part of Criminal Court. Where misdemeanor cases are tried before six-man juries. Despite its name, Jury 1 is a calendar part; Juries 2, 3, and 4 are trial parts.

***Miranda* warning** In *Miranda* v. *Arizona,* 384 U.S. 436 (1966), the U.S. Supreme Court required police to advise prisoners of their right to remain silent, right to counsel, etc.

Murder-one (murder-two, manslaughter-one, etc.) Murder in the first degree.

161 A prosecutor's handwritten summary of a case, prepared for presentation to the judge setting bail, so called from the number of the form, no longer used, on which it was once typed.

Open E (open D, etc.) A guilty plea with the sentence still to be determined, usually by the defendant's future actions.

P.J. See Appellate Division.

P.P.I. Pre-pleading investigation, a probation report prepared before a plea is entered, usually requested for first offenders facing minor charges in the expectation that probation will be recommended.

Paratroop (or paralegal) A non-lawyer who handles non-legal (and non-secretarial) chores for attorneys, such as compiling documents in a case, summarizing testimony, and so on.

Part 30 The original arraignment part of Supreme Court. During the period of this book the courtroom, largest in the building, was occupied variously by Parts 31, 35, 40, and 44, but courthouse old-timers still referred to the courtroom as "Part 30."

Pelican lawyer See 18B lawyer.

Predicate felon A second-felony offender.

R.O.R. Released on own recognizance, i.e., without bail—mispronounced by many defendants "released on own reconnaissance."

***Rosario* material** In *People* v. *Rosario,* 9 N.Y.2d 286 (1961), the Court of Appeals directed the prosecution to show the defense all prior statements made by a witness. Usually this is done between direct and cross-examination, but a judge may direct that the material be turned over the day before or even before the start of the trial.

Rubber-gun squad Policemen who have been denied the right to carry firearms, usually for psychiatric reasons, and generally assigned to clerical duty—so called because many of them carry dummy weapons in their holsters.

***Sandoval* motion** To preclude a prosecutor from asking a defendant about his criminal record, on grounds that such questioning goes not to credibility but to the defendant's propensity to commit the crime charged—from the Court of Appeals' ruling in *People* v. *Sandoval,* 34 N.Y.2d 371 (1974). In a "modified *Sandoval*" the prosecutor may elicit the record, but not the details of the crimes.

730 form The psychiatric report on a defendant's mental capacity to stand trial, mandated by §730 of the Penal Law.

Supreme Court —of the State of New York. Despite its name, it is a trial court, similar to other states' circuit or superior courts. In New York City it is the trial court for felonies. Its judges are called "justices" and are elected for fourteen-year terms. Those who sit in Manhattan are elected from Manhattan and the Bronx.

The criminal parts of the Supreme Court–Manhattan are: Parts 31 through 46; Part 48, the Special and Extraordinary Term, which hears the corruption cases brought by the special prosecutor; Parts 70 through 72, the federally funded parts handling cases of defendants jailed six months or more; Parts 101 through 109; and the narcotics parts, A through H. Parts 31, 35, 40, 44, 101, and 106 are calendar parts.

The Tombs The Manhattan House of Detention for Men, so called because the original jail, built in the nineteenth century, resembled an Egyptian tomb.

Thirteenth jurors Retired men who pass their days watching trials.

***Wade* hearing** A pre-trial hearing mandated by the U.S. Supreme Court in *Wade* v. *U.S.*, 388 U.S. 218 (1967), to determine the admissibility of eyewitness identification of a defendant.

Y.O. Youthful offender. If a defendant is adjudged a youthful offender, the conviction will not appear on his record and the judge may impose probation where prison is mandatory for an adult.

Zip Zero, as in a "zip-six sentence"—zero to six years.

Index